II CHRONICLES

THE ANCHOR BIBLE is a fresh approach to the world's greatest classic. Its object is to make the Bible accessible to the modern reader; its method is to arrive at the meaning of biblical literature through exact translation and extended exposition, and to reconstruct the ancient setting of the biblical story, as well as the circumstances of its transcription and the characteristics of its transcribers.

THE ANCHOR BIBLE is a project of international and interfaith scope: Protestant, Catholic, and Jewish scholars from many countries contribute individual volumes. The project is not sponsored by any ecclesiastical organization and is not intended to reflect any particular theological doctrine. Prepared under our joint supervision, THE ANCHOR BIBLE is an effort to make available all the significant historical and linguistic knowledge which bears on the interpretation of the biblical record.

THE ANCHOR BIBLE is aimed at the general reader with no special formal training in biblical studies; yet, it is written with the most exacting standards of scholarship, reflecting the highest technical accomplishment.

This project marks the beginning of a new era of co-operation among scholars in biblical research, thus forming a common body of knowledge to be shared by all.

William Foxwell Albright
David Noel Freedman
GENERAL EDITORS

EDITORIAL BOARD

Frank M. Cross	Old Testament
Raymond E. Brown	New Testament
Jonas C. Greenfield	Apocrypha

Following the death of senior editor W. F. Albright, The Anchor Bible Editorial Board was established to advise and assist David Noel Freedman in his continuing capacity as general editor. The three members of the Editorial Board are among the contributors to The Anchor Bible. They have been associated with the series for a number of years and are familiar with its methods and objectives. Each is a distinguished authority in his area of specialization, and in concert with the others, will provide counsel and judgment as the series continues.

THE ANCHOR BIBLE

II CHRONICLES

INTRODUCTION, TRANSLATION, AND NOTES
BY
JACOB M. MYERS

Doubleday & Company, Inc.
Garden City, New York

TRANSLATOR'S NOTE

The biblical book of Chronicles is actually one book which, because of its length when translated from Hebrew into Greek, was divided into what we now know as I and II Chronicles. The division into two volumes has been retained here, but the interrelatedness of the two precluded two separate introductions that would, by avoiding repetition, tend to mislead the reader into thinking that I and II Chronicles were two distinct works.

Therefore, the general introduction to the Chronicler's work appears at the beginning of I Chronicles, and a shorter introduction—relevant specifically to II Chronicles—appears here. The appendixes for all of Chronicles are to be found at the end of II Chronicles. Appendix I gives a complete list of the parallel and comparative passages that the Chronicler drew upon for both I and II Chronicles; Appendix II contains genealogical charts based upon the first nine chapters of I Chronicles. Each volume also includes an index of place and personal names that appear *in the biblical text of that volume,* but if a name occurs in any other of the Chronicler's works (I and II Chronicles and Ezra-Nehemiah), all of these occurrences are cited in order to illustrate the basic unity of the narrative contained in these volumes.

J.M.M.

CONTENTS

APPENDIXES

PRINCIPAL ABBREVIATIONS

1. PUBLICATIONS

AASOR   Annual of the American Schools of Oriental Research
AfO   Archiv für Orientforschung
AJSL   American Journal of Semitic Languages and Literature
AMJV   *Alexander Marx Jubilee Volume,* English Section
ANEP   *The Ancient Near East in Pictures,* ed. J. B. Pritchard
ANET   *Ancient Near Eastern Texts,* ed. J. B. Pritchard
AOT   *Altorientalische Bilder zum Alten Testament,* ed. H. Gressmann
AP   *Aramaic Papyri of the Fifth Century B.C.,* ed. and tr. A. Cowley
ARAB   *Ancient Records of Assyria and Babylonia,* ed. D. D. Luckenbill
ARI   *Archaeology and the Religion of Israel,* by W. F. Albright
BA   The Biblical Archaeologist
BASOR   Bulletin of the American Schools of Oriental Research
BBLA   Beiträge zur biblischen Landes—und Altertumskunde
BH   Biblia Hebraica, ed. R. Kittel
BJPES   Bulletin of the Jewish Palestine Exploration Society
BJRL   Bulletin of the John Rylands Library
BMAP   *The Brooklyn Museum Aramaic Papyri,* ed. E. G. H. Kraeling
BP   "The Biblical Period," by W. F. Albright
BRL   *Biblisches Reallexikon,* 1937
BZAW   Beihefte zur Zeitschrift für die alttestamentliche Wissenschaft
CAD   The Assyrian Dictionary, Oriental Institute of the University of Chicago
CBQ   Catholic Biblical Quarterly
EJ   *Die Entstehung des Judenthums,* by Eduard Meyer
FAB   *Festschrift für Alfred Bertholet*
FSAC   *From the Stone Age to Christianity,* by W. F. Albright
GA   *Geschichte des Altertums,* by Eduard Meyer
GVI   *Geschichte des Volkes Israel,* by Rudolph Kittel

IB	The Interpreter's Bible
ICC	The International Critical Commentary
IDB	The Interpreter's Dictionary of the Bible, 1962
IEJ	Israel Exploration Journal
IPN	*Die israelitischen Personennamen im Rahmen der gemeinsemitischen Namengebung,* by M. Noth
1QH	Qumran Hymns of Thanksgiving
1QM	Qumran War Scroll
1QS	Qumran Manual of Discipline
JAOS	Journal of the American Oriental Society
JBL	Journal of Biblical Literature and Exegesis
JBR	Journal of Bible and Religion
JNES	Journal of Near Eastern Studies
JPOS	Journal of the Palestine Oriental Society
JTS	Journal of Theological Studies
KS	*Kleine Schriften zur Geschichte des Volkes Israel,* by A. Alt
LCQ	Lutheran Church Quarterly
LGJV	*Louis Ginzberg Jubilee Volume,* English Section
MGWJ	Monatsschrift für Geschichte und Wissenschaft des Judentums
MVAG	Mitteilungen der vorderasiatisch-aegyptischen Gesellschaft
OIC	Oriental Institute Communications
OTS	Oudtestamentische Studien
PEQ	Palestine Exploration Quarterly
PJB	Palästinajahrbuch des deutschen evangelischen Instituts für Altertumswissenschaft des heiligen Landes zu Jerusalem
QDAP	Quarterly of the Department of Antiquities in Palestine
RB	Revue biblique
SVT	Supplements to Vetus Testamentum
TLZ	Theologische Literaturzeitung
TZ	Theologische Zeitschrifte
ÜS	*Überlieferungsgeschichtliche Studien,* by M. Noth
VT	Vetus Testamentum
WO	Die Welt des Orients
ZAW	Zeitschrift für die alttestamentliche Wissenschaft
ZDPV	Zeitschrift des deutschen Palästina-Vereins

For references to books, see Selected Bibliography.

2. Versions

Aq.	Ancient Greek translation of the Old Testament by Aquila
ATD	Das Alte Testament Deutsch
LXX	The Septuagint
MT	Masoretic Text
RSV	Revised Standard Version
Syr.	Syriac version, the Peshitta
Targ.	Targum, Aramaic translation or paraphrase
Vrs.	Ancient versions generally
Vulg.	The Vulgate

3. Other Abbreviations

Akk.	Akkadian
Ar.	Arabic
Aram.	Aramaic
Bab.	Babylonian
Eg.	Egyptian
Eng.	English
Fr.	French
Ger.	German
Gr.	Greek
Heb.	Hebrew
Kh.	Khirbet
Lat.	Latin
OT	Old Testament
Phoen.	Phoenician
Sem.	Semitic
Sum.	Sumerian

INTRODUCTION

THE WORK OF THE CHRONICLER IN THE BIBLE

In many respects the work of the Chronicler—I Chronicles, II Chronicles, Ezra, and Nehemiah—has been one of the most neglected portions of the Old Testament. Where it had to be dealt with, it was done grudgingly, often with misunderstanding, misgiving, or downright hostility. However, archaeological and historical studies have now rendered it more respectable and have shown it to be at times more accurate than some of its parallel sources. Naturally the Chronicler had a particular purpose in mind and, where he found more than one source to draw from for a story he wanted to use, he followed the one more harmonious with and adequate for his purpose.

Doubtless the position of Ezra, Nehemiah, and Chronicles in both Jewish and Christian canons has had much to do with the attitude of general Bible readers toward them. Their form and content, dictated in large measure by the peculiar interests of the writer(s), makes them rather dull for the modern reader. To those without an understanding and appreciation of the historical milieu and purpose of the work, genealogies, lists, exaggerated statistics, lengthy and detailed descriptions of religious forms and institutions, etc., can be rather depressing. The contrast is striking when the Chronicler's work is compared with the immediately preceding (Christian canon) Deuteronomic history, which reads much better because it appears more in line with the methods of modern historiography.

It seems a bit strange that the Chronicler's efforts should have been dismissed so lightly in view of the fact that his work comes from just that period in Hebrew history about which so little is otherwise known. The spade of the archaeologist is beginning to fill in the gaps of that period and, with a more appreciative and controlled study of the written materials, we can now be fairly certain of a good many of the hitherto obscure references and details. Supplementing the historical materials of Samuel and Kings and carrying the history of the fortunes of the Jews down to the fourth century

B.C., these books become extremely important. Properly understood and interpreted, they throw much welcome light on this confused period.

THE TITLE OF THE HEBREW BOOKS

The title of Chronicles in Hebrew is *dibrē hayyāmīm,* that is, chronicles of events, happenings of the days, records of the days or times. It was a rather widely used expression in Kings where it occurs some thirty-two times, referring to the book or record of the chronicles of the kings of Israel and Judah; it occurs twice in Esther (x 2)—the chronicles of the kings of Media and Persia. In Esther vi 1 it is used to cite the record of the memorable events in the history of Persia. Interestingly enough, the expression is found only twice in the work of the Chronicler—I Chron xxvii 24 and Neh xii 23. The present books of Chronicles were originally reckoned as one book.

THE TITLE IN THE VERSIONS

Our present Greek and Latin versions of Chronicles are called *Paraleipomena,* that is, things left over or omitted in the histories of Samuel and Kings, especially as they involve Judah. The use of the term Chronicles goes back to Luther who took it from St. Jerome's *Prologus geleatus* which has the following notice: *Dabre Aiamim, id est Verba Dierum, quod significatius totius divinae historiae possumus appellare, qui liber apud nos primus et secundus inscribitur* (Dabre Aiamim, that is the events of the days which we might significantly call the meaning of the whole sacred history, which book is entitled first and second by us). The Syriac follows the Hebrew.

PLACE IN THE CANON

In the Hebrew canon, the work of the Chronicler stands in the third division—the *Kethubim* (writings)—and last in that division. In our present canonical arrangement, Ezra-Nehemiah appears to be the sequel to Samuel and Kings. Though that was not originally the case, it may have been the origin of the division at the end of II Chronicles. Hence the history of Ezra begins just after the end of II Kings. This also explains the order of the books, that is, Chronicles after Ezra-Nehemiah, and accounts for the repetition of the ending of II Chronicles at the beginning of Ezra (indicating that the present order of the books is awkward). The separation of Ezra from Chronicles may have resulted from the incorporation of Ezra-Nehemiah into the Bible as a supplement to the story of Samuel and Kings, which occurred after Samuel and Kings had been canonized and therefore could no longer be tampered with. Chronicles, then, was added later. It is the last book in the Hebrew Bible and may have been viewed as a kind of appendix to the writings. The Greek Bible placed Chronicles, Ezra, and Nehemiah in the historical section in the following order: Chronicles, Esdras A, Esdras B (our Ezra-Nehemiah). That was the order followed by St. Jerome and Luther, and hence in our English Bibles, except that Esdras A (apocryphal Ezra) has been relegated to the Apocrypha while Esdras B appears as Ezra and Nehemiah.

THE INTENTION OF THE CHRONICLER[1]

Chronicles, Ezra, and Nehemiah are so closely related in thought, language, and theology that not only must they have come from a single hand, with possibly a few exceptions, but, like the other great literature of Israel, their author must have had in view a purpose that the earlier histories of his people did not meet in the form in which they had been transmitted.

The intent of the Chronicler was neither to rewrite the history of Judah nor specifically to gather together what had not been covered by his predecessors. His work is a lesson for the people of his time and situation drawn from the history of his people.[2] It might be referred to as a series of lectures or sermons on the bearing of that history upon the needs of the hour. Benzinger has said, "The Chronicler is not at all a writer of history in our sense of the term; he does not aim to relate what took place but what serves to edify; he is not a historian but a Midrashist."[3] C. C. Torrey has written in almost the same vein.[4] But just because the Chronicler is a "Midrashist" does not necessarily mean that he is a purveyor of pure fiction; he may look at history with some bias and omit or add material when it suits his purpose.

[1] For a summary of the historicoreligious situation and a discussion of the aim of the Chronicler in the light of his situation, see the comprehensive introduction to the Chronicler's work in *I Chronicles.*

[2] See G. von Rad, "Die levitische Predigt in den Bücher der Chronik" in *Gesammelte Studien zum Alten Testament,* pp. 248–61; *Das Geschichtsbild des Chronistischen Werkes,* pp. 133 f. (For complete references, see Selected Bibliography.)

[3] *Die Bücher der Chronik,* p. x (see Benzinger, Selected Bibliography, Commentaries).

[4] "The Composition and Historical Value of Ezra-Nehemiah," BZAW 2 (1896), 65. Cf. *Ezra Studies,* pp. 153–55, 208–13 (see Torrey, Selected Bibliography).

CONTENTS OF II CHRONICLES[5]

II Chron i–ix is devoted to the activities of Solomon. It begins
with the new king's establishing himself in his position and his
prayer for wisdom (i 1–17) and then proceeds immediately to a
particularization of preparations for the construction of the temple
(ii 1–18) and the formation of the corvée. The plans for the temple
(iii), provision for its equipment (iv) and the dedication (v 1–
vii 10) follow. Solomon's vision, administrative activity—both
secular and religious—(vii 11–viii 18), the visit of the queen of
Sheba (ix 1–12) and an inventory of the royal revenue and trade
activity (ix 13–31) conclude the part. In the estimation of the
Chronicler, Solomon is an extension of David, that is, the one who
carried out the directions issued by the great king, though he did
reflect wisdom and piety in his own right.

II Chron x–xxxvi rehearses the story of Judah as seen by the
writer and enacted through its kings. In some respects, this story is
the fulfillment of the divine promise to David by Nathan (I Chron
xvii 13) and reaffirmed by Yahweh to Solomon (II Chron vii 18).
In line with his method of dealing with history, this part centers
about personalities, generally kings of Judah. The story begins with
an account of the attitude of Rehoboam which led to a division of
the kingdom (x) and a report on the progress of his plans for a
separate administration—dissuasion from attacking Jeroboam, construction of fortress cities, the gravitation of the Levites to his territory (xi). Chapter xii deals with the invasion of Shishak with its
consequences and the Chronicler's emphasis on the submission of
the king in harmony with the demands of prophecy; it closes with
the usual notice of the king's character, years of reign, death, and
burial. The reign of Abijah is covered in a single chapter (xiii)

[5] A full discussion of the literary considerations in Chronicles may be
found in the general introduction to *I Chronicles*.

which limits itself almost entirely to that king's campaign against
Jeroboam which ended disastrously for the latter. The Chronicler's
narrative of Asa includes a note on the ten years of peace at the
beginning of his reign, his active participation in the religious purification of the land, and a more lengthy reference to Asa's defense
against Zerah the Ethiopian (xiv). Chapter xv contains the prophecy of Azariah, son of Oded, and its results. The third chapter (xvi)
devoted to Asa describes his altercation with Baasha of Israel,
which involved an alliance between the former and Benhadad of
Damascus against Baasha, and the prophecy of Hanani against Asa
and its consequences. One of the favorite characters of our author
was Jehoshaphat (xvii 1–xxi 1) whose exploits are set forth at
some length. Chapter xvii begins with a general summation of Jehoshaphat's reign and then enumerates some of the deeds of the
king—the instruction of the people (7–9), the tribute received by
him (10–13) and the garrisoning of the fortified cities of Judah
(14–19). His association with Ahab, king of Israel, in the Ramoth-
gilead campaign, the prophecy of Micaiah ben Imlah associated
with it and the outcome of the battle are related in chapter xviii.
Jehoshaphat was rebuked for participating by Jehu ben Hanani (xix
1–3) a prophet. The judicial reform (xix 11) was of great
significance. The campaign against the Transjordan confederation
composed of Ammonites, Moabites, and Meunites is the subject of
xx 1–30. The summary of Jehoshaphat's reign, his alliance with
Ahaziah, the maritime fiasco at Ezion-geber, and his death and
burial are recounted in xx 31–xxi 1. The remainder of chapter xxi
deals with the reign of the wicked Jehoram, who slew his brothers,
was allied by marriage with the house of Ahab, defeated the Edomites, received a letter from Elijah, suffered an invasion by Philistines and Arabs, and was the victim of a loathsome disease. Chapter xxii presents the story of Ahaziah, his death at the hands of
Jehu, and the usurpation of the throne by Athaliah, his mother.
The purge was not long in coming, as we learn from the success of
Jehoiada in putting Joash on the throne (xxiii). Things went well
while Jehoiada lived (xxiv 1–16), but after his death the king defected. When Zechariah, son of Jehoiada, reprimanded him, Joash
put Zechariah to death. An Aramaean invasion followed and Joash
was killed, the victim of a palace intrigue (xxiv 17–27). Joash
was succeeded by Amaziah who, in accordance with prophetic ad-

vice, rejected Israelite assistance in his war with Edom. But, like his father, he turned away from Yahweh and became proud. The end was defeat, humiliation, and capture at the hands of Joash of Israel. Finally Amaziah was slain, by conspirators, at Lachish (xxv). The reigns of Uzziah and Jotham are of more than ordinary importance. The former was apparently a successful ruler (xxvi 1–15), but, like many others, overstepped his bounds (xxvi 16–23). Jotham's policy was a continuation of his father's (xxvii). The rule of the wicked Ahaz is dealt with most unsympathetically (xxviii). As in the case of Jehoshaphat, four chapters are devoted to Hezekiah (xxix–xxxii). The first act of Hezekiah was to issue orders for the cleansing of the temple (xxix) and the reinstitution of orderly worship. The Chronicler's ascription of a magnificent passover celebration to this king is given in chapter xxx; the following chapter (xxxi) is devoted to the religious reformation of Hezekiah. Chapter xxxii 1–23 is concerned with the invasion of Sennacherib and Hezekiah's reaction to it—his strengthening of the capital and his and Isaiah's prayers about the insults of the Assyrians hurled against the city and people—and the miraculous deliverance of Jerusalem. A summary statement on the achievements of the king follows (xxxii 24–33). Manasseh, the son of Hezekiah, acted haughtily toward Yahweh, followed the Assyrian cult, and desecrated the house of God (xxxiii 1–9). Finally there is the account of his capture by the Assyrians, his repentance and amends, and an evaluation of his reign (xxxiii 10–20). Nothing good is said about Amon who reverted to the evils practiced by his father before his repentance. He was slain by his own servants (xxxiii 21–25). Josiah is portrayed in almost the same glowing terms as Hezekiah. As soon as he reached the proper age he began the general reform (xxxiv 1–7) that led to the repair of the temple and finding the book of the law, which became the program for further cultic reformation (xxxiv 8–35). A spectacular observance of the passover followed (xxxv 1–19). The account of Josiah closes with the king's death at Megiddo where he attempted to thwart Pharaoh Neco in his hasty march to the Euphrates to assist the Assyrians against their opponents (xxxv 20–27). Succeeding reigns are passed over rapidly (xxxvi 1–21). Chronicles ends with a reference to the rise of Cyrus and his benevolent attitude toward the captive Jews in Babylon (xxxvi 22–23).

USE OF THE SOURCES[6]

One of the most difficult problems arising from the study of the literary composition of Chronicles, Ezra, and Nehemiah is the origin and use of the compiler's sources. Can his references to the sources noted in the previous section be taken seriously or were they already present in the anthology employed by him? The answer to that question will, to some extent, determine the evaluation placed on materials transmitted by the Chronicler which are not found elsewhere. R. H. Pfeiffer thinks he draws about one half of his material from earlier biblical books, while the other half consists, for the most part, of more or less historical fiction.[7] B. Maisler thinks that both Kings and Chronicles were dependent on "the words" of the prophets and famous personalities to a very large extent and to a lesser degree on the temple chronicles and official records.[8] The Chronicler's use of his sources is closely related to his purpose, his theology and general point of view,[9] which in turn depend on one's interpretation.[10] In the following resume only the barest facts can be stated, but it is absolutely essential for purposes of evaluation of the problem. For the sake of convenience, the outline follows the one above on content.

Solomon's reign and activity (II Chron i–ix)[11]

i—Solomon's prayer with Yahweh's response (i 7–12 ‖ I Kings iii 5–15; i 14–17 ‖ I Kings x 26–29; i 5 ‖ Exod xxxviii 1 ff.).

[6] Based on M. Noth's analysis in ÜS, pp. 131–50. A complete discussion of the sources of the Chronicler's work is given in the comprehensive introduction to *I Chronicles*.

[7] *Introduction to the Old Testament*, pp. 803 ff.

[8] "Ancient Israelite Historiography," IEJ 2 (1952), 82–88.

[9] See A. M. Burnet, "Le Chroniste et ses sources," RB 60 (1953), 481–508; RB 60 (1954), 349–86.

[10] Cf. Noth, ÜS, pp. 110–80. Also Rothstein and Hänel, *Kommentar zum ersten Buch der Chronik*, pp. ix–lxxxii; Galling, *Die Bücher der Chronik, Esra, Nehemia*, pp. 8–12; Rudolph, pp. x–xxiv; Goettsberger, *Die Bücher der Chronik oder Paralipomenon*, pp. 6–17; Curtis and Madsen, pp. 17–26; and the various introductions (for complete references, see Selected Bibliography, Commentaries).

[11] Noth is certainly correct in assuming that the material of this section is pretty much as it left the hand of the Chronicler—ÜS, pp. 116 f.

Note resort to Gibeon for sacrifice where altar of Bezalel was located at the tent of meeting. Jerusalem had not yet attained its later status. The ark was at Jerusalem, but was associated only with musical service and not with sacrifices.

ii–vii—Temple affairs (ii 3 ‖ I Kings v 3 ff.; ii 7 ‖ v 6; ii 11 ‖ v 7; ii 16–17 ‖ v 13–18, not very close, iii ‖ v, vii, not close; iv 2–5 ‖ vii 23–26; iv 10–22 ‖ vii 39–50; v 1–14 ‖ vii 51–viii 11; vi 1–40 ‖ viii 12–53; vi 41–42 ‖ Ps cxxxii 8–11; vii 1–10 ‖ viii 54–66, not verbally close; vii 11–22 ‖ ix 1–9; vii 1–3a ‖ Exod xl 34 f. and Lev ix 24). Nearly all commentators agree that the writer's source here was the Deuteronomic book of Kings. There may be a few minor additions such as v 11b–13a, vii 6, 9, vii 12b–15. But the author has not lost sight of his aim, that is, the temple, and has omitted matters apparently irrelevant to him (cf. rest of the records and II Chron ix 29); he has transmitted the tradition in his own words.

viii–ix, External matters pertaining to Solomon: his campaign to Hamath-zobah, corvée, fulfillment of religious obligations in accordance with the commands of David, shipping and trade through Ezion-geber, the visit of the queen of Sheba which reminds the writer of the wealth of Solomon made to minister to the glory of God (ix 11). Omissions and inclusions may be seen from the following: viii 1–18 ‖ I Kings ix 10–28; ix 1–28 ‖ I Kings x 1–29 (ix 26 ‖ I Kings v 1); ix 29–31 ‖ I Kings xi 41–43.[12]

Other kings of Judah (II Chronicles x–xxxvi)

x–xii, Rehoboam's reign (x 1–19 ‖ I Kings i–xx [Chronicles omits vs. 20]; xi 1–4 ‖ I Kings xii 21–24; xi 5–17 ‖ xii 25–23). Chronicles expands and omits in last passage. The list of Rehoboam's fortified cities is historically trustworthy.[13] The Levitical exodus from Israel to Jerusalem fortified the Chronicler's

---

[12] On II Chron viii 2–6 see C. H. Gordon, IEJ 5 (1955), 88.

[13] G. Beyer, "Das Festungssystem Rehabeams," ZDPV 54 (1931), 113–34; K. Elliger, ZDPV 57 (1934), 87 ff.; Alt, "Festungen und Levitenorte im Land Juda," KS, II, pp. 306–15; W. F. Albright, "The Judicial Reform of Jehoshaphat," AMJV, pp. 66 f. Whether the fortification took place before or after the Shishak invasion is not clear, but R. Kittel, (GVI, II, p. 223) suggests it was afterward.

conception that only at Jerusalem is true Yahwism to be found and thus is doubtless tendentious, though it rests on a factual basis as may be judged by Jeroboam's construction in his kingdom of religious centers with a more conservative tendency (I Kings xii 27 ff.). The family list of Rehoboam[14] is derived from a special source and is at least partially historical. Chapter xi 23 indicates that he carried out the policies of his father (I Kings iv 8–19). Chapter xii 1–12, the invasion of Shishak, depends on I Kings xiv 25–28; xii 13–14 ‖ I Kings xiv 21–22; xii 15–16 is a variant of I Kings xiv 29–31, but not because different sources are mentioned.

xiii—Abijah. Greatly expanded from I Kings xv 1–8. Abijah's successful war with Israel is probably historical,[15] though it has some typical Chronicler touches. The Northerners were probably more numerous and powerful than the Judeans— as was the case between Samaritans and returnees in the time of the writer. Abijah's victory was due to an alliance with the Aramaeans (cf. I Kings xv 19) and brought Benjamin into the camp of Judah. Observe the theological tendency of Abijah's address to Jeroboam. In the reign of Asa, a portion of Benjamin was in Southern hands, thanks to the intervention of Benhadad (I Kings xv 19–22).[16] The best proof of the Chronicler's assertion is Baasha's attempt to retake some of the lost territory (I Kings xv 17).

xiv–xvi—Asa (xiv 1 ‖ I Kings xv 11; xv 16–19 ‖ I Kings xv 13–15; xvi 1–6 ‖ I Kings xv 17–22; xvi 11–14 ‖ I Kings xv 23–24). The Chronicler has greatly embellished the material found in Kings, for which he had other unutilized sources at his command. Albright thinks an Egyptian colony composed of Cushites was settled between Egypt and Judah by Shishak. This was the force that Asa subdued in part (xiv 9–15), but he did not succeed in taking their capital at Gerar. Since the booty included camels, the Cushites were doubtless assisted by

---

[14] See Noth, ÜS, p. 143, n. 1.

[15] Cf. Kittel, GVI, II, pp. 224 f. Noth, *The History of Israel*, p. 233, attributes it to Rehoboam. Cf. Noth, ÜS, p. 142. Bright, *A History of Israel*, p. 215, and Rudolph, pp. 235–39, also think it is historical.

[16] On Benhadad's first invasion of Israel (II Chron xv 19–xvi 6) see W. F. Albright in BASOR 87 (October 1942), 27 f.

the bedouin.[17] In view of this fact it is within the range of possibility that Asa built, perhaps rebuilt, fortified cities (xiv 6). That he engaged in reforming activity is attested also by Kings.[18] xvii–xx—Jehoshaphat (xviii 1–34 || I Kings xx 1–36; xx 31–37 || I Kings xxii 41–47). The Kings parallels may safely be regarded as representing the Chronicler's views of the received tradition. The judicial reform is factual.[19] The miraculous deliverance of Jehoshaphat from a coalition of Moabites, Ammonites, and Arabs sounds very much like the Israel-Aramaean affair described in II Kings vii. Behind it lies a historical nucleus,[20] though it is difficult to get at the precise facts. As usual the story is shot through with Levitical themes of the Chronicler—the piety of Jehoshaphat, the message of the Levitical prophet (xx 14), the Levitical praises (19 f.), singers appointed to praise Yahweh (21) and the valley of Beracah (blessing). Note the reasons given for the failure of the maritime venture (36–37; cf. I Kings xxii 47–50a).[21]

xxi—Jehoram (xxi 1 || I Kings xxii 51; xxi 2–11 || II Kings viii 16–22). Apparently the Chronicler had another source besides Kings since he reports Jehoram's slaying of his brothers, which is not beyond belief because other kings had done the same and because they may have objected to his policies (cf. II Chron xxi 13). The revolt of Edom and Libnah is reported also in Kings. The defection of Philistine areas (submissive under Jehoshaphat, II Chron xvii 11) and the restlessness of the bedouin in the south is quite possible under such unstable conditions—a legitimate assumption on the basis of other revolts successfully carried out against the king of Judah.[22]

xxii—Ahaziah and Athaliah (xxii 1–6 || II Kings viii 24b–29; xxii 7–9 || II Kings ix 20, 21, 27, 28; xxii 10–12 || II Kings xi 1–3). The slaying of Ahaziah's sons is utilized by the writer as

[17] W. F. Albright, "Egypt and the Early History of the Negeb," JPOS 4 (1924), 146 f.
[18] Albright, ARI, pp. 157–59.
[19] Albright, AMJV, pp. 74–82. I Chron xvii 7–9 may be a doublet describing the reform movement.
[20] M. Noth, "Eline palästinische Lokalüberlieferung in 2 Chron. 20," ZDPV 67 (1944/45), 45 ff.
[21] Cf. N. Glueck in BASOR 79 (October 1940), 8.
[22] Cf. Kittel, GVI, p. 264, n. 6.

retaliation for Jehoram's slaying of his brothers (xxii 1). His enthronement was probably the act of Jerusalem's officialdom who assumed the function of the *am-ha-aretz*. The latter had apparently been pushed into the background by the adoption of Northern policy in Judah because of the close relationship with the Ahab dynasty. That policy was doubtless followed by Athaliah. The rest of the material is from Kings.

xxiii—Jehoiada's acts in behalf of Joash (xxiii 1–21 ‖ II Kings xi 4–20, with some additions by the Chronicler). The additions are interesting; the priests and Levites participate in the plot to thwart Athaliah whereas in Kings only the Carians and guards are mentioned.[23]

xxiv—The reign of Joash (‖ II Kings xii). In addition to the three facts mentioned in Kings, the Chronicler supplies from his source the reference to his family (vs. 3), the death of Jehoiada (vss. 15–16) and the murder of Zechariah, the priest's son (vss. 20–22). In connection with the restoration of the temple, the Levites occupy the center of the stage rather than the priests. The Aramaean invasion is toned down considerably. These additions may well be historical, at least in essence; the Zechariah incident reflects the writer's interest in the prophets though, if historical, was given a peculiar religious twist.

xxv—Amaziah (xxv 1–4 ‖ II Kings xiv 1–6; xxv 11 ‖ II Kings xiv 7; xxv 17–24 ‖ II Kings xiv 8–14; xxv 25–28 ‖ II Kings xiv 17–20). Theologizing is very evident at two points: the prophet forbidding the use of Israelite mercenaries because Yahweh is not with Israel, and the statement that Amaziah served the gods of Edom which he had captured and brought to Jerusalem. There may have been some provocation for Amaziah's challenge of Joash (vs. 13), though the allegory of the thistle and the cedar in both accounts strongly suggests the pride of the former. The defeat of Amaziah and the conspiracy against him are interpreted as punishment for his failure to heed the prophet.

xxvi—Uzziah (Azariah) (xxvi 1–2 ‖ II Kings xiv 21–22; xxvi 3–4 ‖ II Kings xv 2–3; xxvi 20–23 ‖ II Kings xv 5–7). A whole

---

[23] On the whole episode see W. Rudolph, "Die Einheitlichkeit der Erzählung vom Sturz Atalja," FAB, pp. 473–78, and Würthwein, *Der 'amm* . . . , pp. 22 ff.

mass of information is preserved here that is not found in Kings. Archaeological discoveries offer ample evidence of great building activity in this period. Towers were constructed in the wilderness and cisterns carved out.[24] Elath was rebuilt and Jerusalem fortified. The position of the priests is shown by their rebuke of Uzziah for overstepping his bounds in offering incense.[25]

xxvii—Jotham (xxvii 1–3 || II Kings xv 33–35; xxvii 7 || II Kings xv 36; xxvii 9 || II Kings xv 38). The Chronicler notes that Jotham continued the policies of his father. That appears pretty well established by archaeological results. His success is attributed to the fact that "he did what was right in the sight of Yahweh" and did not go into the temple.

xxviii—Ahaz (xxviii 1–5 || II Kings xvi 2–5; xxviii 16 || II Kings xvi 6–7; xxviii 20 || II Kings xvi 9; xxviii 26–27 || II Kings xvi 19–20). Chapter preserves some historical material not in Kings. The Edomite-Philistine uprising is quite plausible in the light of Assyrian inscriptions.[26] The list of Ephraimite chiefs came from the source. Of interest is the notice of the prophet Oded and his declaration of Israel's guilt; so also the reference to the Israelites as brothers of the Judahites (vss. 8, 11, 15), which may be due to his theology.

xxix–xxxii—Hezekiah (xxix 1–2 || II Kings xviii 1–3; xxxi 1 || II Kings xviii 4; xxxii 1–2 || II Kings xviii 13, Isa xxxvi 1; xxxii 9–15 || II Kings xviii 17, 19, 22, 35, 33, 29, Isa xxxvi 2, 4, 7, 14, 20, 18; xxxii 20–21 || II Kings xix 15, 35–37, Isa xxxvii 36–38; xxxii 24 || II Kings xx 1–2, Isa xxxviii 1–2; xxxii 31 || II Kings xx 12–13, Isa xxxix 1–2; xxxii 33 || II Kings xx 20–21). The Chronicler reflects only eighteen verses of Kings; the other material is his own (approximately 100 verses). He regards Hezekiah as more than a descendant of David; he is vir-

---

[24] Cf. F. M. Cross, Jr., and J. T. Milik, BASOR 142 (April 1956), 5–17. They favor the age of Jehoshaphat but admit that the activity in the Judean Buqe'ah could have taken place under Uzziah. Iron II sherds and an inscribed ostracon were found at Qumran (RB 61 [1954], 567); also an Israelite installation and cistern attributed by Father de Vaux to Jotham or Uzziah (RB 63 [1956], 535 f.). Cf. the fortress at Hurvat 'Uzzah; see Y. Aharoni, "The Negeb of Judah," IEJ 8 (1958), 37. For an archaeological summary, see F. Feuillet, VT 11 (1961), 270–91.

[25] See further the discussion in the COMMENT on Sec. 28.

[26] See references in COMMENT on Sec. 30.

tually a second David. The Levites figure prominently in his special material; he combines the musical services with sacrifices at the temple. Emphasis is placed on the king's observance of the commandments of David. There is nothing improbable in the outline of Hezekiah's reforming and missionary activity.[27] The fortification of Jerusalem and preparations for siege are doubtless historical.

xxxiii 1–20—Manasseh (xxxiii 1–10 || II Kings xxi 1–10; xxxiii 18–20 || II Kings xxi 17–18). The Chronicles source included the story of Manasseh's conversion, an attempt to explain the long reign of Judah's worst king.[28] Some of the story may be true, especially that dealing with the Assyrian captivity.

xxxiii 21–25—Amon (|| II Kings xxi 19–24). Source here was Kings, which was somewhat curtailed.

xxxiv–xxxv—Josiah (xxxiv 1–2 || II Kings xxii 1–2; xxxiv 8–28 || II Kings xxii 3–20; xxxiv 29–33 || II Kings xxiii 1–3; xxxv 1 || II Kings xxiii 21; xxxv 18–19 || II Kings xxiii 22–23; xxxv 20 || II Kings xxiii 29; xxxv 24 || II Kings xxiii 30a). Of the fifty verses of II Kings, some thirty are paralleled in II Chron. The Chronicler has expanded the story by using materials unknown or rejected by the Deuteronomist. Josiah's reforming activity began in his twelfth year (ca. 629 B.C.), a few years before the death of Asshurbanipal, and the relative inactivity of the Assyrians in the west. His concern for the people of the north follows that of Hezekiah. His conflict with Neco is correctly interpreted (xxxv 20) and must come from his source.[29] Josiah aspired to become another David and his religio-political activity is, in general, correctly reflected by the writer. He brings in his favorite Levites and mentions the prophetess Huldah. The Levites were the teachers of all Israel (xxxv 3) and participants in the preparations for the passover.

xxxvi 1–4—Jehoahaz (|| II Kings xxiii 30b–34). Source curtailed.

[27] Chapter xxx has been unduly suspected (cf. W. F. Albright, JBL 58 [1939], 185). On the whole situation see Albright, BP, p. 42; Kittel, GVI, II, p. 376.

[28] E. Meyer, GA, III p. 60, n. 1. For other references see COMMENT on Sec. 36.

[29] Cf. Couroyer, "Le litige entre Josias et Nechao," RB 55 (1948), 388–96; M. B. Rowton, "Jeremiah and the Death of Josiah," JNES 10 (1951), 128–30; D. J. Wiseman, *Chronicles of Chaldaean Kings*, 1956, pp. 18 ff.

xxxvi 5–8—Jehoiakim (|| II Kings xxiii 34–37; xxiv 1, 5, 6). Also somewhat shortened. His being bound in chains is connected with a revolt against Nebuchadnezzar after the latter's indecisive campaign against Egypt in 601 B.C.[30]

xxxvi 9–10—Jehoiachin (|| II Kings xxiv 8–10, 16b–17). A greatly condensed version of the essentials as given in Kings and now known from the Weidner texts.[31]

xxxvi 11–21—Zedekiah (11–13a || II Kings xxiv 18–20, Jer lii 1–3). The twenty-five verses of Kings have been condensed to eleven and the historical events theologized. The writer's reference to the duration of the Exile (20) marks a good transition point for the last verses, which were added after the completion of the work.

xxxvi 22–23—The decree of Cyrus (|| Ezra i 1–3a).

Conclusion

The Chronicler had at his disposal the priestly redaction of the tetrateuch and the great history of the Deuteronomist, which included the books of Deuteronomy, Joshua, Judges, Samuel, and Kings. The fact that he omitted much material indicates only that it did not contribute to his purpose—not that he rejected it as untrue; it was clearly available to him, as his use of surrounding matter demonstrates. The inclusion of material supplementary to that of the Deuteronomist does not of itself mean that he wanted to add to the sum total of historical knowledge; it may indicate only that additions or omissions supported his main thesis in a given situation. Where he followed the Deuteronomist exactly, it may be presumed to have represented his point of view.

It is fairly certain that he was in possession of copies of official documents and memoirs (Ezra and Nehemiah), as well as of official lists of various types which he may have completed partly from oral tradition and partly from studies and collections of his own. The availability and use of some independent prophetic materials appear quite plausible. Moreover, sources of information not found elsewhere but which were drawn from the archives of the temple and

[30] He may have bought off Nebuchadnezzar. See Wiseman, *op. cit.,* pp. 29 f.; D. N. Freedman, *The Biblical Archaeologist Reader,* 1961, pp. 113–27.

[31] W. F. Albright, "King Jehoiachin in Exile," BA 5 (1942), 49–55.

were authentic, as can be shown from archaeological discoveries and topographical studies, were utilized.

The matter of recensions is difficult and no firm conclusion is possible. That there were later additions to some stories, perhaps whole stories compiled and inserted, can hardly be doubted, but it seems unwise to conclude that there was wholesale revision or major rewriting of the original work. It would appear that the work is pretty much as it was when it left the hands of the author, with the exception of the additions which may have been intended to bring it up to date or make it applicable to a slightly later period. Furthermore, within the limits of its purpose, the Chronicler's story is accurate wherever it can be checked, though the method of presentation is homiletical. The only valid objection to the foregoing statement could be his numbers which, by any interpretation, are impossibly high. This fact perhaps more than any other has made the Chronicler's work suspect.

The reader may wish to consult the general introduction to the work of the Chronicler, which appears as the Introduction to *I Chronicles,* on THE THEOLOGY OF THE CHRONICLER (The Chronicler's Conception of God, Worship, Israel as God's People, The Prophets and the Torah, and Messianism) and AUTHORSHIP AND DATE.

SELECTED BIBLIOGRAPHY

COMMENTARIES

Barnes, W. E., *The Books of the Chronicles* (Cambridge Bible for Schools and Colleges). Cambridge, 1899.

Benzinger, I., *Die Bücher der Chronik* (Kurzer Hand-Commentar zum Alten Testament). Tübingen und Leipzig: Mohr, 1901.

Cazelles, H., *Les Livres des Chroniques* (La Sainte Bible). Paris: Cerf, 1954.

Curtis, E. L., and Madsen, A. A., *A Critical and Exegetical Commentary on the Books of Chronicles* (The International Critical Commentary). New York: Scribner's, 1910.

Elmslie, W. A. L., "The First and Second Books of Chronicles," *The Interpreter's Bible*, III, pp. 339–548. New York and Nashville: Abingdon Press, 1954.

Galling, K., *Die Bücher der Chronik, Esra, Nehemia* (Das Alte Testament Deutsch). Göttingen: Vandenhoeck & Ruprecht, 1954.

Goettsberger, J., *Die Bücher der Chronik oder Paralipomenon* (Die heilige Schrift des Alten Testaments, XII). Bonn: Peter Hanstein, 1939.

Haller, M., *Chronik* (Die Schriften des Alten Testaments, II, 3, pp. 330–54). Göttingen: Vandenhoeck & Ruprecht, 2d ed., 1925.

Kittel, R., *Die Bücher der Chronik und Esra, Nehemia und Esther* (Handkommentar zum Alten Testament). Göttingen: Vandenhoeck & Ruprecht, 1902.

Noordtzij, A., *De Boeken der Kronieken* (Korte Verklaring der Heilige Schrift). Kampen: J. H. Kok, 2d ed., 1957 (2 vols.).

Rehm, M., *Die Bücher der Chronik* (Echter-Bibel). Würzburg: Echter-Verlag, 1934.

Rothstein, J. W., and Hänel, J., *Kommentar zum ersten Buch der Chronik* (Kommentar zum Alten Testament). Leipzig: A. Deichert, 1927.

Rudolph, W., *Chronikbücher* (Handbuch zum Alten Testament). Tübingen: Mohr, 1955.

Slotki, I. W., *Chronicles* (Soncino Books of the Bible). London: The Soncino Press, 1952.

Van Den Born, A., *Kronieken* (De Boeken van Het Oude Testament). Roermond en Maaseik: J. J. Romen & Zonen, 1960.

Van Selms, A., *I-II Kronieken* (Tekst en Uitleg). Groningen-Batavia: J. B. Wolter, 1939, 1947.

OTHER WORKS

Abel, F. M., *Géographie de la Palestine*. Paris: Gabalda, 1933, 1938.

Albright, W. F., *Archaeology and the Religion of Israel* (abbr. ARI). Johns Hopkins Press, 1942.

————, *From the Stone Age to Christianity* (abbr. FSAC). New York: Doubleday Anchor Books, 1957.

Alexander Marx Jubilee Volume, English Section (abbr. AMJV). New York: The Jewish Theological Seminary of America, 1950.

Alt, A., *Kleine Schriften zur Geschichte des Volkes Israel* (abbr. KS). Munich: Beck, 3 vols., 1953–59.

Bright, John, *A History of Israel*. Philadelphia: Westminster Press, 1959.

Cowley, A., ed. and tr., *Aramaic Papyri of the Fifth Century B.C.* (abbr. AP). Oxford: Clarendon Press, 1923.

Ehrlich, A. B., *Randglossen zur hebräischen Bibel*, VII. Leipzig: Hinrichs, 1914.

Festschrift für Alfred Bertholet (abbr. FAB). Tübingen: Mohr, 1950.

Gressmann, H., ed., *Altorientalische Bilder zum Alten Testament* (abbr. AOT). Berlin and Leipzig: Walter de Gruyter, 2d ed., 1927.

Junge, E., *Die Wiederaufbau des Heerwesens des Reiches Juda unter Josia*. Stuttgart: Kohlhammer, 1937.

Kittel, R., *Geschichte des Volkes Israel* (abbr. GVI). 3 vols., 1923–29: Vols. I, II (Gotha: Leopold Klotz Verlag, 1923, 1925); Vol. III (Stuttgart: Kohlhammer, 1927, 1929).

Kraeling, E. G. H., ed., *The Brooklyn Museum Aramaic Papyri* (abbr. BMAP). Yale University Press, 1953.

Kropat, A., "Die Syntax des Autors der Chronik" (*Beihefte zur Zeitschrift für die alttestamentliche Wissenschaft*). Giessen: A. Töpelmann, 1909.

Kugler, F. X., *Von Moses bis Paulus* (pp. 234–300). Munster: 1922.

Louis Ginzberg Jubilee Volume, English Section (abbr. LGJV). New York: The American Academy for Jewish Research, 1945.

Luckenbill, D. D., ed., *Ancient Records of Assyria and Babylonia* (abbr. ARAB). University of Chicago Press, 1926, 1927.

Meyer, E., *Die Entstehung des Judenthums* (abbr. EJ). Halle: Niemeyer, 1896.

————, *Geschichte des Altertums* (abbr. GA). Darmstadt: Wissenschaftliche Buchgemeinschaft (reprint), 1953–58, 3d ed., 1954.

————, *Kleine Schriften.* Halle: Niemeyer, 2d ed., 1924.

Noth, M., *Die israelitischen Personennamen im Rahmen der gemeinsemitischen Namengebung* (abbr. IPN) (*Beiträge zur Wissenschaft vom Alten und Neuen Testament*). Stuttgart: Kohlhammer, 1928.

————, *The History of Israel.* New York: Harper, 1958.

————, *Überlieferungsgeschichtliche Studien* (abbr. ÜS). Tübingen: Niemeyer Verlag, 2d ed., 1957.

Pritchard, J. B., ed., *The Ancient Near East in Pictures Relating to the Old Testament* (abbr. ANEP). Princeton University Press, 1954.

————, *Ancient Near Eastern Texts Relating to the Old Testament* (abbr. ANET). Princeton University Press, 2d ed., 1955.

Rehm, M., *Textkritische Untersuchungen zu den Parallelstellen der Samuel-Königsbücher und der Chronik* (Alttestamentliche Abhandlungen). Münster: Aschendorff, 1937.

Torrey, C. C., *Ezra Studies.* University of Chicago Press, 1910.

————, *The Chronicler's History of Israel.* Yale University Press, 1954.

Vannutelli, P., *Libri Synoptici Veteris Testamenti seu Librorum Regum et Chronicorum loci paralleli.* Rome: Pontificio Instituto Biblico, 1931.

von Rad, G., *Das Geschichtsbild des chronistischen Werkes* (Beiträge zur Wissenschaft vom Alten und Neuen Testament). Stuttgart: Kohlhammer, 1930.

Welch, A. C., *The Work of the Chronicler.* London: The British Academy, 1939.

————, *Post-Exilic Judaism.* Edinburgh and London: William Blackwood, 1935.

Articles

Albright, W. F., "The Biblical Period" (abbr. BP), *The Jews: Their History, Culture, and Religion,* ed. L. Finkelstein (New York: Harper, 1949), I, pp. 3–69.

————, "The Date and Personality of the Chronicler," JBL 40 (1921), 104–24.

————, "The Judicial Reform of Jehoshaphat," *Alexander Marx Jubilee Volume,* English Section (abbr. AMJV).

————, "The List of Levitic Cities," *Louis Ginzberg Jubilee Volume* I, English Section (abbr. LGJV).

Bea, A., "Neuere Arbeiten zum Problem der biblischen Chronikbucher," *Biblica* 22 (1941), 46–58.

Beyer, G., "Das Festungssystem Rehabeams," ZDPV 54 (1931), 113–34.

Burnet, A. M., "Le Chroniste et ses sources," RB 60 (1953), 481–508; RB 61 (1954), 349–86.

————, "La théologie du Chroniste. Théocratie et messianisme," *Sacra Pagina*, I, 1959, pp. 384–97.

Freedman, D. N., "The Chronicler's Purpose," CBQ 23 (1961), 436–42.

Klein, S., "Kleine Beiträge zur Erklarung der Chronik," MGWJ 70 (1926), 410–16; MGWJ 80 (1936), 195–206.

Noordtzij, A., "Les intentions du Chroniste," RB 21 (1940), 161–68.

North, R., "The Cain Music," JBL 83 (1964), 373–89.

————, "Theology of the Chronicler," JBL 82 (1963), 369–81.

Richardson, H. N., "The Historical Reliability of Chronicles," JBR 26 (1958), 9–12.

Rudolph, W., "Problems of the Books of Chronicles," VT 4 (1954), 401–9.

von Rad, G., "Die levitische Predigt in den Bücher der Chronik," *Gesammelte Studien zum Alten Testament* (München: Kaiser Verlag, 1958), pp. 248–61.

Zimmerman, F., "Chronicles as a Partially Translated Book," JQR 42 (1951–52), 265–82, 387–412.

I. THE REIGN OF SOLOMON

(ca. 962–922 B.C.)

1. SOLOMON TAKES OVER THE KINGDOM
(i 1–17)†

Formal religious ceremony

I 1 Solomon the son of David then established himself firmly over the kingdom and Yahweh his God was with him and magnified him very greatly. 2 Solomon spoke to all Israel, to the captains of the thousands and hundreds, to the judges and to every leader in all Israel, the heads of families. 3 Then Solomon, with the whole congregation, went to the high place at Gibeon because the tent of meeting of God which Moses the servant of Yahweh had made in the desert was there. 4 [But David had brought up the ark of God from Kiriath-jearim to the place which David had provided for it, for he had pitched a tent for it at Jerusalem]. 5 The bronze altar, which Bezalel the son of Uri the son of Hur had made, [was] there*a* before the tabernacle of Yahweh where Solomon and the congregation consulted him*b*. 6 Solomon made an offering there before Yahweh upon the bronze altar of the tent of meeting, offering upon it a thousand burnt offerings. 7 That night God appeared to Solomon and said to him, "Ask, what I shall give to you!" 8 Solomon replied to God, "You have displayed great loyalty to David my father and you have made me king in his place. 9 Now, O Yahweh God, may your promise to David my father be confirmed, in as much as you have made me king over a people as numerous as the dust of the earth. 10 Grant me, therefore, wisdom and knowledge to go out and come in before this people,

† II **Chron i 1–13:** cf. I Kings iii 1–15, iv 1; **14–17:** cf. I Kings x 26–29.

a Heb. "he put" has the same consonants as "there."
b I.e., Yahweh. LXX, Vulg. "it," referring to the altar.

for who can otherwise govern this people of yours that is so great?" 11 Then God said to Solomon, "Because you had this in mind and did not request riches, wealth, honor, or the death of your enemies and did not even request long life but asked for wisdom and knowledge that you may direct my people over whom I have made you king, 12 wisdom and knowledge have been granted to you, and in addition I am giving you riches, wealth, and honor such as no kings before you possessed or such as none after you shall possess." 13 So Solomon came away from the high place at Gibeon, from the tent of meeting, to Jerusalem and assumed his duties as king over Israel.

Solomon's wealth

14 Solomon then amassed chariots and horsemen; he had fourteen hundred chariots and twelve thousand horsemen which he kept in the chariot-cities and at the royal establishment at Jerusalem. 15 The king made silver and gold as plentiful in Jerusalem as stones and cedar as common as sycamore in the Shephelah. 16 Solomon's horses were imported from Cilicia; the merchants of the king acquired them at the prevailing price. 17 They imported a chariot from Egypt for six hundred shekels of silver and a horse [from Cilicia] for one hundred and fifty shekels and thus [at that price] they conveyed them through their agents to the kings of the Hittites and to the kings of Aram.

NOTES

i 10. *to go out and come in.* Originally a military expression (cf. I Sam xviii 13, 16; I Chron xi 2) but here it means to govern the people adequately and with dignity befitting a king.

11. *the death of your enemies.* Literally "the life of those who hate you." Cf. I Kings iii 11 "enemies." In fact, Solomon did remove those who opposed or threatened his position.

15. This verse is the Chronicler's contribution to the description of the quantity of Solomon's wealth. Palestine is one of the stoniest places on earth. Sycamores, not highly esteemed, grew in great numbers in the Shephelah, the low hills between the central highland and the mari-

time plain to the southwest of Bethlehem. Cedar, on the other hand, was rare and greatly prized as may be seen from the many references to the cedars of Lebanon, a few of which grow today as ornamental trees in the Augusta Victoria Hospital compound.

16. *from Cilicia.* Omitting "Egypt" here in harmony with the second part of the verse and because horses were not bred in Egypt. On Cilicia see W. F. Albright, BASOR 120 (December 1950), 22 ff.

the prevailing price. On meaning of *mehīr* see A. Goetze, "The Laws of Eshnunna," AASOR 31 (1956), 111 f.

17. Six hundred shekels is about 15$\frac{1}{10}$ lbs., 150 about 3$\frac{3}{4}$ lbs. Solomon was a great merchant prince who knew how to turn every opportunity to advantage. Among other occupations, he was a dealer in Cilician horses (reported by Herodotus III.90 to be of excellent quality) and Egyptian chariots, equally fine. There can be no doubt on the rendering of *mqwh* ("from Cilicia"). Que (=Cilicia) occurs frequently in Assyrian letters and inscriptions from the time of Shalmaneser III (ninth century). Chariots were four times as expensive as horses, chiefly because wood had to be imported into Egypt and chariot making required great skill and expert workmanship. Moreover, after manufacture the cost of delivering of the product must have been high too. Horses, on the other hand, were simply raised; there is no evidence for pedigrees of any kind. See Albright, ARI, p. 135.

COMMENT

Chapter i serves, for the most part, as an introduction to the work of Solomon which, according to the Chronicler, centers almost exclusively around the building of the temple. Solomon thus carries on the work of his father as it pertains to the religious aspects of the kingdom. Here note is taken of his accession and his wealth, a subject amplified later (ch. ix), probably to emphasize the blessing of Yahweh attendant upon his concern for the cult.

[Assumption of duties as king, i 1–13]: In the background of this story is I Kings iii 1–15, with omission of the elements that did not lend themselves to the purpose the writer had in mind. The observation on Solomon's firm hold on the throne reflects the struggle for power shortly before the death of David (see COMMENT on I Chron xxix). But because God was with him, success crowned the efforts of his partisans. The first move of the new king was to summon the officials and the people to a religious service at Gibeon

—manifestly an official act rather than, as suggested by I Kings iii 4, a personal one. The references to high places in I Kings iii is carefully left out, though a parenthetical statement informs us that while the altar remained before the tent of meeting at Gibeon, the ark was in the tent pitched for it by David at Jerusalem. On the tent of meeting that Moses the servant of God had made special emphasis is laid to protect Solomon from violation of the priestly prohibition (Lev xvii 8, 9). No apology was required as was the case for the Deuteronomist (I Kings iii 3). Perhaps the Chronicler had imbibed something of the spirit of Ezekiel who discovered that the presence of Yahweh was more important than the place; that presence was symbolized by the altar and confirmed by the revelation given to Solomon. To legitimize further the national worship ceremony at the Gibeon high place, the presence of the altar of Bezalel is specifically stressed. Only here do we read of the altar at Gibeon (cf. I Chron xvi 39, 40, xxi 29) being that of Bezalel (Exod xxxi 2–11, xxxviii 1–2). Here it is said to be made of bronze but it was actually made of acacia wood (Exod xxvii 1–2) overlaid with bronze. The holding of this first national religious gathering at Gibeon gains added significance when it is recalled that Zadok was the officiating priest there (I Chron xvi 39–42). On the offerings themselves, cf. the source, I Kings iii 4c–5.

The nocturnal theophany is based on I Kings iii 5–13, 15, iv 1 but is effectively condensed—a fact that demonstrates the literary method of the writer and his use of his sources. God appears to Solomon directly and not in a dream. The Deuteronomist's expatiation on David is omitted because the attention is focused on the man of peace. In place of a discerning mind to judge the people rightly and an ability to distinguish between good and evil, the Chronicler appropriately speaks of wisdom and knowledge, though the significance is the same. Perhaps the most striking omission of all is the appearance of Solomon before the ark and offering sacrifices there (I Kings iii 15b). It is only after these elaborate cultic rites that Solomon assumes his duties as king.

[Amassing of wealth, 14–17]: The wealth and wisdom of Solomon are referred to also in chapter ix and as such can hardly be incidental. The story of the harlots, so vividly told in I Kings iii 16–28 to illustrate his wisdom, is passed over by the Chronicler but the material wealth of the king is accentuated not only here but

throughout the narrative to prove the fulfillment of the divine promise of blessings—riches, wealth, and honor—such as no king before
or after him possessed. This is a cliché not to be applied literally.
Though the divine promise veers away a bit from the Deuteronomic
formula—blessing equals prosperity and wealth and riches may de-
rive from wisdom—the end result is the same: Blessing equals wisdom equals wealth. It is striking that this little pericope stands at the
beginning of the story and that to the horses, chariots, horsemen,
silver, and cedar, gold is added; otherwise I Kings x 26–29 is followed practically verbatim. The writer has in mind two things as
he proceeds with his account of Solomon: (a) the fact that Yahweh
had blessed him beyond parallel and (b) that his interest in the
temple—religious institutions—must not be obscured by other matters however important. That is why he disposes of the other matters pertaining to Solomon's kingdom so quickly.

2. BUILDING THE TEMPLE: PREPARATIONS
(i 18 [ii 1E], ii 1–17 [ii 2–18E]†

I 18 Then Solomon gave the order to build a house for the name of Yahweh and a palace for himself.

II 1 Solomon allotted seventy thousand burden-bearers, eighty thousand quarrymen in the mountain and thirty-six hundred overseers over them. 2 Then Solomon sent the following message to King Huram[a] of Tyre: "As you did for David, my father, when you sent him cedars to build for himself a house to dwell in—3 For you see, I am going to build a house to the name of Yahweh my God, dedicating it to him that perfumed incense may be burned before him, the layer bread set out continually, burnt offerings offered in the morning, in the evening, on the Sabbaths, at the time of the new moons and the festivals of Yahweh our God, as prescribed eternally for Israel. 4 The house I am building must be great, for our God is greater than all [other] gods. 5 Yet who can summon strength to build a house for him when heaven and the highest heavens cannot contain him? Who am I that I should build a house for him, except to burn incense before him?—6 So send me now a man trained to work in gold, silver, bronze, iron, purple, crimson, and violet materials, and who knows how to make engravings; he is to work with my trained men in Judah and Jerusalem whom David my father has provided. 7 Send me also cedar, cypress, and algum lumber from Lebanon, for I know that your servants are experienced in cutting Lebanon timber; indeed, my servants will assist your servants 8 to prepare timber in abun-

† **II Chron i 18–ii 17**: cf. I Kings v 1–18 (v 15–32H), vii 13–14.

[a] Some manuscripts, Vulg., LXX read "Hiram."

dance for me, because the house that I am building is to be wondrously great. 9 I will provide one hundred thirty thousand bushels of wheat, one hundred thirty thousand bushels of barley, one hundred twenty thousand gallons of wine, and one hundred twenty thousand gallons of oil for the board of your servants, the woodsmen cutting the timbers." 10 Huram*a* king of Tyre sent to Solomon the following written reply: "Because Yahweh loves his people, he has made you king over them." 11 Huram said further, "Praised be Yahweh God of Israel, who made heaven and earth and has given David a wise son, endowed with such insight and understanding, to build a house for Yahweh and a palace for his kingdom. 12 I have just now sent a trained man, endowed with good judgment, namely Huramabi, 13 who is the son of a Danite woman but his father is a Tyrian. He is trained to work in gold, silver, bronze, iron, stone, and wood, and in purple, violet, linen and crimson materials; also to do all kinds of engraving and to work out any artistic design that may be entrusted to him in conjunction with your artists and the artists of my lord David, your father. 14 Now let my lord send the wheat, the barley, the oil, and the wine to his servants as he promised, 15 and we will cut all the timber you need from Lebanon and ship it to you in sea rafts as far as Joppa, but you must transfer it from there to Jerusalem." 16 Then Solomon took a census of all the foreigners in the land of Israel similar to the census which David his father had taken and one hundred fifty-three thousand six hundred were found. 17 He made seventy thousand of them burden-bearers, eighty thousand of them quarrymen in the mountain, and three thousand six hundred of them overseers to keep the people at work.

NOTES

ii 1. See NOTE on vs. 17 below.

3. *layer bread*. Also known as show bread, presence bread, continual bread. The loaves of bread placed on the acacia table standing before Yahweh in the temple (cf. Heb ix 2 ff.; Exod xxv 30).

9. Since a kor contained about 6½ bushels, there were about 130,000 bushels each of barley and wheat. A bath was slightly more than 6 gallons, thus making 120,000 gallons each of oil and wine.

the board. Reading *makkōlet* with Vulg. for *makkōt* "crushed" (cf. I Kings v 25, with syncopation of *aleph*).

12. *Huramabi.* The Kings parallels (I Kings vii 13, 40, 45) all have Hiram (originally Ahiram). The text could be read "Huram my father," but King Hiram's father was Abibaal. Rudolph (*Chronikbücher,* p. 200 [see Selected Bibliography, Commentaries]) suggests "Huram, my master" and points out that *'ab* sometimes means adviser, master, as in Gen xlv 8; Judg xvii 10; I Maccabees xi 32. If that is correct, the meaning here might be "Huram, my master (craftsman)."

13. *the son . . . Tyrian.* Rudolph, p. 225, thinks this tradition may be based on an oral source.

15. A copper axhead found in Syria belonged to an ancient Egyptian boat crew possibly engaged in procuring cedar from Lebanon. See BJRL 44 (1961–62), 110.

17. According to I Kings v 13 ff., Solomon raised a levy of forced laborers from "all Israel." The Chronicler modified the claims of his source by limiting the levy to foreigners in Israel. The Deuteronomist has the levies working in relays of three months. Corvées in early Egypt also served in relays of three months, the system being based on the duration of the inundation of the Nile. Cf. Herodotus II.124 and H. Kees, *Ancient Egypt* (London, 1961), p. 55. How to interpret the numbers is a question. If they are based on the unit principle, there would be 153 units, each with 600 persons, yielding a total of 91,800. The 150 units (perhaps a round number) would comprise 90,000 workmen, assuming the same number of persons per unit (i.e., 600). For these 90,000 workmen, there were three units of overseers which (on the same basis) would comprise 1800 individuals, or one overseer for 50 workmen.

COMMENT

[Preparations for the construction of the temple, i 18]: Despite the fact that the amassing of wealth and the formation of a "mechanized" army stationed in chariot-cities in various centers of the kingdom took some time and required no little effort and planning, these developments are passed over hurriedly because the author was concerned about getting to the most significant aspect of Solomon's reign—the construction of the temple and the palace for which the order was given forthwith. That order meant simply the carrying out of the blueprints submitted to Solomon by David as set forth in I Chron xxviii 11–19. While the building of a palace is mentioned by the Chronicler, here and elsewhere (ii 11, vii 11, viii 1, ix 11), he nowhere gives details about it. Perhaps we are to think of the whole complex of buildings of which the temple was itself but the royal chapel (cf. K. Möhlenbrink, *Der Tempel Salomos,* 1932; E. Renan, *Histoire du peuple d'Israel,* II, 1891, p. 142; A. Parrot, *The Temple of Jerusalem,* 1957, pp. 51–55), or it may be that knowledge of the temple from other sources (I Kings vii 1–12) is taken for granted.

[Preparations for the construction of the temple (continued), ii 1–17]: The order of the king to proceed at once with the building of temple and palace, could not be carried out without a great deal of preparation. Such a gigantic enterprise required more than wealth and wisdom; arrangements had to be made with Hiram (Huram) of Tyre, and manpower and organization provided for the actual work. Verse 1 is a repetition of vs. 17, both of which are dependent upon the census of foreigners referred to in vs. 16 (cf. I Kings v 13 ff. (v 27H ff.) where the forced labor is drawn from all Israel). The Chronicler has thus toned down the Kings report in both scope and applicability. He has, in effect, recast the whole story to bring it into harmony with his ideas, omitting some aspects of the Deuteronomic narrative and supplying others. Solomon is a much more independent king here since he takes the initiative in carrying out the obligations to build the temple laid upon him by his father. Kings (I Kings v 1) says Hiram sent ambassadors to Solomon after David's death to console him and to congratulate him upon his own accession. Through these ambassadors of good will Solomon then made his request for men and materials. In the message conveyed to Hiram, I Chron xiv 1 is recalled and made a precedent for that of Solomon, though no mention is made of the reason for David's failure to build the temple—not a thing is said about the latter's plan for the venture, possibly because it was so fully dealt with in earlier chapters. So far as this chapter is concerned, the credit for initiative in the project belongs to Solomon. The purpose for the temple as envisioned by Solomon is worship in all its forms; it must be congruous with the greatness of Yahweh who is above all gods, though he cannot really be confined to a house made by man. Solomon's depreciation of himself conforms to the writer's view of the majesty of God in comparison with whom even the great and wealthy king pales into insignificance.

In contrast with the Kings chapter, the first request is for a man trained in the decorative crafts to direct Solomon's own craftsmen in their work—they had been provided by David, but the plans of the latter are only hinted here. In addition to the request for a skilled workman, there is the order for lumber—cedar, cypress, and algum (cf. *elammakku* in CAD, IV, pp. 75 f.). Algum was a precious wood used for furniture, palace, and temple construction; it occurs in an inventory list from Ugarit (120:10). II Chron ix 10 thinks of it as one of the products of Ophir, but it more likely came from Syria. The Kings parallel does not include it, having only cedar and cypress. Along with the order for lumber comes an offer of assistance from Solomon whose workmen are unskilled in logging (I Kings v 6 [20H]); this offer evidently was made because of the magnitude of the task. In return for Hiram's products and labor, Solomon offers to provide food and drink for the workmen. I Kings v 11 (25H) apparently thinks of the wheat and oil as tribute since it is for Hiram's household. Here barley and wine are added to the wheat and oil, a typical expansion of the Chronicler.

The reply of Hiram begins with a paean of praise to Yahweh who loves his people as shown by his selection of Solomon, David's wise son, to build the temple and palace. This marks an alteration of the Kings parallel which rather coldly, but more realistically, observes "blessed be Yahweh today who has given to David a wise son . . ." and offers to supply the needs of Solomon. Without delay, Hiram sent Huramabi, the son of a Tyrian father and a Danite mother, and urged the king to send on the supplies and laborers. Huramabi's (Hiram from Tyre in I Kings vii 13) abilities have been greatly expanded. Kings refers to him only as a worker in bronze. It has been pointed out that this expansion was due to the requirements of Solomon's temple (iii 7 ff., 14) and that the author thought of him as another Bezalel (Exod xxxi 2–5, xxxv 30–33) who was associated with two Danites. That may be the source of the Danite connection mentioned here, whereas Kings says Hiram was the son of a Naphtali widow.

The Chronicler is more definite in the agreement of Hiram to cut and ship the lumber to Joppa than is the Kings narrator. The former was aware of the port (Ezra iii 7; Jon i 3), which was the nearest to Jerusalem. According to Josh xix 46, Joppa was opposite the territory of Dan (its original allotment among Ephraim, Judah, and Philistia). It is mentioned in Egyptian documents and lists in the time of Thutmose III (fifteenth century B.C.)—see ANET, pp. 22, 242. It was one of the cities besieged by Sennacherib during his campaigns to the west—ANET, p. 287.

3. BUILDING THE TEMPLE: CONSTRUCTION
(iii 1–17)†

III ¹ So Solomon began to build the house of Yahweh in Jerusalem on Mount Moriah *which David his father had selected*—the place which David had prepared—on the threshing floor of Ornan the Jebusite. ² He began to build it on the second day in the second month of the fourth year of his reign. ³ Now these are *the measurements* which Solomon fixed for the building of the house of God: its length in cubits, according to the old standard, was sixty cubits and its width was twenty cubits; ⁴ the portico in front of the house was as long as the width of the house, that is, twenty cubits, and the height was one hundred and twenty cubits. On the inside he overlaid it with pure gold. ⁵ The nave he paneled with cypress wood which he overlaid with fine gold and ornamented with palm and chain designs. ⁶ He decorated the house beautifully with precious stones and with gold from Parvaim. ⁷ Thus he overlaid with gold the house, the rafters, the thresholds, its walls and its doors, and engraved the walls with cherubs. ⁸ He made the holy of holies, its length corresponding to the width of the house, twenty cubits long and twenty cubits wide and overlaid it with genuine gold weighing six hundred talents. ⁹ The weight of the nails was fifty shekels of gold. He also overlaid the upper rooms with gold.

† **II Chron iii 1–17** ‖ I Kings vi 1–38, cf. vii 15–22.

ᵃ⁻ᵃ Vulg. reads *qui demonstratus fuerat David patri eius*. LXX reads "where the Lord appeared to David his father," but "Yahweh" does not appear in either MT or Vulg. See NOTE.
ᵇ⁻ᵇ Insert, with Targ., to bring out meaning. Targ. takes *hwsd* as an abbreviation for *hmdwt 'šr ysd*, "the measures which he fixed."

10 He made two molten[e] cherubs for the holy of holies which he likewise overlaid with gold. 11 The wings of the cherubs had a spread of twenty cubits; one wing of each (being five cubits) touched the wall of the house and the other wing (also of five cubits) touched the wing of the other cherub. 12 On the other hand, one wing of the second cherub touched the other wall of the house, while the other wing, also of five cubits, touched the wing of the first cherub. 13 The wings of these cherubs had a spread of twenty cubits. They stood on their feet with their faces toward the house. 14 He made the curtain of violet, purple, and crimson materials and linen and worked a cherub design upon it. 15 He made two pillars thirty-five cubits long for the front of the house; the capitals on top of them were five cubits. 16 He made chain designs like a necklace and placed them at the top of the pillars; he also made a hundred pomegranates which he put on the chain designs. 17 He set up the pillars in front of the temple, one on the right and the other on the left, and called the name of the one on the right Jachin and the name of the one on the left Boaz.

[e] The word is uncertain but probably refers to a figure of precious metal. LXX has "wood"; Vulg. *statuario opera;* I Kings vi 32 "fir" or "pine"; RSV "olivewood"; Rudolph "plastic"; Goettsberger (see Selected Bibliography, Commentaries) "sculptured work."

Notes

iii 1. *had selected.* So with Ehrlich (*Randglossen zur hebräischen Bibel,* VII; see Selected Bibliography) and Rudolph. For this meaning of Heb. *rā'āh* see Gen xxii 8, xli 33.

—*the place . . . prepared.* This is an explanatory clause.

3. *fixed.* Reading pi. pf. for hoph.; dittography of *h.*

cubits. The cubit was 17.49 inches; that of Ezekiel (xl 5, xliii 13) was about 20.405 inches.

the old standard. The old standard was that adopted by Ezekiel and used in the time of Solomon.

4. *the portico . . . width of the house.* Cf. I Kings vi 3. A difficult verse and not very smooth Hebrew. Translation is based on LXX in

part; literally "the portico which [was] in front of the house was the length in front of the width of the house." What is apparently meant is that the length of the portico extending across the front of the house was 20 cubits. Cf. Möhlenbrink, *Der Tempel Salomos*, p. 27.

one hundred and twenty cubits. Certainly exaggerated. Original may have read 20 cubits, for which there is some evidence in the versions; *mē'āh* may be a corruption of the term for cubit. Cf. vs. 8 and iv 1. But the same figure appears in LXX.

5. *chain designs.* Cf. Akk. *šaršarratu* "chain." Chain designs were also used on the capitals (I Kings vii 17; vs. 16) of the two pillars; these were probably Phoenician. Cf. G. E. Wright, *Biblical Archaeology*, 1957, p. 140.

6. *Parvaim.* "Parvaim" is unknown; perhaps the "el Farwaim" of the Arab historian Hamdani. See H. E. del Medico, "ZAHAB PARWAYIM: L'or fructifère dans la tradition juive," VT 13 (1963), 156–86.

8. *six hundred talents.* Something over 22½ tons.

9. *fifty shekels.* Approximately 1¼ lbs.

11. *twenty cubits.* About 30 ft.

five cubits. Slightly more than 7½ ft.

12. *other.* So for clarity.

16. *like a necklace.* So with most commentators for "inner room, sanctuary," which is hardly possible here.

17. *Jachin . . . Boaz.* For possible interpretation of the names see R. B. Y. Scott, JBL 58 (1939), 143 ff.

COMMENT

Although the Chronicler has a dominant interest in the temple and its institutions, he has considerably curtailed the account now standing in I Kings. There appears to be a greater concern for the cultus than for the building itself which may be explained by the fact that the postexilic temple was evidently less elaborate than the old Solomonic one had been (cf. Josephus *Antiquities* XV.xi).

[The site and the beginning of the construction, iii 1–2]: Solomon built the temple on the site selected by David, not specified by the Kings narrative. Mount Moriah is not elsewhere connected with it. The writer thus associates the site with the land of Moriah where Abraham was to offer Isaac (Gen xxii 2), doubtless because it was designated as the mount of Yahweh (Gen xxii 14). He may have been influenced in part by Isaiah who has a great deal to say about the mountain of Yahweh (ii 2, 3, xxx 29, lxv 25, lxvi 20; cf. also Joel iii 17; Mic iv 1; Zech viii 3). The threshing floor of Ornan is not mentioned in the Kings parallel though it is possibly assumed. The date for the beginning of the building corresponds exactly with that in I Kings, though it is not so broad (for date of Solomon's temple see M. B. Rowton in BASOR 119 [October 1950], 20–22 and references cited there to others who disagree; Parrot, *The Temple of Jerusalem,* pp. 21 f.). The reference to the exodus from Egypt is not included, nor is the name of the month (I Kings vi 1 has "Ziv," i.e., "April–May"). Delay in beginning until the fourth year of his reign was due to the organizational preparations, arrangements for and transport of materials to Jerusalem and the procurement of technicians.

[The temple itself, 3–17]: The full measurements of the temple are not given. The length of the building without the portico was sixty cubits. According to I Kings vi 3, 17, 20, the dimensions of the portico were 20×10 cubits, of the nave 20×40, of the *debir* 20×20, or an over-all length of seventy cubits and breadth of twenty cubits. The *d^ebīr* was the "holy of holies." It means literally, "oracle," since it was the special dwelling place of the Lord. The temple consisted of three parts: the *'ūlām*—portico or vestibule, the *hēkāl* —the "holy place" or the main room of the sanctuary, and the *d^ebīr*. The size of these parts of the temple, in terms of feet, using the long cubit, was approximately 34×17, 34×68, 34×34. For descriptions of the temple see Parrot, *The Temple of Jerusalem;* Möhlenbrink, *Der Tempel Salomos;* G. E. Wright, BA 4 (1941), 17–31, BA 18 (1955), 41–44; P. L. Garber, BA 14 (1951), 2–24. The height is given as thirty cubits for the nave in I Kings vi 2; the *debir* was a cube of 20×20×20, possibly on a platform of ten cubits so that the height of both the nave and *debir* would be the same (see Parrot, *The Temple of Jerusalem,* p. 33, and n. 5; Garber, BA 14 [1951], 18 f. and references there; Möhlenbrink, *Der Tempel Salomos,* pp. 131–41).

The portico was overlaid on the inside with pure gold (cf. I Kings vi 22). The nave paneled with cypress—I Kings vi 15 has cedar, with floor of cypress—was overlaid with gold decorated with palm and chain designs (only here). The decoration of the house with precious stones is explained by Vulg. as follows: "He laid the floor of the temple with costly marble." David had collected precious stones which may have been used in mosaics on the floor of the nave. The cherubs engraved on the walls are referred to also in I Kings vi 29 where, in addition to the designs mentioned in 5b, open flower patterns are specified.

With the exception that the height is not given, the measurement of the *debir* corresponds to that in the Kings parallel. The enormous amount of gold used in encasing the inside of the *debir* is commensurate with I Chron xxix 4, though there is no reference to it in Kings. Nor is there any parallel to the golden nails (really spikes), though the golden hooks of the tabernacle (Exod xxvi 32, 37) may have been in the mind of the writer. The "upper rooms" of the *debir* are not referred to elsewhere. The cast cherubs with a total wingspread of twenty cubits—five cubits for each of their two wings—were placed side by side with tips touching the wall and the other cherub and facing toward the nave (on Cherubs see BA 1 [1938], 1–3).

The curtain between the *debir* and the nave is not noticed in I Kings, nor does it appear in Ezekiel's description of the temple. Some think it was originally present in I Kings vi 21b but fell out through a similarity of consonants (in Hebrew) between *curtain* and *chains*. See Rudolph, pp. 204 f. The Kings parallel has wooden doors between them. The reference here is based on the tabernacle curtain (Exod xxvi 31–35) whose description is identical with this one. According to Josephus (*Wars* V.v) there was a curtain between *debir* and nave in the Herodian temple.

The most interesting feature of the two pillars is that they stood "in front of the temple" and were thus not built into it as an integral part of the structure (cf. Möhlenbrink, *Der Tempel Salomos,* pp. 111 f.). Albright (ARI, pp. 144–48) has shown that they were cressets similar to those connected with Phoenician temples and obviously had special symbolic significance for the worshipers; their possible significance is outlined by Albright on p. 148. Cf. S. Yeivin, "Jachin and Boaz," *Eretz Israel,* V, 1958, pp. 97–104 (in Hebrew).

4. BUILDING THE TEMPLE: FURNISHINGS
(iv 1–22, v 1)†

IV 1 He made a bronze altar twenty cubits long, twenty cubits wide and ten cubits high. 2 He made the cast-metal sea which was circular in shape, ten cubits from brim to brim, five cubits high, and thirty cubits in circumference. 3 Something like oxen under it went the whole way around it, ten per cubit around the entire sea; there were two rows of oxen cast into a solid piece with it. 4 It stood upon twelve oxen, three looking north, three looking west, three looking south, and three looking east, while the sea rested upon them and the hindquarters of all of them were turned inward. 5 It was a handbreadth in thickness, its brim was shaped like the brim of a cup, like a lily blossom, and its capacity was three thousand baths. 6 He made ten basins, placing five on the right and five on the left, in which to wash; they were to rinse the articles for the burnt offering in them, but the sea was for the priests to wash in. 7 He made ten golden lampstands according to pattern which he placed in the temple, five on the right and five on the left. 8 He made ten tables which he set up in the temple, five on the right and five on the left; he also made a hundred golden bowls. 9 He made the court of the priests and the great court together with doors for the court, which doors he overlaid with bronze. 10 He placed the sea on the right side *of the house* toward the southeast. 11 Huram made the ash containers, the shovels, and the bowls; so Huram completed the work on the house of God which he had agreed to do for King Solomon; 12 the two pillars and the basins and the capitals on top of the two pillars, the two gratings to cover

† **II Chron iv 1–22** ‖ I Kings vii 23–50; **II Chron v 1** ‖ I Kings vii 51.

a–a So with LXX and I Kings vii 39.

both of the basins of the capitals which were on top of the pillars, 13 the four hundred pomegranates for the two gratings —two rows of pomegranates per grating—to cover the two basins of the capitals which were upon the pillars, 14 the ten wheel bases and the ten basins for the wheel bases 15 the one sea with the twelve oxen under it, 16 the ash containers, the shovels, and the forks. Huramabi made for King Solomon all the utensils for the house of Yahweh of polished bronze. 17 The king cast them in the territory of the Jordan in the earthen foundries between Succoth and Zarethan. 18 Solomon made all these utensils in very great quantities, for the weight of the bronze was incalculable. 19 Solomon made all the utensils designed for the house of God, together with the golden altar and the tables upon which was the show bread, 20 the lampstands with their lamps, to be lighted before the *debir* according to plan, of fine gold; 21 the blossom ornaments, the lamps, and the tongs were of gold, the most precious gold. 22 The snuffers, the sprinkling bowls, the [incense] ladles, and the pans were made of genuine gold; as for the entrance to the house, its inner doors to the holy of holies as well as the doors of the house itself, that is of the temple, also were made of gold.

V   1 When all the work that Solomon did for the house of Yahweh was completed Solomon brought in the consecrated gifts of David his father: the silver, the gold, and all the utensils he had put into the treasuries of the house of God.

NOTES

iv 1. Roughly 30×30×15 feet.

3. *Something like oxen.* I Kings vii 24 "gourd-like ornaments." Note the attempt to avoid direct equation with oxen because of their resemblance to the golden bulls of the Northern Kingdom that were so obnoxious to the writer.

ten per cubit. With I Kings vii 24.

5. *a handbreadth.* Approximately three inches.

three thousand baths. I Kings vii 26 has two thousand baths. A bath= 6+ gallons.

6. *right . . . left.* I.e., of the molten sea.

rinse. This word occurs elsewhere in the OT only three times (Isa iv 4; Ezek xl 38; Jer li 34). From Isa iv 4 we know it means "to wash." Only here and in Ezekiel is it used in connection with the burnt offering.

11. *the bowls.* For a description of the type, see A. M. Honeyman, PEQ (1939), 83 f.

12. *the basins.* See Zech iv 3; cf. W. F. Albright, BASOR 85 (February 1942), 25; the *gullāh* was the basin on top of the pillar.

14. *the ten . . . the ten.* Reading *'śr* and *'śrh* ("ten") for *'śh* ("he made"), with I Kings vii 43. LXX has "ten bases." For a discussion of the basins and bases, see L. H. Vincent in *Miscellanea Biblica B. Ubach,* 1953, pp. 147–59.

16. *the forks.* I Kings vii 45 "bowls," as in vs. 11. For occurrence of word elsewhere see BA 4 (1941), p. 29, n. 6.

Huramabi. See NOTE on ii 12.

all the utensils. So for "all their utensils" because of verse division. For description see Wright, *Biblical Archaeology,* pp. 141 f.

17. *in the earthen foundries.* For this translation see N. Glueck, BASOR 90 (April 1943), 13 f., where he discusses the difficulties involved in the generally accepted reading. His suggested reading is: "in the earthen foundries (or in the thickened earthen moulds) between Succoth and Zarethan." For W. F. Albright's views see "The Administrative Divisions of Israel and Judah," JPOS 5 (1925), 33, n. 37.

Zarethan. MT has *Zeredah.* With I Kings vii 46, since Zarethan, the birthplace of Jeroboam I (I Kings xi 26), was probably in the hill country of Ephraim. Cf. F. M. Abel, *Géographie de la Palestine,* II, p. 457 (see Selected Bibliography).

20. *fine gold.* On *zhb sgwr* as red gold see G. R. Driver, *Ephemerides Theologicae Lovanienses,* 1950, p. 352.

22. Note the Chronicler's glorification of the temple.

ladles. On the subject of incense spoons see W. F. Albright, *Tell Beit Mirsim III: The Iron Age,* AASOR 21–22 (1943), par. 42; Y. Yadin et al., *Hazor,* II, 1960, p. 63, and Pls. CVIII and CLXIV, 12, where the object is referred to as an incense ladle.

COMMENT

[The bronze altar, iv 1]: There is no direct reference in I Kings to the construction of an altar of bronze, though its existence is demonstrated by reference thereto in I Kings viii 64, ix 25; II Kings xvi 14. The omission here is surely accidental and not deliberate, as its appearance in those passages indicates. Whether this verse is a secondary insertion is a matter for conjecture. Rudolph, p. 207, thinks it came originally from I Kings vii, where it stood between vss. 22 and 23, but fell out through homoioarkton. Both I Kings vii 23 and II Chron iv 1 begin with the same word in MT. Rudolph points out that the order in which the dimensions are given follows the Kings practice, that is, the number of cubits precedes the dimensions, whereas the Chronicler has the dimensions followed by the numbers. Then, two different words are used for height—Kings, *qūm;* Chronicles, *gbh.* Here there is no elaborate description of the block-levels of the altar as in Ezekiel. Only the top is detailed. (For a good illustration of the platform altars of Mesopotamia see ANEP, Fig. 627.)

The bronze altar of Bezalel that was in Gibeon before the tabernacle and upon which Solomon offered sacrifices (II Chron i 5–6) is certainly in the background. In the Yehawmilk inscription (fifth–fourth centuries B.C.) we read of a bronze altar made by the king of Byblos and presented to the Lady of Byblos who was, however, a goddess. (See ANET, p. 502.) The top of the altar was square, as was that of Ezekiel's temple (xliii 16). Its height was about fifteen feet, the same as that of Ezekiel, and it must have been approached by steps. For further information on the altar, see H. Wiener, *The Altars of the Old Testament,* 1927; J. de Groot, *Die Altäre des salomonischen Tempelhofes,* 1924; K. Galling, BRL, cols. 13–22; Albright, ARI, pp. 150 f.

[The cast-metal sea and the basins, 2–6]: Here the Chronicler follows Kings with only a few minor deviations, except for vs. 6. The description of the sea is clear and requires little interpretation. On the expression "something like oxen" for which Kings has "gourds were under its brim," see NOTE on vs. 3. The purpose of the sea was for the priests to wash in. The arrangement of the oxen probably had a

symbolical as well as a decorative significance. See ARI, pp. 148 f.;
Parrot, *The Temple of Jerusalem,* pp. 45 f., and drawing Fig. XI.
A connection of the twelve oxen with the twelve tribes of Israel
seems clear. The arrangement of the oxen may have something to do
with that of the tribes around the tabernacle in the desert, which
were also arranged in groups of three (Num ii). The connection of
the bull with fertility is well known; he was the symbol of Hadad,
the storm-god who was responsible for the life-giving waters. The
writer modifies the Canaanite associations by referring to the oxen
(bulls) as "something like" them. Their arrangement in groups of
three facing in the four directions may point to the four seasons,
though this is disputed by Parrot. While the Canaanite pattern is
obvious, its real meaning was probably forgotten by the writer's time,
but his description may be more accurate than the gourd pattern of
the Deuteronomist because of the latter's abhorrence of the golden
bulls of Jeroboam I.

The other variant is the capacity of the sea: Kings, two thousand
baths, Chronicles, three thousand. C. C. Wylie, BA 12 (1949),
86–90, explains the difference as due to the hemispherical shape
visualized by Kings and the cylindrical shape visualized by the
Chronicler. (For figure of forms cf. BA 4 [1941], 17, but cf.
Rudolph, p. 206; for calculations of capacity see R. B. Y. Scott in
JBL 77 [1958], 209–12, and BA 22 [1959], 29–32.) The ten
basins, placed five on the right and five on the left of the sea, were
for the washing of the burnt offering. The ten basins with their
stands are described in great detail in I Kings vii 27–39, especially
the stands. The basins were made for each stand (vs. 38). The
decorations of the stands were undoubtedly symbolic (for recon-
structions see AOT, Figs. 505, 507, 508; Parrot, *The Temple of
Jerusalem,* pp. 48 f.) and it may be that their description was omitted
by the Chronicler because of their character. The word for basin,
kiyor, derives ultimately from Sumerian and is used frequently
in the inscriptions of Sargon II in the sense of kettle or caldron
(see ARI, pp. 153 f., with notes there; and Honeyman, PEQ [1939],
82 f.).

[The lampstands, tables, bowls, 7–8]: The lampstands were
made according to pattern, which means according to the plan de-
vised for them. The tabernacle had only one lampstand with six
branches, that is, with seven light faucets (cf. Exod xxv 31 ff., xxxvii

17 ff.). That was also the case in later times (cf. I Maccabees i 21, iv 49). But I Chron xxviii 15 and Jer lii 19 refer to lampstands (plural). II Chron xiii 11 also refers to one lampstand with its lights. Nowhere else is there mention of ten tables. Ezek xl 38–43 mentions the use of tables for the slaying of sacrificial animals and the instruments of the priests are mentioned but the text is not clear as to the number, though probably there were only eight. The reference cannot be to the table of the layer bread since only one table is referred to in xiii 11, xxix 18; but the plural is used in I Chron xxviii 16 and in vs. 19 of this chapter. It has been suggested that the number ten is an exaggeration here, as the ten lampstands may be. The tables could have been used for the lampstands since they are in similar position and are equal in number. The hundred sprinkling bowls may have been used to catch the blood of the sacrificial victims for later sprinkling.

[The courts and the placement of the sea, 9–10]: The reference to two courts here is based on Ezekiel and the usages of the second temple. The term "the great court," *ha'zarah hag^{e}dolah,* is used only in Chronicles and Ezekiel. The inner court of I Kings vi 36, vii 12 is the space immediately adjacent to the temple, and the great court of vii 12 is the whole area around the complex of Solomon's buildings. The second temple had two courts; an outer court for the general public and an inner one restricted to those who were ritually clean (cf. E. Bikerman, "Une proclamation séleucide relative au Temple de Jérusalem," *Syria* 25 [1946–48], 67–85). The doors are not mentioned in Kings. The reiteration of the placement of the sea is due to the source for the following verses, which is I Kings vii 39b–50.

[The work of Huram, 11–18]: The ash containers were for the ashes from the altar offerings (cf. Exod xxvii 3). Shovels, forks, and wheel bases have been discovered in a number of excavations (cf. Wright, *Biblical Archaeology,* pp. 141 f., and Fig. 96 on p. 142; for wheel bases, see AOT, Pls. cciii, cciv). The pillars have been discussed in the preceding chapter. The capitals of the pillars were decorated with lily designs (I Kings vii 19); above the basins were gratings decorated with pomegranate designs, two rows around each one. See tripod in C. F. A. Schaeffer, *The Cuneiform Texts of Ras Shamra-Ugarit,* 1939, Pl. xxiii, Fig. 2, for illustration of pomegranate design. The casting was done on the other side of the Jordan between Sukkoth and Zarethan. The bronze probably came from the mines in the wadis of Timna and Amram in the fifteen-kilometer-long valley north of Elath on the Gulf of Aqabah. For the exploration and description of the location see *Illustrated London News,* September 3, 1960, pp. 383–85.

[Summary of utensils, 19–22]: With few changes, this list of temple equipment follows that of I Kings. Of special interest is the golden altar used for burning incense. It was modeled after that of the tabernacle in Exod xxx 1 ff. R. de Langhe in *Biblica* 40 (1959), 476–94, gives a full discussion of the golden altar.

Under the influence of vs. 8, the writer speaks of altars for the show bread. All of the utensils were made of gold. So also were the inner doors of the *debir* and the doors of the temple itself.

[Gifts moved into the temple, v 1]: This verse marks the transition between the story of the construction and that of the dedication of the temple. It observes that when the temple was finished, the consecrated gifts of David (cf. I Chron xviii 11, xxvi 26) were moved into the treasuries, though the Chronicler says nothing about the latter in the preceding account of the building of the temple. The treasuries are probably to be connected with the "upper rooms" of iii 9 and the side chambers of I Kings vi 5 ff. The writer has followed his source in I Kings vii 51 almost exactly.

5. BUILDING THE TEMPLE: REMOVAL OF THE ARK. GOD'S APPROVAL (v 2–14)†

Removal of the ark to the temple

V ² Then Solomon assembled at Jerusalem the elders of Israel and all the heads of the tribes, the Israelite family princes, for the purpose of bringing up the ark of the covenant of Yahweh from the city of David which is Zion. ³ All the men of Israel assembled themselves before the king at the time of the feast, that is the seventh month. ⁴ When all the elders of Israel had arrived, the Levites took up the ark; ⁵ they brought up the ark, the tent of meeting, and all the sacred utensils which were in the tent. The Levitical priests brought them up. ⁶ King Solomon and the whole congregation of Israel present with him before the ark sacrificed sheep and oxen in such abundance that they could neither be numbered nor counted. ⁷ The priests brought the ark of the covenant of Yahweh to its appointed place under the wings of the cherubs in the sanctuary of the house, in the holy of holies. ⁸ The cherubs spread out both their wings over the location of the ark, that is the cherubs formed a canopy for the ark and its poles. ⁹ However, the poles were so long that the ends of the poles of the ark could be seen in front of the sanctuary though they could not be seen from the outside; *it remains there to this day.*ᵃ ¹⁰ There was nothing in the ark except the two tables [of the law] which Moses had placed in it at Horeb when Yahweh made a covenant with the Israelites at the time of their exodus from Egypt.

† **II Chron v 2–14** ‖ I Kings viii 1–11.

ᵃ⁻ᵃ See NOTE.

The appearance of the glory of Yahweh

11 When the priests left the holy place—for all the priests present had sanctified themselves regardless of divisions, 12 and all of the Levitical singers, Asaph, Heman, Jeduthun, and their sons and their brothers garbed in linen were standing on the east side of the altar with cymbals, harps, and zithers; with them stood one hundred and twenty priests blowing the trumpets; 13 the harmony between the trumpeters and singers was [so perfect] that only one melody was audible when they praised and gave thanks to Yahweh—and the music began, accompanied by trumpets, cymbals, and [other] instruments of song, to render

> praise to Yahweh
> for he is good,
> and eternal his devotion

*b*the house was filled with a cloud,*b* 14 so that the priests were unable to remain to perform their service because of the cloud, for the glory of Yahweh filled the house of God.

b–b So, omitting "the house of Yahweh." May be an explanatory note. Cf. LXX "the house was filled by a cloud of the glory of Yahweh" and Vulg. "the house of God was filled by a cloud." The writer may have had in mind Isa vi 4 or the thought of Ezek x 4.

NOTES

v 9. *of the ark.* I Kings viii 8 reads "from the holy place."

it remains . . . day. Kings reads: "they [the poles] remain there until this day"; so also LXX and many manuscripts here. The meaning of the statement is the same since the presence of the poles would at the same time indicate the presence of the ark itself. The writer quoted his source, for the ark was no longer in existence when he wrote.

10. *when . . . covenant.* Required by context. Cf. vi 11.

12. *one hundred and twenty priests.* I.e., five for each of the twenty-four divisions (cf. I Chron xxiv).

13. *trumpeters.* The priests were the trumpeters (I Chron xv 24).

COMMENT

[The transfer of the ark from Zion to the temple, v 2–10]:
The solemn assembly took place at the feast of the seventh month,
unnamed here since the name was not in use in postexilic times.
The name of the month Ethanim (I Kings viii 2) is Canaanite.
The seventh month among the Hebrews was Tishri. The feast in the
autumn was that of tabernacles. The removal of the ark to the
temple certainly presupposes the completion of the work of building; but according to I Kings vi 38, construction was finished in the
eighth month. That may, however, refer to the structure only and
not to the other paraphernalia perfected by Huramabi. In any case,
Solomon was assisted by all the officials of Israel, political and
religious. The ark had been kept in the temporary structure (the
tent) provided for it when David brought it to Jerusalem (I Chron
xvi 1). I Kings viii 3 has the priests taking up the ark; the Chronicler
follows the regulation laid down by David (I Chron xv 2) on the
basis of the law of Moses (Deut x 8, xxxi 25; Num iii 31). The
sharp distinction between priests and Levites was not always observed. The Chronicler has exalted the latter but in so doing does
not encroach upon the prerogatives of the former. Thus he follows
the P and D tradition of having the Levites bear the ark but the
priests place it in the sanctuary. The Kings tradition follows that of
Joshua (iii–iv). The combination of Levitical priests (or the priests,
the Levites) follows Deuteronomy; however the Kings parallel has a
conjunction: "the priests and Levites."

Just what is meant by vs. 5 is not quite certain. It could mean the
religious articles in the tabernacle at Gibeon, though the context
suggests it to have been concerned with the tent pitched for the ark
by David. The term "tent of meeting" is used only of the tabernacle
that was at Gibeon. It may be that both are meant to be included
since no official religious service is recorded as taking place at
Gibeon after the great sacrifice and subsequent revelation to Solomon there (II Chron i). Sacrifices naturally accompanied the event,
their number and character in keeping with the magnitude of the
occasion.

The ark itself was placed in the *debir* of the temple under the cherubs, whose wings formed a canopy over it. It is not clear how the structure was planned or oriented so as to make it possible to see them (see K. Galling, "Das Allerheiligste," JPOS 12 [1932], 43 ff.). It must mean that the ark was hidden behind the curtain (iii 14) but the poles stuck out on both sides. The cherubs must have covered everything from the top because their wings extended from wall to wall (iii 11–13). The contents of the ark were the tables of the *torah,* always closely associated with the ark of the covenant (cf. Deut x 2, 5). The Chronicler followed Kings closely here, and Kings was the work of the Deuteronomist. Later tradition suggested that the ark also contained a pot of manna and Aaron's rod (Heb ix 4), probably on the basis of Exod xvi 32–34, which does not say that it was put into the ark but that it was kept before the testimony ('*ēdūt*). Cf. Josephus *Antiquities* III.vi.5. For the Rabbinic tradition see H. L. Strack and P. Billerbeck, *Kommentar zum Neuen Testament aus Talmud u. Midrash,* III, 1926, pp. 737–40.

[The appearance of the glory of Yahweh, 11–14]: Here the Chronicler has substantially expanded the simple statement of his source. There it is said that when the priests withdrew from the *debir* where the ark had been deposited, the cloud filled the house so that they could not remain to perform their service. The cloud as a symbol of the presence of Yahweh is quite common (Exod xiii; Num ix; Ezek x 3–4) and here is intended to show the acceptance of the house dedicated to his name and now occupied by him. The origin of the passage is uncertain since the appearance of the glory of Yahweh is mentioned again after the dedication of the temple (vii 1–2). Here it may be connected with the festival rite conducted on the occasion of the transfer of the ark which appears to be a special ceremony. The ark played a vital role in Chronicles (the term occurs some fifty times). The auspicious rites conducted when it was brought to its final abode rivals those attending David's removal of it from the house of Obed-edom to Jerusalem. The Levitical singers were there, as were representatives of the twenty-four priestly divisions (on the musical guilds see I Chronicles, COMMENT on Sec. 25). Chronicles is the first to refer to the linen garb worn by the Levites (cf. I Chron xv 27), which was the material for the priestly vestments. That is another indication of the high regard for the Levites held by the writer whoever he was. These verses are generally denied to the Chronicler, possibly belong to the same hand responsible for I Chron xxiii–xxvii. Rudolph, p. 211, thinks they are a mechanical addition from I Kings vii. The rendition of such perfect music is to be observed and follows the repeated assertion of David's organization of the musical guilds. The passage may be an insertion but, if so, it follows the Chronicler's tradition.

6. BUILDING THE TEMPLE:
SOLOMON'S DEDICATION AND PRAYER
(vi 1–42)†

Solomon's dedicatory address

VI ¹ Then Solomon said,

> "Yahweh said he would dwell in darkness;
> ² And I have built for you an exalted house,
> An eternal dwelling place for you."

³ The king then turned around to bless the whole congregation of Israel while the whole congregation of Israel was standing. ⁴ He said, "Blessed be Yahweh God of Israel who by his deeds has fulfilled what he promised David my father orally when he said, ⁵ 'At no time since I brought out my people from the land of Egypt, did I select a city out of all the tribes of Israel to build a house where my name should dwell, or choose a man as leader for my people Israel, ⁶ but I did select Jerusalem where my name should dwell and chose David to be [ruler] over my people Israel.' ⁷ David my father had set his heart on building a house for the name of Yahweh God of Israel, ⁸ but Yahweh said to David my father, 'When you set your heart upon building a house for my name, you did well in that you had it in your heart [to do so], ⁹ nevertheless you shall not build the house, but your son, your bodily descendant, shall build the house for my name.' ¹⁰ Yahweh has fulfilled now the promise which he made and I have risen to the place of David my father; I am occupying the throne of Israel as Yahweh promised and I have built the house for the name of Yahweh God of Israel ¹¹ where I have placed the ark wherein is the covenant of Yahweh which he made with the people of Israel."

† **II Chron vi 1–42** ‖ I Kings viii 12–52.

Solomon's prayer

12 Then he stood up before the altar of Yahweh in the sight of the whole congregation of Israel and spread out his hands— 13 For Solomon had made a bronze platform five cubits long, five cubits wide, and three cubits high which he placed inside the court and upon which he stood. He knelt down upon his knees in the sight of the whole congregation of Israel and spread out his hands toward the heavens—14 and said, "O Yahweh God of Israel, there is no God like you in the heavens or upon the earth who keeps covenant faith with your servants who walk before you with all their heart 15 and which you observed with your servant David my father as you promised him. You have spoken it with your own mouth and have fulfilled it as is evident this very day. 16 Now, O Yahweh God of Israel, for the sake of your servant David, my father, keep your promise to him when you said, 'You shall never lack a descendant to sit upon the throne of Israel before me, if only your sons will guard their conduct, to conform to my instructions, as you have conducted yourself before me.' 17 Now, O Yahweh God of Israel, may your word which you spoke to your servant David prove true! 18 But can God, in truth, dwell among men upon the earth? Behold, the heavens and the highest heavens cannot contain you, how much less this house I have built! 19 Consider, therefore, the prayer and supplication of your servant, Yahweh my God, listen to the entreaty and the prayer your servant is offering before you; 20 that your eyes may be open to this house day and night, to the place where you promised to put your name, so that you may hear the prayer your servant offers toward this place. 21 Listen also to the entreaties of your servant and your people Israel. Whenever they pray toward this place, do listen from your dwelling place, from the heavens, and when you hear [it], forgive. 22 If anyone has sinned against his neighbor and an oath is required of him to confirm it and the oath is taken before your altar in this house, 23 then listen from the heavens and render justice to your servants; requiting the guilty by making

him responsible for his conduct and justifying the righteous in accordance with his righteousness. 24 If your people Israel are defeated before their enemy because they have sinned against you but then repent, confess your name, pray, and implore favor before you in this house, 25 then listen from the heavens, forgive the sin of your people Israel and bring them back to the land which you gave to them and to their fathers. 26 When the heavens remain closed so that there is no rain because they have sinned against you and they pray toward this place, confess your name and turn from their sin because you *humble them*, 27 then listen from the heavens, forgive the sin of your servants, your people Israel—for you are continually teaching them the good way which they are to follow—and let it rain upon the land which you gave to your people as an inheritance. 28 Should there be a famine in the land or pestilence, or should there be blight, or mildew, or locusts, or caterpillars, or their enemies besiege them in their own land, or any plague, or any sickness, 29 whatever prayer or entreaty is made by any one or by all of your people Israel, when each one is acutely aware of his affliction and pain, and he spread out his hands toward this house, 30 then listen from the heavens, your dwelling place, forgive and deal with each one, whose mind you know, in accordance with all his deeds—for you alone know the mind of the sons of men— 31 that they may revere you by following your directions, which you gave to our fathers, throughout all the days of their life on the face of the earth. 32 Also when the foreigner, who is not a member of your people Israel and who comes from a distant land, attracted by your great name, your powerful hand, and your outstretched arm, comes and prays toward this house, 33 then listen from the heavens, your dwelling place, and act in accordance with all that the foreigner implores you to do, in order that all the peoples of the earth may acknowledge your name, revere you as your people Israel do, and know that this house which I have built bears your name. 34 When your people go out to battle against their enemies, on whatever mission you

a–a So with LXX, Vulg.; Hebrew reads "answer them" or "afflict them."

send them, and they pray to you in the direction of this city which you have chosen and the house I have built for your name, 35 then listen from the heavens to their prayer and entreaty and maintain their cause. 36 If they sin against you—for there is not a man who does not sin—and you are angry with them, and abandon them before the enemy so that their captors carry them away to a distant or nearby land; 37 but then they wholeheartedly repent in the land where they have been taken as captives and entreat you once more in the land of their captivity, saying, 'We have sinned, we have done wrong; we have rebelled,' 38 and return to you with all their mind and their soul in the land of their captivity to which they were carried away as captives, and pray in the direction of their land which you gave to their fathers and the city which you chose, and toward the house that I have built for your name, 39 then listen from the heavens, your dwelling place, to their prayer and their entreaties, maintain their cause and forgive your people who sinned against you. 40 Now, O my God, may your eyes be open and your ears attentive to the prayer [offered] in this place.

41 And now go up, O Yahweh, God, to your resting place,
    you and your mighty ark;
Let your priests, O Yahweh, God, put on salvation,
Let your devotees rejoice in that which is good.
42 O Yahweh, God, do not reject your anointed ones;
Remember the loyalties of David your servant."

Notes

vi 2. *exalted.* Cf. W. F. Albright, JPOS 16 (1936), 17–20, on the meaning of *zᵉbūl*.

an eternal dwelling place. For idea see 1QH 18:29.

3. *turned around.* Literally "turned his face and blessed."

11. *where I . . . ark.* I Kings viii 21, "I have made a place for the ark."

the people of Israel. Kings parallel reads "our fathers."

23. *making . . . conduct.* Literally "to put his way [deed] upon his head."

28. *their enemies . . . land.* Literally "his enemies besiege him in the land of his gates." I.e., lay siege to his cities.

29. *his affliction and pain.* Cf. 1QH 9:6, where the order of words is reversed.

33. *bears your name.* Literally "that your name has been called over . . ."

41. Cf. Ps cxxxii 8–11.

42. *anointed ones.* Some manuscripts and Ps cxxxii 10 have singular. For RSV expression "the face of," see 1QH 16:18. The "anointed ones" refers to kings and priests.

Remember . . . servant. Based on Isa lv 3—loyalties of David.

COMMENT

This section closely follows its source in I Kings viii 12–52. It contains two addresses, one to the people and the other to God in the form of a lengthy prayer just as appropriate for the Chronicler's time as for that of Solomon.

[The address to the people, vi 1–11]: Verses 1, 2 are apparently meant to be a part of the preceding episode and are Solomon's comment upon the appearance of the glory of Yahweh that descended upon the sanctuary when the ark of the covenant was moved into it. The king and the congregation of Israel followed the procession from the east; they stood behind the Levitical singers facing the altar and looking toward the temple. In response to the withdrawal of the priests from the sanctuary because of the presence of the glory of Yahweh, Solomon uttered these lines. That sequence of events connects the dedication with the placing of the ark in the *debir* (but see COMMENT on Sec. 5, v 5).

With some additions the address to the people reiterates the same principles enunciated by David in I Chron xxviii 2 ff. The passage begins with the note that Solomon turned from facing the altar toward the people who had been standing behind him. He observes that Yahweh has now fulfilled his promise to David by his deeds, that is, by permitting the house to be constructed and showing his approval by the appearance of his glory. I Kings viii 16 omits, by homoioteleuton, 5b–6a which the Chronicler has preserved for us.

[Solomon's prayer, 12–42]: Having addressed the people, Solomon turned toward the altar of Yahweh that was before him and offered up this prayer. According to the Chronicler, he stood upon a bronze platform—or knelt upon it—in full view of the assembled congregation. The Chronicler alone records the detail of the bronze platform. The *kiyyōr* (platform) is fairly well attested as a cult object used by dignitaries. Albright calls attention to a number of such representations from Egypt and Syria (ARI, pp. 152 f.; cf. also Parrot, *The Temple of Jerusalem,* pp. 44 f.). A king offering prayer to Baal is depicted on a stele from Ugarit (C. F. A. Schaeffer, *Ugaritica* 2 [1949], Pls. xxiii, xxiv; cf. H. Bossert, *Altsyrien,* 1951, Fig. 960, which shows a priest on a high platform with legs presenting an offering to the deity. The stele is from Daphne).

Both standing and kneeling positions are shown on the monuments. Pritchard (ANEP, p. 192, Fig. 576) has one of Tukulti-Ninurta I standing and kneeling before a cult socket. H. Schmökel (*Ur, Assur und Babylon,* 1955, Pl. 66) shows a bronze statue of a man kneeling in prayer. The statue comes from Larsa. Just why Solomon stood or knelt upon this platform is uncertain; it could have been that such a position made him more readily visible to the congregation or enabled the people to hear him better. For another view cf. G. von Rad, *Gesammelte Studien zum Alten Testament,* 1958, p. 207. The temple is, according to this theory, both the dwelling place of Yahweh and the place where he is worshiped. Yahweh is present in the temple, also in heaven.

The first portion of the prayer is characterized by praise for Yahweh who always remains faithful to his covenant, and by thanksgiving for the fulfillment of his promises to David. This is coupled with a petition that the promises made to David may remain forever true. An ascription of majesty to Yahweh follows, pointing out that since the very heavens cannot contain God, the temple, which is so infinitesimal, cannot hope to do so. That may be the reason for the Chronicler's frequent references to Yahweh's hearing "from heaven" (seven times in the chapter). Though the writer follows his source closely, it is significant that he stresses the house of Yahweh as the place where prayer is both offered and answered. It is thus the meeting place of God and man, for not only is Yahweh implored to hear the prayer of the king but also the prayers of "your people Israel." Also of special importance is the recognition of the people's need for forgiveness—an outstanding characteristic of the whole prayer of the king.

The seven petitions in vss. 22–39 deal almost exclusively with national affairs. Though the first petition appears to be individual in import, it is a matter of maintaining community order. It deals with the confirmation of the oath so as to vindicate the innocent and to requite the guilty. The second petition concerns Israel's recognition of its sin in its defeat at the hands of an enemy. If the people repent, God is implored to hear their prayer and restore them to their land. The third petition deals with drought; the fourth with famine, pestilence, and other calamities; the fifth with the foreigner who may be drawn to Israel's God by the observation of his mighty acts. It is significant that no condition is laid upon the foreigner; he is neither required to confess his faith nor to confess his sins, though both may be implied by an attraction to Yahweh. The sixth petition requests assistance from Yahweh for any military mission upon which he may have sent Israel. The final petition is on behalf of those who are in captivity and who recognize their sin by repentance and contrition. The broad application of the principle involved (vs. 36) is extraordinary. The petitionary portion of the prayer closes with the plea that Yahweh may ever hear those who pray "in this place." Verses 39–40 are a curtailed parallel of I Kings viii 50–52.

The conclusion of the prayer was added by the Chronicler from Ps cxxxii 8–11 and Isa lv. Since this conclusion is missing in the Kings parallel, the writer must have included it for a specific purpose. Psalms cxxxii is one of the royal psalms and as such centers about the idea of the enthronement of the king (see H. Gunkel and J. Begrich, *Einleitung in die Psalmen,* 1933, pp. 140–71, and S. Mowinckel, *Psalmenstudien,* II, 1922, pp. 112 ff.; for recent literature bearing on the Psalm see H. J. Kraus, *Psalmen,* II, 1960, p. 876). Amid the vicissitudes of the age, recalling the Deuteronomic theme of the rest of the people of God, the Chronicler has Solomon pray that Yahweh may take up his resting place with them (cf. von Rad, *Gesammelte Studien zum Alten Testament,* pp. 104 f.). Rest could be assured only if the mighty ark were present because it was the symbol of power. But that is not enough: the priests would have to put on salvation and the devotees delight in the good—a motif not present in the Psalm parallel. Once more the king prays, in the words of the Psalm, for the continuity of the Davidic line, which for the writer would have messianic significance. Only thus could the Davidic hope be realized and the promise to him be fulfilled (I Chron xxiii 25)—a blessing devoutly to be wished for in his time.

There may be a connection here between the dedication of the temple by Solomon and the second temple of Zerubbabel. The use of Ps cxxxii would be particularly suitable for such an occasion as the dedication of the second temple. Zerubbabel was the last pretender of whom we know until after the time of Ezra and Nehemiah. The variations from Ps cxxxii, based on Isa lv, look like a formulation of the Chronicler. If, therefore, the addition has Zerubbabel's temple as a frame of reference, the hope expressed is both messianic and historical.

7. BUILDING THE TEMPLE: THE DEDICATION CEREMONY
(vii 1–10)†

VII 1 As soon as Solomon had concluded his prayer, fire descended from the heavens and consumed the burnt offering and the sacrifices, and the glory of Yahweh filled the house, 2 so that the priests were unable to enter the house of Yahweh because the glory of Yahweh filled the house of Yahweh. 3 When all the Israelites saw the descent of the fire and the glory of Yahweh upon the house, they bowed down with their faces to the ground on the pavement, worshiped and praised Yahweh with

"For he is good and his loyalty eternal."

4 Then the king and all the people offered a sacrifice before Yahweh. 5 King Solomon offered a sacrifice of twenty-two thousand oxen and one hundred twenty thousand sheep when the king and all the people dedicated the house of God. 6 The priests occupied their posts and the Levites had the musical instruments of Yahweh which David the king had provided to [render]

"Give thanks to Yahweh, for eternal is his loyalty"

whenever David offered praise with their help; the priests on the other side blew trumpets while all Israel stood. 7 Solomon also dedicated the middle section of the court that was in front of the house of Yahweh, for he offered the burnt offerings and the fat pieces of the peace offerings there, because the bronze altar which Solomon had made could not hold the burnt offering, the meal offering and the pieces of fat. 8 At that time Solomon together with all Israel who had come from the entrance

† II Chron vii 1–10 ‖ I Kings viii 54, 62–66.

at Hamath to the wadi of Egypt—a very large congregation—celebrated the feast for seven days. 9 On the eighth day they had the final celebration, for they had devoted seven days to the dedication of the altar and seven days to the feast. 10 On the twenty-third day of the seventh month he sent the people to their tents, rejoicing and delighted because of the goodness Yahweh had shown to David, to Solomon, and to Israel his people.

NOTES

vii 3. *the pavement.* Cf. Ezek xl 17–18, xlii 3 which locate the pavement in the outer court.

"For he . . . eternal." The title of the hymn.

6. *"Give thanks . . . loyalty."* The title of the hymn.

on the other side. Literally "in front of them." Could also be rendered "responsively." While there may well have been an antiphonal arrangement, the reference here appears to be to a position in view of the priests' posts mentioned at the beginning of the verse. According to v 12 the Levitical musicians stood on the east side of the altar. The priests "in front of them" would then have been on the west side, between the altar and the temple proper.

8. *the entrance . . . Egypt.* The traditional limits of the holy land; in other sources, the limits are more tightly drawn (from Dan to Beersheba).

COMMENT

The source in I Kings is followed fairly closely, though there are some deviations and some rearrangements. This section is concerned with the actual dedication of the house of Yahweh, and the following section with Yahweh's response to Solomon's work in connection with the temple and his prayer.

The response of Yahweh to Solomon's dedication of the temple was a gigantic holocaust ignited by fire from heaven, which confirmed his acceptance of both temple and offerings that had been waiting (cf. v 6). The same phenomenon occurred when David offered sacrifices on the threshing floor of Ornan to stay the plague (I Chron xxi 26). Verses 1c–3 replace Solomon's blessing of the people in I Kings viii 54b–61. The glory of Yahweh now filled the

temple as it had filled the *debir* when the ark was placed therein
(v 13 f.). The people bowed reverently before Yahweh and worshiped him; they burst into praise with the hymn sung on the other
occasion just noted. The sacrifices referred to were those consumed by the heavenly fire (vs. 1). Verse 6 may be a later
insertion since it does not occur in Kings. But such a hymnal response
to the accompaniment of Levitical musicians and priestly trumpeters
may well have been part of the service, if, as is believed, musical
guilds were organized by David (for a discussion of David's provision of musical instruments and organization of musical guilds see
COMMENT in *I Chronicles,* Sec. 25).

The place where the sacrifices were offered, in the center of the
court, was consecrated especially for the purpose as the bronze altar
was too small for such enormous offerings. This was, in all probability, the rock upon which David offered the oxen purchased from
Ornan. According to the Chronicler, the bronze altar was made by
Solomon (vs. 7, iv 1). The Kings parallel says nothing about the
construction of such an altar, nor is it referred to elsewhere in
Chronicles. Evidently the Deuteronomist assumed that the bronze
altar of the tabernacle was moved into the temple complex where it
remained until it was displaced by Ahaz (II Kings xvi).

The feast of tabernacles was celebrated in connection with the
consecration of the altar as the phrase "at that time" (vs. 8) indicates. This was one of the feasts requiring the presence of all male
Israelites (Deut xvi 16). Not only does the writer repeat the assertion of I Kings viii 65 that all Israel from the Hamath entrance
to the wadi of Egypt was present but stresses the great size of the
congregation in attendance by adding "very." According to the
Kings parallel, Solomon dismissed the people on the eighth day;
here the eighth day marked the climax of the whole festival, a later
practice (cf. Lev xxiii 36b; Num xxviii 25 f.; Neh viii 18) not
mentioned in the earlier law (Deut xvi 13–15). The combined
time for dedication and the feast then was a total of fifteen days
plus one day for the dismissal of the people. As Rudolph, p. 217,
has pointed out, since the dismissal of the people took place on the
twenty-third day of the seventh month, the feast of dedication occupied the eighth to the fourteenth days, and the dedication, the
fifteenth to the twenty-second days. That the dedication of the temple
is here referred to as that of the altar is explained in vs. 12: the
place of sacrifice is the communion center of the temple complex.

8. BUILDING THE TEMPLE: YAHWEH'S RESPONSE (vii 11–22)†

VII 11 When Solomon had completed the house of Yahweh and the palace and brought to a successful conclusion all that was in the mind of Solomon to do with reference to the house of Yahweh and his own house, 12 Yahweh appeared to Solomon that night and said to him, "I have heard your prayer and have chosen this place for myself as a house of sacrifice. 13 If I shut up the heavens so that it does not rain and command the locust to crop the land, or if I send a pestilence on my people, 14 and then my people over whom my name is called humble themselves, pray, seek my presence, and turn away from their evil ways, I will listen from the heavens, forgive their sin, and restore their land. 15 Now my eyes shall be open and my ears attentive to the prayer offered at this place. 16 Now I have chosen and consecrated this house where my name shall remain forever and where my eyes and my heart shall be continually. 17 If you walk before me as David your father did, strive to do everything that I command you, and keep my statutes and judgments, 18 I will uphold your royal throne as I covenanted with David your father, saying, 'You shall not lack one to rule Israel.' 19 But if you turn away, abandon my statutes and my commandments which I have laid down for you, and go to serve other gods and worship them, 20 I will uproot *you* from my land which I gave to *you,* and I will cast out of my sight this house which I have consecrated for my name and make it a derision and taunt among all the peoples. 21 And everyone who

† II Chron vii 11–22 ‖ I Kings ix 1–9.

a–a So with some of the versions, for Heb. "them" influenced by the pronoun at the end of the preceding vs. I Kings ix 7 reads "I will cut off Israel."

passes by it shall be appalled at this house which was so exalted
and remark, 'Why has Yahweh done so to this land and to this
house?' 22 Then shall they reply, 'Because they abandoned
Yahweh God of their fathers who brought them up out of the
land of Egypt, joined themselves to other gods, worshiped and
served them; on that account he brought all this evil upon
them.'"

NOTES

vii 18. *I covenanted.* I Kings ix 5 reads "I promised."

COMMENT

The appearance of Yahweh to Solomon is indicative of the acceptance of his work, as the descent of fire had been for the offerings and the glory of Yahweh for the *debir* when the ark was placed
in it. While there is no special passage dealing with the palace or
other structures (cf. I Kings vii), it must be remembered that they
were all part of the same complex of buildings. In fact, the temple
itself was in all probability a royal chapel in the days of Solomon
and as such would be only one of the buildings involved in the
gigantic enterprise. For a sketch of the buildings see Parrot, *The
Temple of Jerusalem*, p. 20 (from Galling, BRL, cols. 411–12). For
the royal chapel idea see Parrot, *op. cit.*, pp. 51 f.; Möhlenbrink,
Der Tempel Salomos, pp. 48 ff.; Alt, KS, II, pp. 100–15. The king
occupied a special place in Israel and hence the house of Yahweh
adjacent to the house of the king is quite appropriate. In any case,
Yahweh appeared to Solomon that night (Kings indicates this was
the second time, the first at Gibeon) to reassure him that his
work and prayer have been noted in heaven. The communication
of Yahweh in the first statement follows the same line taken by the
prayer of the king. Yahweh promises to be attentive to "this place,"
which may have more in it than the temple itself, referring to both
the place of worship and the center of the rule of his anointed one.

So much is implied by vss. 17–18. There is certainly a messianic overtone in the phrase "one who rules over Israel" (cf. Mic v 2). The influence of the prophets is apparent here. The threat in vs. 20 is stronger here than in I Kings ix 7.

9. OTHER ACHIEVEMENTS OF SOLOMON
(viii 1–18)†

VIII ¹ At the end of twenty years during which Solomon had built the house of Yahweh and his own house, ² and *ᵃrestored the cities which Huram had given to himᵃ* and colonized them with Israelites, ³ Solomon went to Hamath-zobah and seized it. ⁴ He also fortified Tadmor in the desert, as well as all the store cities he had built in Hamath. ⁵ He built Upper Beth-horon and Lower Beth-horon, fortress cities with walls, gates, and bars; ⁶ Baalath and all Solomon's store cities; all the chariot-cities and the cities for his teams of horses; and everything heᵇ wanted to build in Jerusalem, in the Lebanon, or in any [other] area under his dominion. ⁷ All the people left of the Hittites, the Amorites, the Perizzites, the Hivites, and the Jebusites who did not belong to Israel—⁸ that is, those of their descendants remaining in the land after them and whom the Israelites had not exterminated—Solomon reduced to slavery as they are to this day. ⁹ However Solomon did not make slaves of any of the Israelites for his work; for they were soldiers, chiefs of his adjutants, and chiefs of his chariots and his horsemen. ¹⁰ These were the chiefs of King Solomon's garrisons: two hundred and fifty of them who were in charge of the people. ¹¹ Then Solomon brought up the daughter of Pharaoh from the city of David to the house he had built for her because, he said, "My wife must not live in the house of David the king of Israel, for the precincts*ᶜ* to which the ark of Yahweh has come are sacred."

† **II Chron viii 1–18** ‖ I Kings ix 10–28.

ᵃ Text repeats the name Solomon as subject of "restored" and as the object "him" in the relative clause.
ᵇ Text has "Solomon."
ᶜ Hebrew reads "these," referring to the total complex of buildings.

12 Then Solomon offered burnt offerings to Yahweh, upon the altar of Yahweh which he had erected before the portico, 13 in accordance with the regular prescriptions for offering as commanded by Moses, on the Sabbaths, the new moons, the festivals, and the three yearly feasts: the feast of unleavened bread, the feast of weeks, and the feast of tabernacles. 14 Following the prescription of David his father, he set up the divisions of priests for their service and the Levites for their duties of praise and ministration before the priests, in conformity with the daily requirements; also the porters according to their divisions for each gate, for such was the command of David the man of God. 15 Nor did they deviate in any respect from the command of the king concerning the priests, the Levites, and the storehouses. 16 Thus all the work of Solomon was carried out from*d* the day of the foundation of the house of Yahweh until its consummation—the house of Yahweh was complete in every detail. 17 Then Solomon went to Ezion-geber and to Eloth, on the seashore in the land of Edom. 18 Huram sent him ships through his agents as well as experienced seamen who went to Ophir with Solomon's servants where they took on four hundred and fifty talents of gold which they brought to King Solomon.

d So with the Vrs. for Heb. "until."

NOTES

viii 4. *Tadmor*. I Kings ix 18 has Tamar but vocalizes Tadmor.

6. *area*. Literally "land."

8. *slavery*. Cf. I Kings ix 21 where the phrase for total slavery occurs. See I. Mendelsohn, *Slavery in the Ancient Near East*, 1949, p. 97.

16. *the house of Yahweh was complete in every detail*. Based on I Kings ix 25c.

18. *experienced seamen*. Literally "servants who know the sea."

ophir. See COMMENT on vss. 17–18.

four hundred and fifty talents. I Kings ix 28 has "420 talents."

COMMENT

In most respects the Chronicler follows his source though he modifies certain points and expands others. This section is a good illustration of his method.

[Building and fortification of cities, viii 1–6]: The most striking thing in the section is vs. 2, which does not agree with the situation narrated in I Kings ix 10 ff. There it is stated that Solomon gave to Hiram twenty cities in Galilee in exchange for lumber and gold. Here it is said that Hiram gave to Solomon certain cities, presumably in Galilee though the location is not given, which Solomon colonized. If Kings is right about Hiram's reaction, Chronicles may have the sequel to the story. Hiram may have returned the cities to Solomon as worthless, which might explain why he "restored" them. There may be more involved in the transaction than meets the eye. Solomon may have made good on the original deal, with payment in gold or in some other way; in that case the cities may have been collateral until the time when payment could be made in gold. It has been suggested that the Chronicler refers to another situation than the one in I Kings ix 10 ff., but that seems unrealistic (cf. Rudolph, p. 219) in view of the context. Some feel that Hiram may have returned the cities, which may be correct, but that might reflect on the financial condition of Solomon.

The seizure of Hamath-zobah is not mentioned in I Kings ix. Hamath-zobah, which are brought together twice by the Chronicler (I Chron xviii 3 and here), reflect the situation in the Persian period when Zobah was part of the province of Hamath (see K. Elliger in PJB 32 [1936], 56; M. Noth, PJB 33 [1937], 47; C. H. Gordon, JNES 14 [1955], 56–58; Noth, ÜS, p. 159). David had trouble with Zobah (II Sam viii 9, x 8; I Chron xix 6), perhaps on more than one occasion. It is possible that the difficulty reappeared in Solomon's time or the Chronicler may have attributed David's conquest to Solomon. Zobah may have rebelled after David's death but it is hard to understand how Hamath would be involved; its friendship with David (II Sam viii 9–10) doubtless continued into Solomon's reign. A. Malamat thinks there may be a historical kernel present in the story of Hamath-zobah (cf. BA 21 [1958], 101, n.

22, and references there). Gordon thinks Israelites were settled there as enclaves during the period of the united monarchy (IEJ 5 [1955], 88).

Tadmor does not occur in the parallel (I Kings ix 18); the name given there is Tamar, which was a small village southwest of the Dead Sea (cf. Ezek xlvii 19, xlviii 28; the Thamara of Eusebius, presently identified with Qurnub, was some twenty-five miles south-east of Beer-sheba. For further discussion see J. A. Montgomery and H. S. Gehman, *The Book of Kings* [in ICC], 1951, p. 208). The alteration of Tamar to Tadmor is usually attributed to the Chronicler's attempt to glorify Solomon, since Tadmor was an important center east of Zobah on the caravan route to Mesopotamia (Tadmor later became Palmyra). It is to be noted that the Kings reference appears in a different context and thus the Chronicler may indeed preserve another tradition since he places it immediately after Hamath-zobah in whose territory Tadmor was located. There is no evidence that David did much fortifying; but there are numerous references to Solomon's fortifications, which are supported by archaeological explorations. See A. Dupont-Sommer, *Les Araméens,* 1949, pp. 28 f. But also see remarks of W. F. Albright, "The Judicial Reform of Jehoshaphat," AMJV, p. 69; in ARI, p. 133, he speaks of Solomon's control of the outlying district of Zobah, etc. Cf. also John Bright, *A History of Israel* (see Selected Bibliography), p. 192, n. 66. There is just a possibility that Solomon may have constructed some kind of fortification at or in the vicinity of Tadmor to check the Aramaeans, who threatened the outskirts of his empire. If we admit his endeavor to control Aramaean pressures then the fortifying of Tadmor or its environs is not impossible. See M. Gichon, "The Defences of the Solomonic Kingdom," PEQ (July–December 1963), pp. 116–19.

Beth-horon was some ten miles west northwest of Jerusalem on the boundary between Ephraim and Benjamin (Josh xviii 13) and a Levitical city (Josh xxi 22). Later it became Upper Beth-horon and Lower Beth-horon (Beit 'Ur el-Foqa and Beit 'Ur et-Tahta). It was a gateway into the hill country (cf. I Sam xiii 18). The I Kings parallel speaks only of Lower Beth-horon which was probably the more important of the two. It was a fortified place on the way from the Valley of Aijalon to Gibeon. Baalath was somewhere in Dan (Josh xix 44). Kings mentions in addition Hazor, Megiddo, and

Gezer, which are probably implied here in the phrase "all the chariot-cities and the cities for his teams of horses."

Solomon's building activity is attested by archaeology at Gezer, Megiddo, Hazor, Ezion-geber, and other places. A description of the results at Megiddo in the Solomonic period, including the famous stables, may be found in R. S. Lamon and G. M. Shipton, *Megiddo,* I, 1939, pp. 8–61; for Gezer, see G. E. Wright, BA 21 (1958), 103 f.; for Hazor, see Y. Yadin, BA 21 (1958), 46 f. See also Y. Aharoni's attribution to Solomon of casemate walls at Hazor, Gezer, Tell Qasile, Beth Shemesh, and Tell Beit Mirsim (BASOR 154 [April 1959], 35–39).

[Labor battalions, 7–10]: This passage follows I Kings ix 20–23 (fairly) closely. Both authors assert that forced labor was confined to the descendants of the peoples living in the land when Israel took over. The Chronicler says Israel did not exterminate them; the Deuteronomist says they could not do so. The Israelites were either soldiers or overseers over the labor battalions. But cf. I Kings v 13 ff., which the Chronicler conveniently overlooks earlier. The number of those set over the labor gangs is 250; in I Kings ix 23 it is 550. The former may be a scribal error, though it is to be observed that he has toned down the whole statement a bit by omitting the phrase "over the work."

[Moving day for the daughter of Pharaoh, 11]: I Kings ix 24 says the daughter of Pharaoh *came up* from the palace of David to the house that Solomon had made for her. Elsewhere in I Kings (ix 16) we learn that Gezer (perhaps Gerar) was given by the Pharaoh to Solomon as a marriage dowry for his daughter. All this is carefully excluded by the Chronicler because he wants to play down any relationship with Egypt. Here he stresses two points: (a) that Solomon *brought* the daughter of Pharaoh up to the house prepared for her, and (b) that she is separated from the royal palace because she is his wife and not because she is the daughter of Pharaoh. The reason for the separation was that she was a woman. Women were more frequently unclean in the ritual sense (Lev xv 19 ff.) than men. The Chronicler, in the interests of cult purity, thus endeavored to remove women from proximity to that which was sacred in line with the precepts of the *P* code. This led, later on in the days of the Herodian temple, to the provision of the court of women (cf. E. Schürer, *Geschichte des jüdischen Volkes im Zeitalter*

Jesu Christi, II, 3d ed., 1898, p. 285). The parallel verse of Kings speaks of the building of the Millo, which is not referred to here at all.

[Cultic provisions, 12–16]: The Chronicler has both curtailed and expanded the notice of offerings in his source (I Kings ix 25). The latter mentions burnt offerings and peace offerings as being offered three times a year, that is, at the annual feasts. He also says that Solomon also burned incense to Yahweh. The Chronicler, on the other hand, limits the scope of offerings to the burnt offering and says nothing about the offering of incense. Verses 13–16a are missing in I Kings ix. There it is said that the offerings were in accord with the prescription laid down by Moses (cf. Num xxviii–xxix) which are then detailed as referring to the Sabbath, new moon and festivals, as well as to the three annual feasts. Following the appointment of David, Solomon continued the priestly and Levitical orders (I Chron xxiii–xxvi) and those of the gatekeepers. They were followed exactly. So far as the writer is concerned, the carrying out of those prescriptions marked the completion of the work on the house of God, the fulfillment of the commands of David.

[Maritime mission to Ophir, 17–18]: The maritime venture of Solomon has been greatly illumined by the explorations and excavations of Nelson Glueck (see Glueck, *The Other Side of the Jordan,* 1940, Ch. iv; *Rivers in the Desert,* 1959, pp. 153–63; BA 1–3 [1938–40]; *National Geographic Magazine,* February 1944, 233–56). The Chronicler has the king himself go to Ezion-geber. As the maps indicate, Ezion-geber is near the northern end of the Gulf of Aqaba. The town was apparently known as Elath or Eloth in the time of Kings (I Kings ix 26). (See N. Glueck, "The Topography and History of Ezion-geber and Elath," BASOR 72 [1938], 2–13.) It is identified with present-day Tell el-Kheleifeh, west of Aqaba. Solomon had a seaport and large copper and iron works at Ezion-geber, and to judge from the remains, there was also a naval yard there for the construction and repair of ships. Copper and iron were derived from the surrounding area. On the problem of the source of Solomon's copper and the location of his copper mines see Y. Yadin, *Biblica* 36 (1955), 346, n. 2, and B. Rothenberg, "Ancient Copper Industries in the Western Araba," PEQ (January–June 1962), 5–64. Finished products were apparently exported in barter trade with South Arabia and Ophir, and thus broke the land route monopoly of the South Arabians. Ophir was probably in Somaliland across from South Arabia. (See Albright, ARI, pp. 133 f.; J. A. Montgomery, *Arabia and the Bible,* 1934, p. 38, n. 5, and pp. 176 ff. For further references to Solomon's activity at Ezion-geber and its significance see Montgomery and Gehman, *The Book of Kings,* pp. 211 f.)

The Tyrians were the best seamen of the time and once again Hiram assisted Solomon by sending him shipbuilders and sailors. Through their combined efforts they were quite successful, as the archaeological remains indicate. The enormous quantity of gold (over fifteen tons) is probably exaggerated.

10. SOLOMON'S WISDOM AND WEALTH
(ix 1–28)†

The visit of the queen of Sheba

IX 1 When the queen of Sheba heard about the renown of Solomon, she came to Jerusalem, with a very large company of attendants and camels bearing perfume, a large quantity of gold and precious stones, to test Solomon with perplexing questions. After she arrived, she conversed with Solomon about everything that was on her mind. 2 Solomon answered all her questions and nothing was concealed from Solomon that he could not interpret for her. 3 When the queen of Sheba saw the wisdom of Solomon, the house he had built, 4 his table fare, his servants' quarters, the position and attire of his ministers, his cupbearers and their attire, and the steps*a* by which he went up to the house of Yahweh, she was breathless. 5 She said to the king, "The report I heard in my country about your wisdom in handling affairs of state is true. 6 I did not believe their reports until I came and saw it for myself; yes, the greater half of your wisdom had not been told me; you surpass the report I have heard. 7 Fortunate are *b*your men*b* and fortunate these your servants who stand before you continually and listen to your wisdom. 8 Blessed be Yahweh your God who was pleased with you and put you on his throne as king for Yahweh your God. Because your God loved Israel and wanted to give them eternal support,

† **II Chron ix 1–12** ‖ I Kings x 1–13; **13–28** ‖ I Kings x 14–29, iv 21 (v 1H).

a Hebrew reads "his upper chamber," on the roof of the temple. I Kings x 5 reads "his burnt offering." The interpretation is difficult with either reading. Based on von Rad's suggestion.
b–b LXX of I Kings x 8 reads "your wives," as do some Greek manuscripts here.

he set you over them as king to maintain justice and righteousness." 9 Then she gave the king one hundred and twenty talents
of gold, a great quantity of perfume and precious stones; there
was no perfume like that which the queen of Sheba presented
to King Solomon. 10 The servants of Hiram and the servants of
Solomon who brought gold from Ophir, also brought algum
wood and precious stones. 11 The king used the algum wood for
steps° of the house of Yahweh and the house of the king, and
for zithers and harps for the singers; their like had never
been seen before in the land of Judah. 12 King Solomon gave the
queen of Sheba every delightful thing for which she asked, apart
from [what he gave her in exchange for] what she brought to
the king. Then she returned to her country with her servants.

Solomon's wealth

13 The weight of the gold that Solomon received annually
amounted to six hundred and sixty-six talents of gold, 14 apart
from [what] the traders and merchants brought; all the Arabian
kings and the governors of the land also brought gold and silver
to Solomon. 15 King Solomon made two hundred large shields of
beaten gold, six hundred shekels of beaten gold being inlaid in
each shield; 16 and three hundred shields of beaten gold, three
hundred shekels of beaten gold going into each shield; the king
put them into the house of the forest of Lebanon. 17 The king
also made a large ivory throne which he overlaid with pure gold.
18 The throne had six steps, and a footrest [made] of gold was
attached to the throne and on both sides of the seat were armrests with two lions standing beside the armrests, 19 and twelve
lions standing there, one on each side of the six steps. Nothing
like it had been made for any kingdom. 20 All the drinking cups
of King Solomon were made of gold and all the vessels of the
house of the forest of Lebanon of fine gold; silver was of no
estimation in the time of Solomon. 21 The king's fleet went to
Tarshish with the servants of Huram, making a round trip every

° With LXX, Heb. "streets." The Kings parallel (I Kings x 12) is equally
obscure. Rudolph (p. 222) renders "balustrades" or "banisters."

three years; the Tarshish fleet carried gold, silver, ivory, and two species of monkeys. 22 King Solomon surpassed all the kings of the earth in wealth and wisdom, 23 and all the kings of the earth consulted Solomon to listen to his wisdom which God had put in his mind. 24 Each one of them brought his gift—articles of silver and articles of gold, garments, weapons,*d* perfume, horses, and mules; so it was year after year. 25 Solomon also had four thousand stalls for horses and chariots together with twelve thousand horsemen whom he billeted in the chariot-cities and with the king at Jerusalem. 26 He was the ruler over all the kings from the river to the land of the Philistines as far as the border of Egypt. 27 The king made silver as cheap in Jerusalem as stones, and cedar as plentiful as sycamore in the Shephelah. 28 They brought Solomon horses from Egypt and from all [other] lands.

d LXX reads "oil of myrrh."

NOTES

ix 1. *After she arrived.* Literally "she came to Solomon, she conversed with him."

5. *your wisdom . . . state.* Literally "about your words and about your wisdom."

9. *one hundred and twenty talents of gold.* A little over 4½ tons.

10. *algum wood.* Cf. COMMENT on ii 1–17. Customarily rendered "sandalwood," which is not found in the Lebanon mountains.

12. *every delightful thing . . . asked.* The meaning seems to be that he gave her whatever she admired and said she wished to possess.

[*what he gave her in exchange for*]. Some such clarification is necessary. The mission of the queen of Sheba was mostly commercial, hence the exchange. Some complimentary presents were doubtless exchanged along with the conclusion of commercial agreements. The addition really combines the texts of Kings and Chronicles. If it is correct, we have a case of double haplography because the clauses begin and end in the same way. Thus I Kings x 13 reads: "Except for what he gave her as the hand of the King Solomon"; while the text here says, "Except for what she brought to the king." Putting the two together we read, "Except for what he gave her [according to the authority of King Solomon] for what she brought to the king."

13. *six hundred and sixty-six talents.* Slightly over 25⅛ tons.

14. *the traders.* Literally "from the men of caravan trade." The meaning seems to be the revenue derived from tolls and mercantile trade. See J. Gray, *The Legacy of Canaan,* 1957, p. 157.

15. *large shields.* For drawings of large (*sinnāh*) and small (*māgēn*) shields see Galling, BRL, cols. 457–58; also ANEP, 184, 372.

beaten gold. May be alloyed or inlaid gold; they were for ornamental purposes.

six hunded shekels. About 15 lbs.

16. *shields.* See first NOTE on vs. 15.

three hundred shekels. I Kings x 17 has "3 minas of gold," which equals 150 shekels or about 3¾ lbs.

the house of the forest of Lebanon. So called perhaps because of the extensive use of cedar.

19. *One . . . steps.* Literally "on both sides of the six steps."

20. *silver . . . Solomon.* This is of course oriental hyperbole. There was so much of it that it didn't count. Cf. the request of King Dushratta of Mitanni for Egyptian gold which he says is "as common as dust" (J. A. Knudtzon, *Die El-Amarna Tafeln,* No. 19, line 61).

21. *Tarshish.* On the problem of Tarshish and the Tarshish fleet as the refinery fleet see W. F. Albright, BASOR 83 (October 1941), 22; ARI, p. 136; *Eretz Israel,* V, 7–9. Since Tarshish means "refinery" in Phoenician and the trade was with Ophir and Punt, there can hardly be a reference to Tartessus in southern Spain. Taken literally, i.e., as Tartessus in Spain, a voyage around the tip of Africa would be involved. That is quite unlikely.

making . . . years. The round trip would require something over a year; if it began in a given year it would extend through the next and into the following year. Thus parts of two years plus the one full year between would be reckoned as three years. See ARI, p. 134 and notes.

two species of monkeys. The *qōphīm* and *tukkiyīm* were monkeys of different types, ARI, p. 212, n. 16.

26. *the river.* I.e., the Euphrates.

27. *the Shephelah.* Low hills southwest of Bethlehem.

28. Refers to the horse trade; see NOTES on i 16, 17.

COMMENT

These verses are closely paralleled in I Kings x, the source upon which the writer relied. There was no reason to deviate from the source since it fitted quite well into his scheme for the glorification of King Solomon.

[The visit of the queen of Sheba, ix 1–12]: From the viewpoint of the Chronicler, the two phases of Solomon's achievements—wisdom and wealth—are associated to illustrate his fame and splendor. But the underlying motive of the source he used is undoubtedly trade. The visit of the queen of Sheba can no longer be regarded as fictional. Recent archaeological explorations in South Arabia have added a whole new chapter to the wealth and trade of a hitherto obscure land. While the names of queens as rulers do not appear in the known Assyrian records before the eighth century (one, Samsi, is mentioned in the records of Tiglath-pileser III and Sargon II; ANET, pp. 283 ff.), they must have been prominent in South Arabian affairs before that time. The impact of Arabia upon Palestine was considerable, as may be seen from the numerous references in the Bible (cf. Montgomery, *Arabia and the Bible;* G. W. Van Beek, BA 15 [1952], 2–6; W. F. Albright, "Dedan," *Geschichte und Altes Testament,* 1953, pp. 1–12). Sheba (Saba, Sabaeans) is mentioned frequently (cf., in addition to this section and its parallel, Isa lx 6; Jer vi 20; Ezek xxvii 22, xxxviii 13; Joel iii 8; Job i 15, vi 19; Ps lxxii 10, 15), especially in connection with caravans and the spice trade. To judge from the results of excavations so far published, Marib, the ancient capital of Sheba, was an imposing center of activity. Furthermore, evidence of economic vitality is shown by trade carried on all over the area from South Arabia northward to Phoenicia and Syria. See R. L. Bowen and F. P. Albright, *Archaeological Discoveries in South Arabia,* 1958, especially Pt. II, and the popular account by W. Phillips, *Qataban and Sheba,* 1955, especially Chs. 10, 24. Part of the site of Hadjar Bin Humeid, about sixty miles south of Marib, has been excavated to the bottom of the Tell and shows the existence of a settlement there in the tenth century B.C. The depths of the deposits at Timna and Marib indicate much older settlements and are therefore reflective of an advanced civilization, widespread and prosperous, in South Arabia (see W. F. Albright in *Eretz Israel,* V, 7–9). The tenth century was apparently one of extraordinary growth and expansion from Syria to Ethiopia (W. F. Albright, "Zur Chronologie des vorislamischen Arabien," in *Von Ugarit nach Qumran,* 1958, pp. 1–8).

It is probably no accident that this episode is reported immediately after the reference to the establishment of Solomon's seaport at Ezion-geber, whose traffic with Ophir threatened the lucrative overland trade of the South Arabians. Thus the visit of the queen of Sheba takes on added significance; it is of the nature of a diplomatic and trade mission whose business was to establish a modus vivendi with the great merchant prince of Palestine. What the queen saw confirmed the reports that had reached her of Solomon's wisdom and enterprise. The Chronicler does not refer to the classic description of Solomon's wisdom (I Kings iv 29–34 [v 9–14H]) and the term here appears to include something other than songs and proverbs. As Alt has shown, KS, II, pp. 90–99, Solomon's wisdom as described in I Kings iv 33 (v 13H) is to be explained in the light of Egyptian and Babylonian parallels; Alt characterizes it as "Listenwissenschaft," the art of classification. As viewed here it seems to be the knowledge of how to do things (vss. 3–4), functional knowledge as applied to building, organization, arrangements in his court, etc. Along with these qualities went that of a shrewd trader, as the queen must have learned even before her mission to Jerusalem. In addition to the traditional exchange of gifts there was trade of goods as implied in vs. 12.

The widest departure from the sources occurs in vs. 8 where I Kings x 9 has David occupying the throne of Israel. Here, in line with the writer's general view that the throne is Yahweh's which the king occupies for him, it is his (i.e., Yahweh's) throne occupied by Solomon "as king for Yahweh your God" (cf. I Chron xvii 14, xxviii 5, xxix 23; II Chron xiii 8).

[Solomon's wealth, 13–28]: With few significant variants, the Chronicler follows his source, which is itself composed of an assortment of materials bearing on the general subject of the wealth of Solomon. While there is certainly a great deal of exaggeration connected with almost every item, there is doubtless truth in each one. He did have a tremendous income from various sources, particularly from tolls levied on merchants and as a merchant trader, refiner, and manufacturer (see COMMENT on Sec. 9, viii 17–18). The reference to Arabian kings may reflect trade in Solomon's period but also a later time as Arabian trade continued into post-exilic times and after. The tribute or taxes received from the governors (a late term) of the land may contain a kernel of truth, though couched in late terminology, if the reference is to tolls levied for economic privileges.

The golden shields, made for decorative purposes, may be no more than the persistence of a local tradition and brought into the picture here because of the mention of gold in the preceding verses. The great ivory throne overlaid with gold was a showpiece; the story was repeated here because it reflected the splendor and glory of the Solomonic empire. This is also true of the later exaggeration of the drinking cups and the other ornamental vessels in the house of the forest of Lebanon. For a description of the throne, with a note on Asshurbanipal's, see Montgomery and Gehman, *The Book of Kings,* pp. 221 f. Here, vss. 17–19, is one of the significant variations from Kings. According to the latter, the back of the throne contained the figure of a calf's head, which here is made into either a lamb or armrest (cf. C. North, ZAW 50 [1932], 28 f.), in order to avoid any reference to the golden calves of Jeroboam as already evident in the MT of Kings. For such ornaments see J. W. and Grace M. Crowfoot, *Early Ivories from Samaria,* 1938, Pl. 9, Fig. 1, and G. Loud, *The Megiddo Ivories,* 1939, Pl. 4, Figs. 2a, b. The throne of Bar Rekab had a footstool (ANEP, 460). For a good illustration of a throne, though with different decorations on the back, see H. Carter and A. C. Mace, *The Tomb of Tut-Ankh-Amen,* I, 1923, Pls. LXII–LXIV. For the lion features see M. Pongracz, "Löwendarstellungen an Podesten der Königsthrone," *Mitteilungen des deutschen archäologischen Instituts Alteilung Kairo,* XV, 1957, pp. 213–20.

The maritime adventures of Solomon are significant and again the Chronicler has shown his bias toward the king. His source stated that both Hiram and Solomon had ships plying the waterways between Ezion-geber and Ophir. But Hiram's maritime activity has been toned down, as may be seen from the translation, which fits in well with the following verses describing Solomon's wealth and fame. Verse 24 doubtless refers to mercantile activity, which was conducted on a barter basis. Tolls and taxes were also paid in kind.

What is involved in the reference to chariot-cities with their horse stables and chariot sheds may be seen from the excavations of Megiddo and elsewhere (see Lamon and Shipton, *Megiddo,* I, pp. 32–47). According to the calculations of the archaeologists there was room at Megiddo for about four hundred and fifty horses and one hundred and fifty chariots, along with exercising grounds, water tanks, houses for grooms, etc. The four thousand stalls is probably not an exaggeration (though I Kings iv 26 [v 6H] obviously is; possibly a scribal error) since there were stables of similar character at Tell el-Hesy, Gezer, Taanach, and perhaps at Hazor (see P. L. O. Guy, *New Light from Armageddon,* 1931, pp. 42–48). However, these structures may not have been stables but storage places, as may have been those at Hazor; see Yadin et al., *Hazor,* II, p. 9. On the extent of Solomon's rule see COMMENT on Sec. 9. While there may have been some shrinking of the Israelite empire under Solomon, there cannot have been much (cf. Bright, *A History of Israel,* p. 193, and references there). But Solomon's claims were, in all probability, largely of a commercial nature as is hinted at again and again in the account.

11. CONCLUSION
(ix 29–31)†

IX 29 As for the remainder of the history of Solomon from beginning to end, is it not written down in the records of Nathan
the prophet, in the prophecy of Ahijah the Shilonite, and in the
visions of Iddo the seer concerning Jeroboam the son of Nebat?
30 Solomon was king over all Israel at Jerusalem for forty years.
31 When Solomon slept with his fathers, they buried him in the
city of David his father and Rehoboam his son became king in
his place.

† II Chron ix 29–31 ‖ I Kings xi 41–43.

COMMENT

Omitting the stories of Solomon's defection through catering to
foreign women, the Hadad and Rezon episodes, and the treason of
Jeroboam with the support of Ahijah because they undermined his
views of the king, the writer brings his account of Solomon to a
conclusion. This section follows I Kings xi 41–43 with the exception
of the reference to the sources in 29b. Whether they were actual
sources current at the time or whether they refer to Kings is disputed. Three prophetic records are mentioned as in the case of
David (I Chron xxix 29).

II. THE KINGS OF JUDAH

(ca. 922–587 B.C.)

12. THE REIGN OF REHOBOAM (ca. 922–915 B.C.): THE REBELLION OF ISRAEL (x 1–19)†

X 1 Then Rehoboam went to Shechem, for all Israel had come to Shechem to make him king. 2 When Jeroboam the son of Nebat heard about it—for he was in Egypt whither he had fled from the presence of Solomon the king—he returned from Egypt. 3 So they sent and summoned him. When Jeroboam and all Israel arrived, they said to Rehoboam, 4 "Your father made our yoke heavy; ease now the harsh servitude of your father and the heavy yoke he has imposed upon us and we will serve you." 5 He said to them, "Come back to me again in three days." So the people left. 6 Then King Rehoboam consulted the elders who served his father during his lifetime saying, "What reply do you advise for this people?" 7 They advised him as follows: "If you will be kind to this people, befriend them, and speak charitably to them, they will always remain your servants." 8 But he rejected the advice which the elders gave him and then consulted the younger men who grew up with him and were now his counselors. 9 He said to them, *a*"How do you advise me*a* to reply to this people who have said to me, 'Ease the yoke which your father imposed upon us'?" 10 The younger men who grew up with him gave him the following advice: "This is how you ought to reply to the people who petitioned you:

> 'Your father made heavy our yoke;
> you make [it] easier for us'!

† **II Chron x 1–19** ‖ I Kings xii 1–20.

a–a MT has "how do you advise that we . . ."; LXX "how do you advise that I." May be the royal plural.

This is what you ought to tell them, 'My little finger is thicker than my father's loins; 11 Although my father laid a heavy yoke upon you, I will make it yet heavier;

> My father disciplined you with whips,
> I will [do it] with scorpions.' "

12 When Jeroboam and all the people came to Rehoboam on the third day, as the king had directed, saying, "Come back to me on the third day," 13 the king Rehoboam answered them harshly because the king had rejected the advice of the elders. 14 In accordance with the advice of the younger men, he replied to them as follows:

> ^b"My father made heavy your yoke,^b
> I will add to it;
> My father disciplined you with whips,
> I will [do it] with scorpions."

15 So the king did not listen to the people, for it was a turn of affairs brought about by God that Yahweh might fulfill his word concerning Jeroboam the son of Nebat which he delivered through Ahijah the Shilonite. 16 When all Israel saw that the king would not listen to them, the people retorted to the king as follows:

> "What part have we in David,
> No inheritance with the son of Jesse;
> Each one to your tents, O Israel,
> Now look to your own house, O David."

So all Israel went to their tents. 17 Hence Rehoboam was king only over those of the Israelites who lived in the cities of Judah. 18 When King Rehoboam sent out Hadoram^c the corvée chief, the Israelites stoned him to death but King Rehoboam managed to mount his chariot and escape to Jerusalem. 19 So Israel has remained in rebellion against the house of David until today.

^{b–b} So with many manuscripts. Hebrew reads "I will increase your yoke."
^c LXX^B has "Adoniram." Cf. I Kings xii 18 "Adoram," a spelling variant.

NOTES

x 2. *he returned from Egypt.* I Kings xii 2 "he lived in Egypt." I Kings xii 2–3a is missing in LXX and is in part an intrusion from this passage combined with reminiscences of xi 40.

7. *kind.* I Kings xii 7 "servant."

befriend them. I Kings xii 7 "serve them."

16. *all Israel.* Kings parallel reads "Israel."

saw. Add with I Kings xii 16.

19. The Chronicler was quoting his source here. It has no reference to the later Samaritan schism.

COMMENT

Apparently there was no question of Rehoboam's accession in Judah; the old Davidic structure of a double crown, one of Judah and the other of Israel, was maintained. Hence he had to receive the crown of the latter from the hands of the elders of Israel. To that end he traveled to Shechem, the old amphictyonic center of Israel. (On the amphictyonic character of the Israelite tribes see M. Noth, *Zwölf Stämme Israels,* 1930. The personal union of Israel and Judah initiated by David and continued under Solomon fell apart after the latter's death because of the refusal of Rehoboam to redress the grievances of Israel.) Before anointing him, the authorities demanded the lifting of the grievous burdens imposed upon them by the extravagant building program of Solomon.

The preceding chapter mentions Jeroboam only in connection with the prophecy of Ahijah. The Chronicler, having avoided any reference to discontent during Solomon's reign, does so here only to explain why Jeroboam was in Egypt from whence he returned when he was informed of the proposed accession of Rehoboam. "All Israel" (vss. 1, 3, 16[*bis*]) refers to all the Northern tribes. "The Israelites who lived in the cities of Judah" (vs. 17) and "all Israel in Judah and Benjamin" (xi 3) underline the Chronicler's view that only those elements of Israel that remained loyal to the Davidic line were the true Israel.

In vs. 7 the Chronicler has toned down the source which has "servant" for "kind," obviously too strong a word for him as it applied to the king. For the same reason he changed "serve them" into "please them." Although Solomon is glorified by the writer, he cannot and does not exclude the damaging reflections upon his rule provided by this chapter, which is telling evidence to the effect that he does not completely distort history, painful though it may have been for him.

13. THE REIGN OF REHOBOAM (ca. 922–915 B.C.): ESTABLISHING THE KINGDOM (xi 1–23)†

The prophecy of Shemaiah

XI 1 When Rehoboam arrived at Jerusalem he mustered one hundred and eighty thousand select warriors from the house of Judah and of Benjamin to win back the kingdom for Rehoboam by war with Israel. 2 Then the word of Yahweh came to Shemaiah, the man of God, saying, 3 "Tell Rehoboam the son of Solomon, the king of Judah and all Israel in Judah and Benjamin: 4 'Thus has Yahweh said, you must not go up to fight with your brothers. Let each man return to his house, for this matter is my doing'." When they heard the words of Yahweh, they abandoned their pursuit of Jeroboam.

Cities for defense

5 Rehoboam resided in Jerusalem but built cities for the defense of Judah. 6 He built Bethlehem, Etam, Tekoa, 7 Beth-zur, Soco, Adullam, 8 Gath, Mareshah, Ziph, 9 Adoraim, Lachish, Azekah, 10 Zorah, Aijalon, and Hebron, which were the fortified cities for Judah and Benjamin. 11 He strengthened the fortified places and put commanders and supplies of food, oil, and wine, in them. 12 He also put large shields and spears in every single city and strengthened them very much. Thus Judah and Benjamin were retained by him.

Migration of priests and Levites

13 The priests and Levites from all over Israel came from their domain and placed themselves at his disposal. 14 The Levites left their pasture grounds and their property and went to Judah

† **II Chron xi 1–4**: cf. I Kings xii 21–24; **5–17** ‖ I Kings xii 25–33.

and Jerusalem because Jeroboam and his sons had excluded them from the priesthood of Yahweh, 15 and appointed priests of his own for the high places for the satyrs and for the calves he had made. 16 Those of all the tribes of Israel who had set their minds on seeking Yahweh God of Israel followed them to Jerusalem to sacrifice to Yahweh God of their fathers. 17 They strengthened the kingdom of Judah and supported Rehoboam the son of Solomon for three years, for they followed the way of David and Solomon for three years.

Rehoboam's family

18 Rehoboam took Mahalath the daughter of Jerimoth, David's son, and Abihail the daughter of Eliab, Jesse's son, as wife. 19 She bore him the following sons: Jeush, Shemariah, and Zaham. 20 After her he took Maacah the daughter of Absalom [as a wife] who bore him Abijah, Attai, Ziza, and Shelomith. 21 Rehoboam loved Maacah the daughter of Absalom more than all his [other] wives and concubines—for he had taken eighteen wives and sixty concubines and fathered twenty-eight sons and sixty daughters. 22 Rehoboam named Abijah the son of Maacah as the head and, therefore, leader of his brothers, for he wanted to make him king. 23 He acted wisely by distributing some of his sons to all the territories of Judah and Benjamin, that is to all the fortified cities, where he provided food in abundance for them and sought out wives *for them.*

a–a So for Heb. "multitude"; but cf. LXX. See NOTE.

NOTES

xi 1. *one hundred and eighty thousand.* Possibly the unit basis is involved here too since the reference is to a mustering of armed forces.

20. *Maacah the daughter of Absalom.* Cf. I Kings xv 2.

Abijah. "Abijam" in I Kings xv 1–7 (cf. Albright, AMJV, p. 81, n. 72).

22. *Rehoboam named Abijah . . . as the head.* Abijah was named "eldest" son and heir apparent. The use of the term *nāgīd* suggests the

possibility of a coregency here to secure succession against other claimants.

23. *and sought out wives for them.* Cazelles (*Les Livres des Chroniques* [see Selected Bibliography, Commentaries]) refers to the literal translation, approximately, "he consulted the multitude [of the gods] of his wives" which he takes with the following verse (xii 1). The rendering here adopted is based on the following division of words: *wayyiśśā' lāhem* [ ] *nāšīm*. Rudolph suggests . . . *lāhem hᵃmōn nāšīm* ("for them a multitude of wives").

COMMENT

[Prophecy of Shemaiah, xi 1–4]: To Shemaiah belongs the distinction of having averted further internecine war between Rehoboam and Jeroboam. "All Israel in Judah and Benjamin" in vs. 3 reflects the Chronicler's view, since I Kings xii 23 has "all the house of Judah and Benjamin" (cf. COMMENT on preceding section).

[Cities for defense, 5–12]: This passage is unique with the Chronicler and points clearly to the fact that he had sources at his disposal that were ignored by or unknown to the Deuteronomist. It also shows how he wove this material into his narrative in place of the latter's references to certain activities of Jeroboam.

G. Beyer ("Das Festungssystem Rehabeams," ZDPV 54 [1931], 113–34) has shown convincingly that the system of fortifications belongs to the period of Rehoboam; whether it dates from before the invasion of Shishak, as the Chronicler infers (xii 2), or after cannot now be determined (see also E. Junge, *Die Wiederaufbau des Heerwesens des Reiches Juda unter Josia,* 1938, who thinks the list is Josianic; and Alt, KS, II, pp. 306–15, who thinks it possible that it dates from the time of Rehoboam). Excavations at Azekah, Mareshah, Lachish, Beth-zur, and elsewhere have uncovered fortifications which may date from the period of Rehoboam (cf. Bliss and Macalister, *Excavations in Palestine, 1898–1900,* 1902; O. R. Sellars, *The Citadel of Beth-Zur,* 1933, and BA 21 [1958], 71–76; O. Tufnell, *Lachish III: The Iron Age,* 1953). If Beth-shemesh was in ruins at the time, that would account for its not being included (cf. F. M. Cross, Jr., and G. E. Wright, "The Boundary and Province Lists of the Kingdom of Judah," JBL 75 [1956], 216 f.); on the other hand both Beth-shemesh and Debir, present-day Tell

Beit Mirsim, may have been fortified already by Solomon (see BASOR 154 [April 1959], 38, n. 16). All of the places mentioned have now been identified. See the index in L. Grollenberg, *Atlas of the Bible,* 1956. On Etam, present-day Khirbet el-Khokh, see H. J. Kraus, ZDPV 72 (1956), 152–62. The fortifications were either in the hill country or at the edge of it and were intended for defense primarily against the Egyptians and Philistines, though they may have been erected in part also against the expansions of Edom. There was rebellion in Edom already in the time of Solomon (I Kings xi 14–22, 25), an incident not mentioned in Chronicles. The order of the listing in our passage does not follow the expected geographical sequence and, apart from 1 to 4, cannot be explained. Why Hebron should come last is also difficult to explain, unless it was a secondary fortress to which the hard-pressed defenders of Ziph might retreat if necessary. It is possible that others too were secondary fortifications, a line of fortified places where arms and other supplies were kept for emergency purposes, or for service in case the first line of defense was pierced. Rehoboam either regarded Jerusalem as fortification enough against Israel or he did not regard defense against Israel as imperative as against foreign elements.

[Migration of priests and Levites, 13–17]: The migration of priests and Levites is based on the report of I Kings xii 31–32, xiii 33 to the effect that Jeroboam appointed priests "from the whole people who were not Levites," though that does not imply necessarily that the latter were excluded as the Chronicler seems to think. But, as for the Deuteronomist, everything Jeroboam did was sinful in the sight of the Chronicler, who added satyrs to the high places and calves that he provided in Israel. Because of his feeling for Jerusalem as the worship center, he emphasizes the fact that all the really discerning Israelites followed the priests and Levites to the only legitimate shrine of the nation. Verse 17 may refer to the period before defection set in in the south, or that the Northerners came to Jerusalem for three years, that is, until the shrines of Jeroboam were set up when they, for the most part, worshiped there—a situation deplored by the writer.

[Family relationships of Rehoboam, 18–23]: Mahalath was a great-granddaughter of Jesse through both parents. Her father, Jerimoth, is nowhere else listed as a son of David and thus must have been the son of an inferior wife. Thus Mahalath was a cousin of the king Rehoboam. Maacah was either the granddaughter of Absalom, the son of David, or the daughter of another Absalom. Absalom, David's son, had only one daughter, Tamar, and three sons (II Sam xiv 27) who probably died in infancy (cf. II Sam xviii 18). Since no family connection is given, this appears to have been another Absalom. The oldest son of the beloved wife became the successor of Rehoboam.

Like his father Solomon (I Kings iv 11, 15), Rehoboam placed his sons in strategic centers to maintain his position and to guard against disloyalty.

14. THE REIGN OF REHOBOAM (ca. 922–915 B.C.): ABANDONMENT OF YAHWEH (xii 1–16)†

Shishak invasion

XII 1 **When the kingdom of Rehoboam was established** and he had become strong, he, together with all Israel, abandoned the law of Yahweh. 2 In the fifth year of King Rehoboam, Shishak the king of Egypt came up against Jerusalem, because they were unfaithful to Yahweh, 3 with twelve hundred chariots and sixty thousand horsemen; the people who came with him from Egypt were innumerable—Libyans, Sukkiim, and Ethiopians. 4 They captured the fortified cities belonging to Judah and came as far as Jerusalem. 5 Then Shemaiah the prophet came to Rehoboam and the captains of Judah who had retreated to Jerusalem before Shishak and said to them, "Thus has Yahweh said, 'You have abandoned me and so I have abandoned you to the hand of Shishak.'" 6 Then the captains of Israel and the king humbled themselves and said, "Yahweh is righteous." 7 When Yahweh saw that they humbled themselves, the word of Yahweh came to Shemaiah, saying, "Because they have humbled themselves, I will not destroy them but I will grant them some measure of deliverance; my wrath shall not be poured out upon Jerusalem by the hand of Shishak, 8 but they shall be his servants that they may find out [the difference between] my service and the service of the kings of the [other] lands." 9 So Shishak the king of Egypt attacked Jerusalem and carried away

† **II Chron xii 1–9:** cf. I Kings xiv 25–26; **10–14:** cf. I Kings xiv 27–28, 21–22; **15–16** ‖ I Kings xiv 29–31, xv 6.

a–a Reading *k^ehikkōn* for *k^ehākīn*. MT has "when Rehoboam established the kingdom."

the treasures of the house and the treasures of the king's house. He carried away everything, including the golden shields which Solomon had made.

More on Rehoboam

10 King Rehoboam then made bronze shields to replace them and put them into the hand of the captains of the guard who kept watch over the entrance to the king's house. 11 Whenever the king entered the house of Yahweh the guards would come and take them up and when he retired they would bring them back again into the guard chamber. 12 When he humbled himself, the wrath of Yahweh turned away from him so as not to destroy him completely. There were also some good things in Judah. 13 So King Rehoboam grew strong in Jerusalem and continued as king. For Rehoboam was forty-one years old when he became king and remained king for seventeen years in Jerusalem, the city where Yahweh had chosen, out of all the tribes of Israel, to put his name. His mother's name was Naamah the Ammonitess. 14 But he did wrong in that he did not set his mind to seek Yahweh.

Conclusion

15 As for the history of Rehoboam from beginning to end, is it not written down in the records of Shemaiah the prophet and Iddo the seer; so also is the official genealogy? Wars between Rehoboam and Jeroboam continued throughout the period. 16 When Rehoboam slept with his fathers, he was buried in the city of David and Abijah his son became king in his place.

NOTES

xii 3. *Sukkiim*. There were foreign mercenaries in the Egyptian army at the time. See W. F. Albright in *The Old Testament and Modern Study*, ed. H. H. Rowley, 1951, p. 18.

8. *kings*. So on basis of Phoen. *mmlkt* "kings," rather than "kingdoms."

11. *chamber.* On *t'* as "chamber," see W. von Soden, WO 1 (1950), 356–61.

13. *His . . . Naamah the Ammonitess.* On the status of the queen mother, see H. Donner, "Art und Herkunft des Amtes der Königinmutter im Alten Testament," *Festschrift Johannes Friedrich*, 1959, pp. 105–45 and references cited there.

16. *Abijah.* I Kings xiv 31 has "Abijam." Cf. M. Noth, IPN, p. 234. Probably the given name, while Abijah was the throne name. Cf. Uzziah-Azariah, Eliakim-Jehoiakim, Mattaniah-Zedekiah.

COMMENT

The sources for chapter xii were I Kings xiv 21–28 and a special piece, probably the temple records of the prophecy of Shemaiah. The following table indicates the situation:

II Chron xii	I Kings xiv
1	——
2 ab	25
2 c–9 a	——
9 b–11	26–28
12	——
13–14	21–22
15–16	29–31

The order adopted by the writer points up the fact that he pursued his own methods for the purpose he had in mind.

[The Shishak invasion, xii 1–9]: The Deuteronomist devoted only two verses to this important episode. The Chronicler had access to another source which gave a fuller account and has thus preserved for us data corroborated by archaeological discoveries and Egyptian historical lists. Shishak was the first strong king of the twenty-second dynasty (Bubastite) whose aim doubtless was twofold: (a) to extend Egyptian power and (b) to teach Jeroboam a lesson. His invasion took place in the fifth year of Rehoboam (ca. 918 B.C.) and was a major operation, as indicated by the list of cities claimed as its victims. (See M. Noth, ZDPV 61 [1938], 277–304; Albright, AASOR 21–22 [1943], 38, n. 14; B. Mazar, "The Campaign of Pharaoh Shishak to Palestine," in SVT: *Volume du Congrès: Strasbourg, 1956* [Strasbourg, 1957], pp. 57–66, and IEJ 2 [1952], 82–88; W. F. Albright, BP, pp. 29 f., and BASOR

130 [1953], 4–8.) The names of towns in that list suggest that there was no major invasion of Judah proper, except for Aijalon. However both Kings and Chronicles assert that Jerusalem was attacked and there is evidence from archaeology that some of the cities of Judah were destroyed at the time, notably Lachish. Moreover, the Chronicler says that the fortified cities of Judah were captured and that the military leaders had retreated before the forces of Shishak to Jerusalem. It may be that Judah did escape more serious destruction by the payment of tribute. Despite the utilization of his excellent source, the Chronicler appears to have been concerned chiefly with the theological significance of the event. "All Israel" (Judah was for the Chronicler the true Israel, the only Israel that counted) and her king had abandoned the torah of Yahweh; that is why Shishak came against Jerusalem. Jerusalem was dealt a severe blow but was not destroyed because the leaders humbled themselves before Yahweh whose word was delivered by Shemaiah the prophet.

[Further observations on Rehoboam, 10–14]: The golden ornamental shields had to be replaced with shields of bronze. Again the Chronicler reverts to his theological view that Rehoboam and Judah escaped complete destruction because of his submission. There was still some good in Judah and so the wrath of God was turned away from him. Verse 13 is a concluding observation following the invasion of Shishak; it is placed here at the end of the narrative on Rehoboam rather than at the beginning (as in I Kings xiv 21), probably as a testimony to Yahweh's fulfillment of his promise to spare Jerusalem. Rehoboam became strong in Jerusalem and his reign continued for seventeen years. Verse 14 is an addition, a reminder of what was said in vs. 1.

[Conclusion, 15–16]: The statement on the sources used by the writer follows the pattern set in the references to the records of the reigns of David and Solomon. He thus departs from I Kings xiv 29 which speaks of the chronicles of the kings of Judah as the source for "the rest of the deeds of Rehoboam"; there is no mention of the prophetic records (see Introduction to I Chronicles, "The Sources Referred to by the Chronicler").

15. THE REIGN OF ABIJAH (ca. 915–913 B.C.)
(xiii 1–23 [xiii 1–22, xiv 1E])†

Accession

XIII 1 In the eighteenth year of King Jeroboam, Abijah became king over Judah. 2 He was king for three years in Jerusalem and his mother's name was Micaiah the daughter of Uriel from Gibeah. When war broke out between Abijah and Jeroboam, 3 Abijah began the battle with an army of four hundred thousand choice warriors. Jeroboam engaged him in battle with eight hundred thousand choice warriors.

Address of Abijah

4 Then Abijah stood up on Mount Zemaraim, located in [the region of] Mount Ephraim, and said, "Listen to me, Jeroboam and all Israel: 5 Don't you know that Yahweh God of Israel has given eternal dominion over Israel to David and his sons by a covenant of salt? 6 Yet Jeroboam the son of Nebat, the slave of Solomon the son of David, rose up and rebelled against his master, 7 and worthless men, rascals, joined him and proved too strong for Rehoboam the son of Solomon, in as much as Rehoboam was an inexperienced and timid young man and could not hold his own against them. 8 Now you propose to resist the rule of Yahweh exercised through the sons of David because you are a vast multitude and have with you the golden calves which Jeroboam made as gods for you! 9 But have you not driven out the priests of Yahweh, the sons of Aaron, and the Levites and made for yourselves priests just as the peoples of [other] countries have

† **II Chron xiii 1–3** ‖ I Kings xv 1–2, 6; **22–23** ‖ I Kings xv 7–8.

done? Whoever comes to consecrate himself with a young bull
and seven rams may become a priest of the no-gods. 10 As for
us, Yahweh is our God; we have not abandoned him, and priests
who are sons of Aaron minister to Yahweh and the Levites perform his service; 11 they sacrifice burnt offerings and [offer]
perfumed incense to Yahweh morning after morning and evening after evening, [set] layer bread on the clean table and light
the lamps on the golden lampstand nightly. We keep the decree
of Yahweh our God, but you have abandoned him. 12 Behold,
God is on our side, at our head, and his priests with signal
trumpets are ready to sound the alarm against you. O sons of
Israel, do not fight with Yahweh God of your fathers, for you
will not succeed."

The results of the campaign

13 Now Jeroboam had sent a party around to ambush them
from the rear, so that they were in front of Judah and the
ambush behind them. 14 When Judah turned about, behold they
were attacked from both front and rear; then they cried unto
Yahweh, the priests sounded the trumpets, 15 and the men of
Judah raised the battle cry. When the men of Judah raised the
battle cry, God routed Jeroboam and all Israel before Abijah
and Judah. 16 So the sons of Israel fled before Judah, for God
gave them into their hand. 17 Abijah and his people inflicted a
great slaughter upon them—five hundred thousand selected men
of Israel fell, slain. 18 The sons of Israel were humbled at that
time while the sons of Judah prevailed because they relied upon
Yahweh God of their fathers. 19 Abijah pursued Jeroboam and
took away from him the cities of Bethel with its dependencies,
Jeshanah with its dependencies, and Ephron with its dependencies. 20 Jeroboam could not regain strength again while Abijah
lived. Finally Yahweh struck Jeroboam and he died. 21 So Abijah
grew powerful; he married fourteen wives and fathered twenty-
two sons and sixteen daughters.

Conclusion

22 The remainder of the history of Abijah, his exploits and his words, are recorded in the treatise of the prophet Iddo. 23 When Abijah slept with his fathers, they buried him in the city of David and Asa his son became king in his place. The land remained undisturbed in his time for ten years.

NOTES

xiii 3. Perhaps 400,000 and 800,000 are to be interpreted on the unit basis, i.e., 400 and 800 units. The number per unit is not given.

4. *Mount Zemaraim.* Somewhere in the neighborhood of Beth-el, probably slightly to the northeast. Cf. Abel, *Géographie de la Palestine,* II, p. 454. On possible location and incidental discussion of this incident see K. Koch, "Zur Lage von Semarajim," ZDPV 78 (1962), 19–29, especially 26 ff.; cf. also Z. Kallai-Kleinmann, "The Town Lists of Judah, Simeon, Benjamin and Dan," VT 8 (1958), 134–60.

5. *eternal dominion.* This reference to the eternal dominion (kingdom) of David is independent of Samuel and of Kings, which the Chronicler usually follows and which is ambiguous; i.e., the kingdom is sometimes eternal, sometimes contingent on the behavior of the kings of the Davidic line. While this is a statement by Abijah and therefore not necessarily the same as a word from God, through a prophet, it is interesting that it should be in special Chronicles material used with approval by the Chronicler.

7. *rascals.* Literally "sons of Belial."

10. *his.* Suffix added for clarity.

12. *signal trumpets.* On the significance of trumpets see P. Humbert, *La Terou'a,* 1946. The priestly summons to battle signified Yahweh's entrance into the fray. In the face of such tremendous odds, the subsequent victory was his alone.

18. *they relied.* *niš'an* is parallel to "believe" or "trust" in Isa x 20, xxx 12, xxxi 1. Cf. also II Chron xiv 10, xvi 7–8.

19. *dependencies.* Literally "daughters." The chief city was called the "mother," i.e., metropolis, and the villages its "daughters."

20. *struck Jeroboam.* So for clarity. MT has "him." Two events may have been combined by the Chronicler. The last reference in Kings to Jeroboam is the death of his son. It may be that the stroke here against

Jeroboam fell upon his son. The king apparently died soon afterward
and was succeeded by another son, Nadab.

22. *treatise*. The Hebrew "midrash," i.e., a study or presentation, with
embellishments, of an earlier work. In the canonical books of OT, the
term occurs only here and II Chron xxiv 27.

23. *in his time*. According to LXX this phrase refers to Asa. In any
case, Abijah seems to have died soon after the war with Jeroboam.

COMMENT

The Chronicler's assessment of Abijah and his reign varies considerably from that of the Deuteronomist. The latter has nothing
good to report about him and says that he was tolerated only for
David's sake. The Deuteronomist notes the fierce struggle between
him and Jeroboam which continued throughout his reign.

[Accession of Abijah, xiii 1–3]: The Chronicler obviously followed another tradition in the matter of the name of Abijah's
mother. According to xi 20 and I Kings xv 2 his mother was
Maacah, the daughter of Absalom (Abishalom). The problem is
further complicated by the name of Asa's mother (I Kings xv 10;
II Chron xv 16). To alter Micaiah to Maacah, with LXX, does not
help very much in view of the family pedigree, "the daughter of
Uriel from Gibeah." The problem is, whose mother was Maacah?
There may have been divergent records, hardly surprising in view
of the many wives, concubines, and children Rehoboam and Abijah
are supposed to have had. In the present state of our knowledge,
any solution can only be speculative. The following suggestions have
been put forth: (a) Abijah and Asa were brothers; (b) Uriel was
the husband of Tamar the daughter of Absalom; (c) the wife of
Asa also bore the name of Maacah; (d) Chronicles is correct and
the name of Maacah in I Kings xv 2 is secondary due to the
influence of vs. 10 (Noth, ÜS, p. 143, n. 1); (e) Maacah was the
grandmother of Asa. It may be observed here that the regular
formula giving the year of accession, the length of the reign and the
name of the mother in the case of Asa is missing in Chronicles.
Only in xv 16 is the mother of Asa referred to as Maacah. It is
possible that in Kings the real name of Abijah's wife was submerged
by the strong personality of his mother, Maacah. (See Montgomery

and Gehman, *The Books of Kings,* pp. 274 f.; Bright, *A History of Israel,* p. 220, n. 35; Albright, ARI, pp. 158, 219, n. 105; Donner, *Festschrift Johannes Friedrich,* pp. 105–45.)

The writer speaks of war between Jeroboam and Abijah—Kings has it between Jeroboam and Rehoboam—which favored Abijah, probably because of an alliance between him and the Aramaeans of Damascus (xvi 3; I Kings xv 19). The strength of Jeroboam's forces corresponds exactly with the figures for the Northern tribes in II Sam xxiv 9. The lowering of the number by a hundred thousand for Judah is due to the desire to stress the magnitude of the victory by a force only half the size of the enemy.

[Abijah's sermon on the mount, 4–12]: Abijah's sermon on Mount Zemaraim is typical of the Chronicler. It is an excellent specimen of Levitical preaching directed at the situation prevailing at the time of the writer and illustrated by a telling example from history. Verse 5 states that God has given eternal dominion over Israel to David, which was made clear through the covenant of salt; this is another way of saying that it is Yahweh's kingdom presided over by Yahweh's king. (On the covenant of salt, see Lev ii 13 and H. C. Trumbull, *The Covenant of Salt,* 1899.) The North was thus in rebellion (vss. 6–7) against Yahweh and not simply against Rehoboam (and his successor) as a man. Despite the material advantage of Israel—a well-known fact—they could not prevail against the kingdom of Yahweh and his anointed (vs. 8). The rebels do have a cult of sorts—golden calves (the golden calves were originally pedestals for "the glory of God" and fulfilled the same function for Israel as the ark with the cherubs did for Judah. For illustrations see F. Thureau-Dangin, A. Barrois, G. Dossin, and M. Dunand, *Arslan Tash,* 1931, Pl. II, Fig. 1; *Orientalia* 15 [1946], 1–45, with plates; *Orientalia* 18 [1949], Pl. 28; Bossert, *Altsyrien,* Pls. 446, 498, 960; BA 1 [1938], 2 f.), an illegitimate priesthood in the service of no-gods—but the true cult and priesthood are in Jerusalem (vss. 10–11). There true, legitimate, acceptable sacrifices were offered regularly and the decrees of Yahweh kept properly. The writer was thinking not only of the time of Abijah, but of his own time; he thus appealed to the people of Samaria, as Abijah had appealed to Jeroboam and "all Israel," to give up their rebellion against Yahweh. The South had the true God, the true kingdom, the true cult.

Especially significant is the fact that the rebels are still referred to as "sons of Israel" (vs. 12).

[The results of the campaign, 13–21]: According to the writer, when the priests blew the alarm God intervened and routed Jeroboam and his army. The latter's strategy (vss. 13–14), however brilliant, was no match against Yahweh who fought on the side of his devotees. The victory was his. Verse 19 is certainly based on authentic information, as is shown by the inclusion of a good portion of Ephraimite territory in the Judah-Benjamin list (Josh xviii 21–27) dating from the age of Jehoshaphat. For a discussion of the problem see Cross and Wright, JBL 75 (1956) 222 f. The thrust northward by Abijah resulted in the inclusion of this territory in what the authors refer to as the eleventh administrative district of Judah in the ninth century. Cf. their sketch map on p. 213 and Van Selms, *II Kronieken* (see Selected Bibliography, Commentaries), p. 112. Bethel (modern Beitin) is ten miles north of Jerusalem; Jeshanah (Burj el-Isāneh), about four miles south of Shiloh; Ephron-Ophrah (et-Taiyibeh), about four miles northeast of Bethel. Jeroboam may not have recovered the lost territory but Baasha certainly did since Asa had to retake it later (xv 8, xvii 2; cf. GVI, II, p. 226). Kings knew nothing of a violent death for Jeroboam; the statement here is due to the Chronicler's belief that resistance to Yahweh demanded it and may have been based on the prophecy of Abijah concerning the son of Jeroboam (I Kings xiv). Reference to the wives and progeny of Abijah is the writer's way of indicating the blessing of the Lord.

[Conclusion, 22–23]: Once again the writer refers to a prophetic treatise probably included in the records at his disposal, perhaps part of a larger work used by him (cf. I Kings xv 7). After Abijah's deliverance, the land was at peace for ten years into the reign of Asa. The formula is suspiciously like that following the deliverances of the judges.

16. THE REIGN OF ASA (ca. 913–873 B.C.):
THE EARLY YEARS
(xiv 1–14)†

The early years

XIV ¹ Asa did what was good and right in the sight of Yahweh his God. ² He removed the foreign altars and high places, broke down the Masseboth, cut the Asherim to pieces, ³ and urged Judah to seek Yahweh God of their fathers and to observe the law and the commandment. ⁴ Because he removed the high places and the incense altars from all the cities of Judah, the kingdom under him was undisturbed. ⁵ He built fortified cities in Judah because the country was undisturbed and no one was at war with him during these years, for Yahweh had given him rest. ⁶ He had said to Judah, "Let us build these cities and surround them with walls, towers, gates, and bars while the land is yet at our disposal; because we sought Yahweh our God, ªhe sought usª and gave us rest all around." So they built and enjoyed success. ⁷ Asa had an army of three hundred thousand Judeans armed with shields and spears and two hundred eighty thousand Benjaminite shield-bearers and bowmen, all of whom were mighty warriors.

The Ethiopian war

⁸ Zerah the Ethiopian, with an army of a million [men], in addition to three hundred chariots, went out against them and reached Mareshah. ⁹ Asa went out to meet him and they prepared for battle in the Valley of Zephathah near Mareshah. ¹⁰ Then Asa called to Yahweh his God and said, "O Yahweh,

† **II Chron xiv 1–7** ‖ I Kings xv 11–12.

ª⁻ª deⁿrāšānū, with LXX. MT "we sought."

you do not take into account numbers or strength when you come to assist: help us, O Yahweh our God, for we have relied upon you and come against this multitude in your name. O Yahweh, you are our God; mortal man cannot prevail over you." 11 When Yahweh vanquished the Ethiopians before Asa and before Judah, the Ethiopians fled. 12 But Asa and his associates pursued them as far as Gerar; so many of the Ethiopians fell that they were unable to rally; they were cut to pieces before Yahweh and his army. They carried off a very great deal of booty. 13 They destroyed all the cities around Gerar—for the dread of Yahweh was upon them—and plundered all the cities because there was much booty in them. 14 They also struck down *b*those who had cattle*b* and carried away large numbers of sheep and camels when they returned to Jerusalem.

b–b Hebrew reads "tents of cattle," which probably signifies "possessors of cattle." Cf. Ar. root *'hl* "people," "possessors."

NOTES

xiv 2. *Masseboth.* Rough, unhewn stones usually set up for cultic purposes. (See Galling, BRL, cols. 368–71.)

Asherim. Cult objects of some sort, perhaps exemplifying some of the characteristics of Asherah, originally a Canaanite sea-goddess. Cf. W. F. Albright, "The High Place in Ancient Palestine," SVT: *Volume du Congrès: Strasbourg, 1956* (Strasbourg, 1957), pp. 242–58.

4. *incense altars. Ḥammānīm.* For discussion of the meaning with illustrations see H. Ingholt, "Le sens du mot Hammān," in *Mélanges Syriens offerts à Monsieur René Dussaud,* II, 1939, pp. 795–802; K. Elliger, "Chammanim=Masseben?", ZAW 57 (1939), 256–65; Albright, ARI, p. 215, n. 58.

7. On numbers see NOTE on xiii 3.

9. *Zephathah.* Place is unknown. LXX "north of." It has nothing to do with the Zephath of Judg i 17.

10. *you do not take . . . assist.* Literally "it is not with you to help between the great and the strengthless." The meaning is that the strong as well as the weak need Yahweh's assistance to gain victory.

prevail over you. For *'al* with indicative here, cf. Gray, *The Legacy of Canaan,* p. 203.

12. *unable to rally*. Literally "that no life remained to them." Cf.
C. Brockelmann, *Hebräische Syntax,* 1956, p. 145a.
army. Literally "camp."
They. Asa and his followers.
13. *for the dread . . . them*. Indication of the "holy war" tradition
(cf. G. von Rad, *Der heilige Krieg im alten Israel,* 1951, p. 12), which
Chronicles continues (II Chron xv 1 ff., xvi 7 ff., xx 15 ff., xxxii 7 ff.), as
G. von Rad has pointed out in *Studies in Deuteronomy,* 1953, pp.
45–59. The Chronicler is perhaps more consistent in his application of
the theory than Kings.

COMMENT

The last verse of chapter xiii is really the incipit of the following
three chapters which deal with the reign of Asa. The Chronicler
has greatly expanded the account of Asa's reign both by additions
of his own and material from sources not used by the Deuteronomist.

[The early years, xiv 1–7]: The peace won by Abijah's defeat
of Jeroboam carried over into the reign of Asa. Here that period
of rest seems to be attributed to the fervent religious activity of the
new king (vss. 4–6). It was doubtless due, in large measure, to the
activity of the Aramaeans inspired by Abijah (xvi 3) and the
troubles that beset Israel immediately after the death of Jeroboam.
Of the reforming activity of Asa there can be no doubt, though
that probably did not come in the first years of his reign because
he was only a boy when he became king. The chronology of Asa is
rather complicated. For a discussion see W. F. Albright, BASOR
100 (December 1945); E. R. Thiele, *The Mysterious Numbers of
the Hebrew Kings,* 1951, Index; Rudolph, pp. 239 ff. Just when in
his reign the cities of Judah were fortified cannot be determined
but that some such activity did take place cannot be doubted in
view of the unsettled condition of the times (cf. I Kings xv 32;
cf. ÜS, pp. 140 f.). It may have followed the Ethiopian war. It is
also quite credible that Asa maintained a standing army, though
the numbers are exaggerated. The proportionately large number of
Benjaminites suggests that Asa held on to most of the eastern region
of the tribe taken by Abijah. Several scholars have advanced the
idea that the Chronicler had access to a history of the Judean army

from which these notes were taken. See Junge, *Der Wiederaufbau* . . . , pp. 38 f., 77 ff.; Noth, ÜS, p. 141, n. 2.

[The Ethiopian war, 8–14]: The account of Asa's brush with Zerah can hardly be a fabrication because of the prominence of the place names involved. However, it was not so imposing as the figures indicate; they result from the writer's tendency to magnify the victory of Yahweh. How the Ethiopians got to Gerar is not known. They were probably Egyptian mercenaries with their families, though they could have been Arabs (cf. Hab iii 7; Num xii 1). That Bedouin were at least associated with them is indicated by the presence of camels (vs. 14). The Egyptian mercenaries may have been settled there by Shishak in a kind of buffer state after the campaign against Rehoboam (so W. F. Albright, JPOS 4 [1924], 146 f., and as is suggested by the combination of Ethiopians and Libyans (xvi 8); on the location of Gerar, see Y. Aharoni, "The Land of Gerar," IEJ 6 [1956], 26–32). The episode related here may have been a movement by Zerah into better pasture grounds at the expense of Judah. On the other hand, Zerah could have been inspired by his Egyptian sovereign, Osorkon I, the successor of Shishak.

The battle took place near Mareshah (Tell Sandahannah), some twenty-five miles southwest of Jerusalem. The invaders were chased back to Gerar, which was apparently the capital of their district since the surrounding cities point to outlying centers of the metropolis. There is no indication that Gerar itself was taken. Beyond those facts we cannot go. Though the account is given essentially for theological purposes, it is one more indication of the significance of many of the peculiar stories of the Chronicler. The main interest of the writer was not the presentation of the bare facts of history. The victory over Zerah was Yahweh's, a powerful illustration of what could be expected by those who relied upon him. No forces of mortal man can withstand Yahweh.

17. THE REIGN OF ASA (ca. 913–873 B.C.): THE REFORMATION
(xv 1–19)†

The sermon of Azariah

XV 1 Then the spirit of God came upon Azariah the son of Oded, 2 as he went to meet Asa and said to him, "Listen to me, Asa and all Judah and Benjamin; Yahweh will be with you so long as you are with him; if you seek him he will let himself be found by you but if you abandon him he will abandon you. 3 For a long time Israel did not have the true God, or a priest teacher, or a torah, 4 but when in their distress they turned to Yahweh God of Israel and sought after him, he let himself be found by them. 5 At that time there was no security for those who went and came, rather there was much unrest among the inhabitants of the lands. 6 Nation was crushed by nation, city by city, for God caused confusion among them by every kind of distress. 7 Be strong and do not be discouraged, for there is a reward for your work."

The reformation

8 When Asa heard these words and ªthe prophecy of Oded the prophetª, he took courage, removed the abominations from the whole land of Judah and Benjamin as well as from the cities he took inᵇ Mount Ephraim and renewed the altar of Yahweh which stood before the portico of Yahweh. 9 He convoked all Judah, Benjamin, and those from Ephraim, Manasseh, and Simeon who sojourned with them—for many from Israel had deserted to him when they saw that Yahweh his God was with

† II Chron xv 8–15: cf. I Kings xv 12; **16–19** ‖ I Kings xv 13–15.

ª–ª Vulg. "the prophecy of Azariah the son of Oded."
ᵇ With LXX. MT "from."

him. 10 They came together at Jerusalem in the third month of
the fifteenth year of Asa's reign 11 and sacrificed to Yahweh
that day some of the booty they brought, seven hundred oxen
and seven thousand sheep. 12 Then they entered into a covenant
to seek Yahweh God of their fathers with all their minds and
with all their soul, 13 and that anyone who would not seek
Yahweh God of Israel should be put to death, whether young
or old, man or woman. 14 They swore to Yahweh with a loud
voice, with a shout of joy, with trumpets, and with rams' horns.
15 All Judah rejoiced over the oath, for they had sworn it with
all their mind and sought him with utter delight so that he let
himself be found by them; Yahweh gave them rest all around.

Removal of Maacah

16 Asa the king even removed his mother Maacah from the
status of queen mother because she had made a horrible representation of Asherah. Asa cut down her horrible representation,
smashed it and burned it in the Kidron Valley. 17 But the
high places did not disappear from Israel, though the mind of
Asa was loyal throughout his whole life. 18 He brought his
father's and his own dedicated gifts of silver, gold, and [other]
articles into the house of God. 19 There was no war up to the
thirty-fifth year of Asa's reign.

Notes

xv 3. *a torah.* I.e., a body of instruction; better left untranslated
since "law" here is too narrow.

5. *those who went and came.* Literally "for him who went out and him
who came in"; cf. Judg v 6 f.

there was much unrest. For phrase see 1QH 3:25.

11. *some of the booty they brought.* The booty from the campaign
against Zerah (ch. xiv).

16. *queen mother.* See COMMENT on Sec. 15, xiii 1–3. The queen
mother apparently occupied a position of honor and influence, especially
in a harem where there would be numerous wives; but only the one
whose son was designated heir would be "queen." During the minority

of her son she apparently exercised considerable authority. Athaliah probably ruled as queen mother and regent during the minority of Joash. Joash was kidnaped by the priests not because his life was in danger (Athaliah may have killed others, but if she killed the last surviving son, she could not reign either), but because that was the only way to challenge her power. So long as he remained in her hands she controlled the kingship.

horrible representation. Mipleṣet only here and I Kings xv 13. Cf. Josiah's burning of Asherah, II Kings xxiii 6.

COMMENT

Verses 1–15 deal with the same situation described in xiv 1–4, where the initiative for rededication of king and people lies in the act and word of the king. Here, on the other hand, it is inspired by the preaching of Azariah.

[The sermon of Azariah, xv 1–7]: The definitive way in which the name of the prophet is set down seems to indicate its presence in the source material utilized by the writer. The sermon itself, however, is an excellent illustration of Levitical preaching (see von Rad, *Gesammelte Studien* . . . , pp. 251 f.). It is thoroughly biblical, drawing upon Judges and the prophets (see Rudolph, p. 245). It has three main points: (a) the declaration that Yahweh will be with the people so long as they are with him (vs. 2); (b) illustrations from history, especially from Judges (vss. 3–6); (c) exhortation and promise (vs. 7). The people addressed, Judah and Benjamin, are characteristic for the Chronicler.

[The reformation, 8–15]: The effectiveness of the sermon of Azariah, so far as the writer is concerned, was beyond dispute. The account of the reformation follows the notice in I Kings xv 12, which speaks of the purging of the male prostitutes (*haqqᵉdēšīm*) and the abominable objects (*haggillūlīm*) his fathers had constructed. The Chronicler says nothing of the former, but he apparently refers to the latter as *haššiqqūṣīm,* usually rendered as detestable (pagan) abominations. Along with this religious house cleaning went the renewal of the altar which had been desecrated by illicit offerings, probably at the instigation of Maacah, the queen mother. The whole movement was thoroughgoing and took in the territory of Judah and Benjamin as well as the cities Asa had taken from Ephraim. The reference to Ephraim seems to indicate that his father's conquests were of short duration; the cities mentioned in xiii 19 appear to have fallen into the hands of Baasha, perhaps during Asa's minority. Asa was supported in his reformation by all the people of Judah, Benjamin, and by those who had taken refuge there from Ephraim, Manasseh, and Simeon. Why Simeon is included is not clear. It may have been, as Beyer has suggested, that the inhabitants of Simeon (i.e., southern Judah) were forced out by the expansion of the Edomites. The Chronicler attributes the presence of the refugees in Asa's realm to their recognition that Yahweh was with him. The convocation was attended by a great sacrifice for which part of the booty taken in the campaign against Zerah was used. The entire transaction was accompanied by a convenant renewal into which the people entered wholeheartedly. That the covenant was a sovereignly imposed affair may be seen from the threat accompanying it (vs. 13). The ceremony was conducted with proper decorum and ritual, though without mention of the participation of Levitical choirs. In harmony with his theory, the writer observes that this fervent response of king and people to Yahweh brought a period of rest and peace.

[The Maacah affair, 16–19]: The deterioration of the religious situation in Judah is attributed to Maacah, the queen mother (cf. I Kings xv 13), who is said to have made a *mipleṣet,* that is, a horrible representation having something to do with the Tyrian goddess Asherah (cf. ARI, pp. 157 f.). The name Maacah is associated with pagan elements in Israel as may be seen from the fact that she came from the family of Absalom whose mother, a princess of Geshur, bore the same name. Her position enabled her to exercise a strong influence in Judah in the early years of Asa's reign. But under the pressure of such religious leaders as Azariah, the king was led to take drastic action as soon as he was in a position to do so. Maacah was removed from her commanding position and the cult object set up by her cut down and burned. But even Asa's best efforts were insufficient to eradicate the pagan practices entirely, as the Deuteronomist attests (I Kings xv 14). The deposit of Asa's and his father's dedicated gifts in the temple is obscure. The absence of war from the time of Zerah until the invasion of Baasha supports the Chronicler's contention of an era of peace; perhaps the statement that there was *no war* indicates that the Zerah affair was no more than a skirmish and that the only major war was that dealt with in the following chapter, despite the statement in I Kings xv 16. There could have been border clashes from time to time but no all-out war.

18. THE REIGN OF ASA (ca. 913–873 B.C.): THE LATER YEARS (xvi 1–14)†

Baasha moves against Asa

XVI ¹ In the thirty-sixth year of Asa's reign, Baasha the king of Israel came up against Judah and fortified Ramah to prevent Asa the king of Judah from going out or coming in. ² So Asa took out silver and gold from the storehouses of the temple and the palace, which he sent to Ben-hadad the king of Aram who resided at Damascus, with the following proposal: ³ "Let us make a treaty between me and you, like the one that existed between my father and your father; look, I have sent you silver and gold; go, renounce your treaty with Baasha the king of Israel that he may withdraw from me." ⁴ Ben-hadad listened to King Asa and sent the captains of his army to the cities of Israel; they destroyed Ijon, Dan, Abel-maim, and all the storage cities of Naphtali. ⁵ When Baasha heard about it, he stopped building operations at Ramah and suspended his work [there]. ⁶ Then Asa the king had all Judah carry away the stones and timber of Ramah which Baasha had used in building and fortified Geba and Mizpah with them.

The prophecy of Hanani

⁷ At that time Hanani the seer came to Asa the king of Judah and said to him, "Because you relied on the king of Aram and did not rely upon Yahweh your God, the army of the king of ᵃIsraelᵃ has escaped from your hand. ⁸ Did not the Ethiopians

† **II Chron xvi 1–6** ‖ I Kings xv 17–22; **11–14** ‖ I Kings 23–24.

ᵃ⁻ᵃ With LXXᴸ, noted by neither Kittel (*Biblia Hebraica*, 3d ed.), nor Swete and Rahlfs. (H. B. Swete, *The Old Testament in Greek*, II, 3d ed., reprinted 1930; A. Rahlfs, *Septuaginta*, I, 3d ed., 1949.) MT "Aram." F. M. Cross, Jr., has shown that LXXᴸ often has better readings than other witnesses to the and Libyans have a large army, with chariots and horsemen in great abundance? But when you relied on Yahweh he gave you victory over them. 9 For the eyes of Yahweh move to and fro through all the earth to support those who are wholeheartedly committed to him. You have acted foolishly in this respect, for from now on you will have wars." 10 Asa, however, was provoked at the seer and put him in the stocks because he was angry with him about this. At the same time Asa also mistreated some of the people.

Conclusion

11 Now, the history of Asa from beginning to end is recorded in the chronicles of the kings of Judah and Israel. 12 In the thirty-ninth year of his reign Asa developed a foot disease which became very severe; yet in his illness he did not consult Yahweh but [he did consult] the physicians. 13 So Asa slept with his fathers; he died in the forty-first year of his reign. 14 They buried him in his grave chamber which he had cut out for himself in the city of David. They laid him in the crypt which was filled with perfume blended from all sorts of oils, and they made for him a very great funeral fire.

Vorlage of LXX in connection with the Samuel MS of Qumran (cf. JBL 74 [1955], 165–72; and *The Ancient Library of Qumran* [Anchor Books, revised ed.], 1961, pp. 173 ff.). Maybe the same is true here. Certainly the reading suggested by LXX^L is required by the context.

NOTES

xvi 2. *the temple . . . the palace.* Literally "the house of Yahweh," "the house of the king."

Ben-hadad. Ben-hadad I. I Kings xv 18 "Ben-hadad, the son of Tabrimmon, the son of Hezion." See COMMENT on vss. 1–6.

4. *Ijon . . . Naphtali.* For identification of sites see Abel, *Géographie de la Palestine,* II, pp. 233, 302, 352.

8. *he . . . them.* Literally "he gave them in your hand."

9. *For . . . through all the earth.* Cf. Zech iv 10.

14. *grave chamber.* To be rendered singular, since the grave had

more than one chamber (A. Kropat, "Die Syntax des Autors der Chronik," BZAW 16 [1909], 10).

all sorts. Z*enīm* in the original Hebrew text is a word borrowed from the Persian, meaning "all sorts."

COMMENT

[Baasha's hostile move toward Judah, xvi 1–6]: The only significant conflict between the rival kingdoms during this period, so far as we know, took place in the thirty-sixth (LXX, "thirty-eighth") year of Asa. On the vexed question of the date see W. F. Albright, BASOR 87 (October 1942), 27 f., and BASOR 100 (December 1945), 20, n. 14; he thinks the thirty-sixth year of Asa was ca. 879 B.C. This is another of the points at which the Chronicler has preserved authentic material, as can be seen from the famous stele of Ben-hadad treated by Albright in the above noted article. Cf. also H. L. Ginsberg, LGJV, p. 160, n. 4.

The conflict was precipitated by Baasha's fortification of Ramah, about ten miles north of Jerusalem on the main highway. The chief purpose for Baasha's action was to prevent movement of the Judahites; no one belonging to Asa was allowed to enter or leave. It appears to have been an interdiction of the roads leading north from Judah, thus cutting off trade and communication. A secondary aim may have been to prevent defection of Northerners or to cut off the stream of religious devotees going to Jerusalem to worship. Asa was not in a position to carry on offensive war with Israel and so stripped his treasuries to buy the intervention of Ben-hadad I against Baasha. The plan succeeded: Ben-hadad terminated his treaty with Baasha and invaded the northern area of Israel. While only a harassing action, it had the effect of causing Baasha to drop his fortifications at Ramah and to withdraw to Tirzah. The foray of Ben-hadad's men followed a path south between the Lebanon ranges to Ijon, then on to Abel-maim and Dan. Ijon has been connected with the Merj Ayyun, north of Abel-maim (Abel-beth-maacah in I Kings xv 20) which was some four miles west of Dan. Both the latter places were approximately 10 miles north of Huleh. For discussion see Abel, *Géographie de la Palestine,* II, pp. 233, 302, 352; W. F. Albright, AASOR 6 (1926), 16, n. 6. Apparently they moved as far as the district of Chinneroth (Galilee); cf. I Kings xv 20. The Chronicler has "store-cities" for Chinneroth which Abel (*op. cit.*, I, p. 495) says became Genneseret in the postexilic period; this explains the change by the Chronicler.

When Baasha abandoned his project at Ramah, Asa conscripted his fellow countrymen to pull down the fortifications and constructed fortifications of his own at Geba and Mizpah. Just what locations were involved is uncertain; it depends on whether Asa's reaction to Baasha's move was offensive or defensive. If the former, then Mizpah might be at Tell en-Nasbeh and Geba at Jeba; if the latter, then Mizpah could be Nebi Samwil and Geba Tell el-Ful (the Gibeah of Saul). For the former view see arguments of James Muilenberg in *Excavations at Tell en-Nasbeh,* ed. C. C. McCown, I, 1947, pp. 28–30 (see map on p. 51) and W. F. Badé in *Werden und Wesen des AT,* eds. P. Volz, F. Stummer, and J. Hempel, 1936, pp. 30–36; for the latter, W. F. Albright, AASOR 4 (1924), 38 ff. The excavations at Tell el-Ful revealed reused stones and timber and the third fortress bore evidence of hasty construction (*ibid.*, pp. 20, 39). Jeremiah xli 9 refers to a cistern made by Asa at the time "for fear of Baasha," which suggests defensive tactics on the part of the king of Judah.

[The prophecy of Hanani, 7–10]: The story of Hanani the seer (*hārō'ĕh*) is theologically motivated and follows closely the tradition of the prophets (Isa vii; Zech iv 6). The seer is represented as appearing before the king after the intervention of the Aramaeans, whose pressure upon Israel served to remove its threat against Judah. That was to the seer a direct reversal of the policy followed in the Zerah affair in which case Yahweh was besought to intervene. However, that situation was not so serious as this one; Asa faced political realities and in so doing took a leaf from Jeroboam's book. Thus, from the seer's point of view Asa acted foolishly since he took matters into his own hands when the eyes of Yahweh were scanning the earth, watching over those who were loyal to him (cf. Zech iv 10). Asa's reaction to Hanani's rebuke was swift and fateful; Hanani was put in the stocks and his partisans crushed. The reference to the persistence of wars (vs. 9) is probably a reflection of I Kings xv 16, since Asa's years were few after the Ramah affair and there was more or less peace between the kingdoms until the unwise move of Amaziah three-quarters of a century later (xxv 20 ff.).

[Conclusion, 11–14]: As has been observed by commentators generally, the writer here gives the full title of the sources he used in his work. From the materials concerning Asa said to have been taken from them, it is obvious that it is not equivalent to our book of Kings.

Asa's death was caused by a foot disease (dropsy?) which set in two years before and which may have incapacitated him. If there was a coregency for the period of his illness, nothing is said about it. The chief interest of the writer centers in the observation that he consulted physicians, rather than Yahweh, about healing. This must not be construed as a condemnation of the healing art as such; there are hints of its approval and use in the OT (Exod xxi 19; Jer viii 22; Isa xxxviii 21). In general, however, Yahweh is the healer (e.g., Ps ciii 3b). The objection here may be due to the tendency to associate magic with healing processes or to the concept that the human media alone are not enough, as the case of Asa illustrates. The point of the passage (vs. 12b) is that Asa consulted only physicians, without consulting Yahweh at all. The underlying thought is the same as that expressed in the prophecy of Hanani. Moreover, it is possible that Asa's illness may have been regarded as the result of what he did to the prophet and his friends following the rebuke administered to the king for his lack of faith. In any case, the failure to consult Yahweh pointed to a tragic lack of confidence in him, at least in the view of the writer.

The burial notice evidences the utilization of an expanded source, unknown to or unused by the Deuteronomist. Asa had prepared his own grave chamber. The festivities connected with his entombment reflect the esteem in which he was held by the people, though the expressions are those of the Chronicler.

19. THE REIGN OF JEHOSHAPHAT (873–849 B.C.): CHARACTER AND ORGANIZATION (xvii 1–19)†

Character and rule of Jehoshaphat

XVII 1 When Jehoshaphat his son became king in his place, he proceeded to fortify himself against Israel 2 by stationing troops in all the fortified cities of Judah and placing garrisons in the land of Judah and in the cities of Ephraim which Asa his father had captured. 3 Yahweh was with Jehoshaphat because he followed the earlier ways of *his father* and did not consult Baal, 4 but sought the God of his father, followed his commandments and did not act as Israel did. 5 So Yahweh firmly established the kingdom under his control, while all Judah gave gifts to Jehoshaphat until he had an abundance of wealth and honor. 6 His mind was so firmly set on the ways of Yahweh that he again removed the high places and the Asherim from Judah.

Teaching mission

7 In the third year of his reign he sent his captains, *outstanding men*—Obadiah, Zechariah, Nethanel, and Micaiah—to teach in the cities of Judah. 8 With them went the Levites— Shemaiah, Nethaniah, Zebadiah, Asahel, Shamiraimoth, Jehonathan, *Adonijah, and Tobiah,* the Levites; Elishama and Jehoram the priests accompanied them. 9 They taught in Judah, taking with them the book of the law of Yahweh; they went around to all the cities of Judah and taught the people.

† **II Chron xvii 1–6** ‖ I Kings xv 24c.

a–a So with six manuscripts and LXX. MT reads "in the ways of David his father." See NOTE.

b–b So with LXX. Others read "Ben-hail," a personal name, not occurring elsewhere.

c–c Weṭob 'aḏōniyyāh ("and Tob-adonijah") is dittography.

Tribute

10 The dread of Yahweh was upon all the kingdoms of the lands around Judah so that they did not go to war with Jehoshaphat. 11 Some of the Philistines brought gifts and a load of silver to Jehoshaphat; the Arabians also brought flocks to him—seventy-seven hundred rams and seventy-seven hundred he-goats. 12 So Jehoshaphat kept on growing greater; he built fortified towns and store-cities in Judah 13 and accumulated an abundance of supplies in the cities of Judah.

Classification of military officials at Jerusalem

He also had warriors, outstanding men, in Jerusalem. 14 This was their official classification according to their families: Over the captains of the thousands of Judah was Captain Adnah with three hundred thousand soldiers; 15 at his side was Captain Jehohanan with two hundred eighty thousand; 16 at his side was Amasiah the son of Zichri, who volunteered for Yahweh, with two hundred thousand soldiers. 17 Officer Eliada represented Benjamin with two hundred thousand men equipped with bow and shield, 18 and at his side was Jehozabad with one hundred eighty thousand men equipped for war. 19 These were the ones who were in the service of the king apart from those whom the king put in the fortified cities all over Judah.

NOTES

xvii 3. *the earlier ways of his father*. See textual note *a*. The reference must be to Asa because a distinction is made between his earlier and later practices, while the Chronicler never makes such a distinction in the case of David. I Kings xxii 43 does refer to Asa, but without the time division made by the Chronicler. Perhaps David was copied directly from the source, since it is easier to explain the dropping of the name than its insertion.

Baal. The reference is to the Baal of Canaan and not to local representations. The plural, when used of the god, is parallel to Elohim= God. Wherever the term *ba'al* is used of owner or master with the suffix, it is the plural form of the noun that is used, despite its clearly singular reference. Cf. J. M. Myers, LCQ 19 (1946), 398 f.

5. *under his control.* Literally "in his hand."

6. *again.* As his father had done.

12. *he built . . . Judah.* See F. M. Cross, Jr., and J. T. Milik, "Explorations in the Judaean Buqê'ah," BASOR 142 (1956), 5–17.

14. The numbers are doubtless to be explained on the basis of units (see NOTES on Sec. 15). Then we have a total of 1160 units, still pretty large in comparison with the Davidic census of 1100 units for all Israel. The size of the units is not given.

COMMENT

Jehoshaphat was one of the Chronicler's favorite kings of Judah, along with Hezekiah and Josiah. There is remarkably little criticism of his alliance with the Northern Kingdom; the caveat raised by Jehu, son of Hanani, is rather mild (xix 2–3).

[Character and rule of Jehoshaphat, xvii 1–6]: In view of Asa's difficulties with Baasha, the rapid movements in Israel leading to the enthronement of Omri, the soldier king, who was consolidating his position, and the uncertainties of the situation, Jehoshaphat took immediate steps to secure his position in Judah. Rudolph, pp. 249 f., thinks a source other than Kings is involved here since "Israel" in vs. 1 refers to the Southern Kingdom and "Ephraim" in vs. 2 to the Northern Kingdom, because the cities taken by Asa (xvi 6) were not in the tribal territory of Ephraim but in Benjamin. His translation then would differ somewhat from ours. "When Jehoshaphat his son became king in his place he established his authority *over* Israel. . . ." In vss. 4, 5, then, Israel refers to the Northern Kingdom and Judah to the Southern. Hence vss. 1–2 came from the source used by the Chronicler and vss. 3–6 represent his own work.

The Ephraimite cities taken by Abijah (xiii 19) and maintained, at least most of the time, by Asa (xv 8), were still in the hands of the king of Judah; they were apparently uncontested until the fiasco under Amaziah (xxv 17–24; see Cross and Wright, JBL 75 [1956], 222 f.).

The successful rule of Jehoshaphat, according to the Chronicler, was due to his loyalty to the tradition of his father in following

Yahweh and his consequent rejection of Baal. His devotion to Yahweh brought him wealth and respect—the gifts of peace and prosperity. He continued the reformation instituted by Asa, though he had little more success than his father in completely eradicating the high places (xx 33). The matter of reformation in Israel (Judah) must have been one of long standing and persistent endeavor. It is hard to believe that the reformers of the seventh century (the Deuteronomist) were the first to institute a movement against the high places. There must have been movements in the direction of centralizing worship from the time of David on, sporadic efforts made to clean out the high places by the kings mentioned, if only for practical rather than doctrinaire reasons. Deuteronomy formulated in absolute terms a policy of long standing, generally observed in the breach. Kings and Chronicles are thus in flat contradiction over Asa and Jehoshaphat.

On the date of Jehoshaphat and the synchronization with the Omri dynasty see Albright, BASOR 100 (December 1945); Thiele, *The Mysterious Numbers of the Hebrew Kings,* Ch. IV.

[A teaching mission, 7–9]: This has been viewed as another version of the judicial reform reported in xix 4–11 (Albright, AMJV, p. 82). The Chronicler refers to the mission here as an example of Jehoshaphat's zeal for Yahweh. While some elements in the story are obscure, the main points are clear. In view of the procedure of the reform, there is at least a strong probability that such a teaching mission was established to inform the people of the torah of the Lord. The fact that laymen are mentioned first among the participants points to a tradition older than the Chronicler, who regarded the Levites as the primary functionaries in the matter of teaching (xxxv 3; Neh viii 7–8). In truth vs. 8 may be the Chronicler's own contribution to the story. Perhaps the position of laymen as teachers is quite old since Hos iv 6 speaks of the priests as the handlers of the torah. The names in vs. 7 do not prevent attributing it to the ninth century B.C. Just what is meant here by the "book of the torah" is not clear; the Chronicler generally refers to the priestly work of the Pentateuch under that phrase but that can hardly be so in this instance (cf. Rudolph, p. 251; Rehm, *Die Bücher der Chronik* [see Selected Bibliography, Commentaries], p. 101). Some think it was the Book of the Covenant, or an edition of it. More plausibly it may have been a royal law code along the lines of the Code of Hammurabi and other royal edicts. As such, it may well have been based on premonarchic sources, but for purposes of the monarchy much of the Covenant code would have been outmoded and inapplicable. Royal law is practically nonexistent in the Bible, though there must have been plenty of it to operate the kingdom successfully for so long a time. The biblical writers were not greatly interested in royal law, since their authorities were the earlier premonarchic figures with their utterances and actions. It is possible, then, that this was one of the lost law codes rather than some biblical source, though it probably contained older materials also now preserved in the Pentateuch.

[Tribute, 10–13a]: As the preceding passage was intended to illustrate the direction of the new king's piety, so this one explains the source and use of his wealth. The surrounding nations observed the strength of Jehoshaphat and recognized the presence of Yahweh with him so that they not only refrained from attacking Judah but even brought tribute to him. Their reaction toward him enhanced his prestige and power still further and enabled him to fortify Judah. The Philistines were his southwestern neighbors while the Arabians had pushed into the Negeb, where they may have been associated with the Ethiopians referred to in xiv 9 ff. (cf. xxi 16). If this is a summary assessment of Jehoshaphat's reign, other peoples or groups may have been involved too (ch. xx).

[Military arrangements in Jerusalem, 13b–19]: This interesting little pericope is meant to illustrate further the standing of Jehoshaphat because of his piety. It informs us of the military organization of Jerusalem and the arrangements for the defense of the kingdom. Jehoshaphat had a standing army in the capital as well as garrisons in the fortified cities. Doubtless we are to understand that the central command was also located at Jerusalem. The organization centered about the tribal association of Judah and Benjamin, the former directed by a chief of staff and two assistants, the latter by one chief and one assistant. This appears to be an authentic bit of information, certified by names and quite appropriate to the situation.

20. THE REIGN OF JEHOSHAPHAT (873–849 B.C.): ALLIANCE WITH THE NORTHERN KINGDOM (xviii 1–34)†

Jehoshaphat's visit with Ahab

XVIII 1 Although Jehoshaphat had wealth and great honor, he entered into a marriage alliance with Ahab. 2 So one time when he went down to Ahab at Samaria, Ahab slaughtered sheep and cattle in abundance for him and his followers to elicit his support against Ramoth-gilead. 3 Then Ahab the king of Israel said to Jehoshaphat the king of Judah, "Will you go with me to Ramoth-gilead?" He replied, "I am as you, my people as your people; I'll go to war with you!" 4 Jehoshaphat then said to the king of Israel, "Inquire first what the word of Yahweh is!" 5 So the king of Israel summoned the prophets, four hundred of them, and said to them, "Shall we go to war with Ramoth-gilead or shall I withdraw [my plan]?" "Go up," they replied, "for God has given it into the hand of the king." 6 Jehoshaphat said, "Is there no other prophet of Yahweh here, that we may inquire through him?" 7 The king of Israel said to Jehoshaphat, "Yes, there is one fellow by whom we may inquire of Yahweh, but I hate him because he never prophesies good for me, but always evil; he is Micaiah, the son of Imlah." "Let not the king speak so," replied Jehoshaphat. 8 So the king of Israel summoned a court official and ordered, "Bring quickly Micaiah the son of Imlah." 9 Now the king of Israel and Jehoshaphat the king of Judah were sitting each upon his throne, and clad in robes; they were sitting in a plaza at the entrance to the gate of Samaria where all the prophets were prophesying before them. 10 Zedekiah the son of Chenaanah had made iron horns for himself and said, "Thus, has Yahweh said, you shall gore Aram with these

† II Chron xviii 1–34 ‖ I Kings xxii 1–36.

until they are destroyed." 11 All the other prophets prophesied similarly, saying, "Go up against Ramoth-gilead! Enjoy success, for Yahweh has given it into the hand of the king." 12 The messenger who went to summon Micaiah spoke to him as follows: "Look here, the words of the prophets are uniformly favorable to the king; so let your word be the same as theirs and speak favorably." 13 Micaiah replied, "By the life of Yahweh, I will speak just what my God tells me!" 14 When he came to the king and the king said to him, "Micah, shall we go up to Ramoth-gilead for battle or shall I withdraw [my plan]?"; he said, "Go ahead, enjoy success, for they shall be given into your hand." 15 Then the king said to him, "How many times must I adjure you to tell me only the truth in the name of Yahweh?" 16 He replied,

> "I saw all Israel
> scattered upon the mountains,
> like a flock without a shepherd.
> And Yahweh said, these have no master,
> Let them return each to his house in peace!"

17 The king of Israel said to Jehoshaphat, "Did I not tell you, he will not prophesy good for me but evil?" 18 But he said, "Listen now to the word of Yahweh. I saw Yahweh sitting on his throne with the whole host of the heavens standing on his right and his left. 19 Yahweh said, 'Who will entice Ahab, the king of Israel, to go up and fall at Ramoth-gilead?' One said this and another said that. 20 Then a spirit came forth and stood before Yahweh and said, 'I will entice him!' 'How?' said Yahweh to him. 21 He said, 'I'll go forth and be a deceiving spirit in the mouth of all his prophets.' He replied, 'You will succeed in enticing him; go and do so.' 22 Behold, now, Yahweh has put a deceiving spirit into the mouth of these your prophets, for Yahweh has really decreed evil against you." 23 Then Zedekiah the son of Chenaanah approached and struck Micaiah on the cheek and said, "Which way did the spirit of Yahweh pass from me to speak to you?" 24 "Behold you will see on that day when

you shall go from room to room to hide yourself," replied Micaiah. 25 The king of Israel said, "Seize Micaiah and turn him over to Amon the mayor of the city and Joash the king's son, 26 and say, Thus has the king commanded: Imprison this fellow and put him on meager rations of bread and water until I return in triumph." 27 Retorted Micaiah, "If you do indeed come back safely, Yahweh has not spoken by me." And he said, "Listen, all peoples." 28 So the king of Israel and Jehoshaphat the king of Judah went up to Ramoth-gilead. 29 The king of Israel said to Jehoshaphat, "I will go into the battle in disguise, but you keep on your robes." So the king of Israel disguised himself when they went into battle. 30 Now the king of Aram had given orders to his chariot captains, saying, "Don't fight with anyone, either small or great, except with the king of Israel alone." 31 So when the chariot captains saw Jehoshaphat, they thought he was the king of Israel and surrounded him in order to attack [him]. But when Jehoshaphat shouted, Yahweh helped him and God *drew them away* from him. 32 When the chariot captains saw that he was not the king of Israel, they turned back from pursuing him. 33 But a man drew a bow *at full strength,* and shot the king of Israel *between the joints of the armor.* He commanded the charioteer, "Turn around and take me out of the turmoil of battle, for I have been wounded." 34 Because the battle raged furiously that day, the king of Israel remained *propped up* in his chariot until evening in full view of Aram; but at sunset he died.

a-a LXX "turned them away."
b-b LXX "with good aim." The root of the Heb. *leṭummō* means basically "to be whole or full."
c-c Uncertain. Heb. "between the bands and the armor."
d-d Cf. LXX and I Kings xxii 35 where *hoph.* pt. ("he had to be held up") is used. For syntax see *Gesenius' Hebrew Grammar,* ed. E. Kautzsch, 2d Eng. ed. of A. E. Cowley, 1910, 116 r.

NOTES

xviii 2. *So one time.* Literally "at the end of years."

3. *Ramoth-gilead.* Tell Ramith in north Gilead. Cf. N. Glueck, BASOR 92 (December 1943), 10–16.

9. *a plaza.* For this meaning see J. Gray, VT 2 (1952), 209 f. On the basis of Aqht passage (II Aqht, col. 5, lines 6–8 in C. H. Gordon's *Ugaritic Handbook,* 1947, p. 182), Gray concludes that it means a wide plaza before the city gate rather than a threshing floor.

14. *"Go ahead, . . . your hand."* Observe the irony of the reply.

16. *master.* MT *'ᵃdōnīm,* "masters," "lords." But the parallelism appears to demand a singular. Hence this may be a case of the enclitic *mem.*

18. *standing.* The standing is technical as well as actual. They were in attendance upon the divine King, doubtless in a standing position.

23. Note the irony of the remark, as well as its insulting nature. Behind it lies the usual assumption about the powers of the prophet. Whether Zedekiah is referring to his own action, or whether the action is independent of the statement, which may refer to the same lying spirit as having passed from Zedekiah and his companions to Micaiah, is not clear. The tone of his voice may be sensed but the meaning is hard to determine.

27. *"Listen, all peoples."* Quotation from Mic i 2a, perhaps due to a confusion of names.

COMMENT

Verses 2–33 of this impressive story vary but slightly from their source, I Kings xxii. Since it deals almost exclusively with the Northern Kingdom, there must have been compelling reasons for its inclusion by the writer; these are not difficult to discover in the light of his over-all views of religion. The most obvious reason for the Chronicler's copying of the story is that it concerns itself with a prophet. He was very fond of recalling the records of prophets not mentioned elsewhere (see Introduction to *I Chronicles*) and upon which he depended for much of his information. He was doubtless led to his regard for the prophets by the Deuteronomic historian, who was strongly influenced by them. The story of Elijah-Elisha was not included in Chronicles because in no instance known to us did their activity or message impinge on Judah. In the case of Micaiah the situation is quite different. Not only did the story of Micaiah involve a king of Judah but it had some lessons to teach that were appropriate to the total message of the Chronicler.

Perhaps the outstanding significance of the whole episode to him was the fact that Micaiah unlike the official prophets of Ahab was a true prophet of Yahweh. That the king of the Davidic line insisted upon calling in this prophet of Yahweh must have made a deep impression on the writer—Micaiah the prophet of Yahweh versus "your prophets" (vs. 22). It is quite possible that he also wanted to emphasize the interest in and insistence upon the orthodox religion of Yahweh by the king of Judah as opposed to the unrecognized religion of the north.

The lesson drawn by the Chronicler is worthy of note. Jehoshaphat did not really need a marriage alliance with Ahab because he already possessed wealth and honor (vs. 1). The author follows the source in showing the involvements attendant upon the alliance. Nevertheless, Jehoshaphat was able to extricate himself from the jaws of death because, as the writer significantly asserts, "Yahweh helped him" (vs. 31). Thus, the folly of such an alliance is depicted, from which he was delivered by Yahweh and not just because of what Jehoshaphat did himself, that is, shouted to divert the attention of his pursuers.

In as much as there is no direct interest in Ahab—though the moral is apparent—the reader is given the barest outline of his misfortune and spared the gory details of his death (I Kings xxii 35b–38).

21. THE REIGN OF JEHOSHAPHAT (873–849 B.C.): GOD'S REBUKE AND JEHOSHAPHAT'S REFORMATION
(xix 1–11)

Jehu rebukes Jehoshaphat

XIX 1 However, Jehoshaphat the king of Judah returned home to Jerusalem safely. 2 Jehu the son of Hanani the seer went out to meet him and said to King Jehoshaphat, "Should you help the evil or love those who hate Yahweh? Because of this, there is wrath against you from Yahweh. 3 But some good things are to your credit, for you swept the Asherahs from the land and determined in your mind to seek God."

Reform of Jehoshaphat

4 Jehoshaphat lived in Jerusalem but went about regularly among the people, from Beer-sheba to Mount Ephraim, to convert them to Yahweh God of their fathers. 5 He also appointed judges in the land, in each of the fortified cities of Judah; 6 he admonished the judges: "Be careful what you do because you are not judging for man but for Yahweh who will be*ᵃ* with you in your decisions. 7 And now may the fear of Yahweh be upon you; be careful what you do, for Yahweh our God loathes dishonesty, partiality, or bribery." 8 Jehoshaphat also appointed at Jerusalem some of the Levites, priests, and family heads of Israel to handle cases pertaining to the cult and disputes arising between the citizens*ᵇ* of Jerusalem; 9 he charged them as follows: "Thus you must do, in the fear of Yahweh, in truth, and with the utmost integrity. 10 When any case comes before you involving any of your brothers living in their cities, whether

ᵃ yhy omitted by haplography.
ᵇ So with LXX and Vulg. MT has "and they dwelt."

capital or [civil], and having to do with the interpretation of commandment, statutes, or judgments, you must warn them that they do not incur guilt before Yahweh and [his] wrath fall upon you and your brothers; thus you must do so as not to incur guilt. 11 Look now, Amariah the chief priest shall be over you in all cultic cases, Zebadiah the son of Ishmael, the leader of the house of Judah, [shall be over you] in all civil cases, and the Levites shall be your official bailiffs. Act decisively and may Yahweh be on the side of the right."

Notes

xix 8. *cases*. Literally "matter of Yahweh."
9. Cf. 1QH 16:17 for similar expression.
10. *you must warn*. I.e., in addition to rendering the judicial decree in the case.
11. *cultic cases*. Literally "matter(s) of Yahweh."
civil cases. Literally "matter(s) of the king."
bailiffs. Cf. Albright, AMJV, p. 75, n. 56; he translates "official agent." Their duty was apparently to carry out the orders of the court and assist in the maintenance of civil order. See S. R. Driver, *A Critical and Exegetical Commentary on Deuteronomy* (in ICC), 1916, pp. 16 f.
may Yahweh . . . the right. Literally "may Yahweh be with the good."

Comment

[Prophetic opposition to Jehoshaphat's alliance with Ahab, xix 1–3]: Chapter xviii 1 f. already disclosed the writer's view of Jehoshaphat's marriage alliance with Ahab. The prophecy of Jehu is much more pointed, though the rebuke he administered to the king is relatively mild. The prophet is pictured as going out to meet Jehoshaphat on his way back to Jerusalem after the debacle at Ramoth-gilead. His message emphasizes two points: the judgment of Ahab—and therefore the Northern Kingdom—as evil and a hater of Yahweh, and the statement that Jehoshaphat's good deeds outweigh his mistake. Here the prophet expresses the view of the Chronicler.

[The reform of Jehoshaphat, 4–11]: But the most important portion of the chapter is the account of the judicial reform of Jehoshaphat, whose inception may have been due in part to his desire to strengthen the Southern Kingdom in view of the internal corruption and deterioration of the Northern Kingdom. The reforming activity proceeded along two lines: the teaching mission (vs. 4; cf. xvii 7–9) and the reorganization of the judiciary. Both were really two aspects of the same movement of whose general historicity there can hardly be any doubt. The Deuteronomist has little to say about the internal affairs of Judah in the reign of Jehoshaphat; they were lost sight of largely because of his main interests in Elijah and Elisha who were so deeply involved in the activities of Ahab. But the fact that Jehoshaphat's assistance was sought by Ahab (I Kings xxii) and Jehoram (II Kings iii), and the respect which Elisha is said to have had for Jehoshaphat (II Kings iii 14) add weight to the Chronicler's story about him.

The administrative organization of Solomon was continued, probably with necessary modifications, in both kingdoms (Albright, JPOS 5 [1925], 17–54, especially 36 ff., 44 ff.). The extent of Jehoshaphat's kingdom is said to be "from Beer-sheba to Mount Ephraim," which is no doubt coextensive with Judah in the story. The Solomonic structure was administrative in character, but that did not exclude the judicial function which was retained by the king, at least in Judah (I Kings iii 16 ff.). The important point here is the addition of Levites and priests, whose duty it was to preside over cultic cases coming before the court (cf. Albright, AMJV, p. 76). Jehoshaphat probably catered to local tradition in his appointment of judges from the elders or outstanding men of the community. See further, Cross and Wright, JBL 75 (1956), 202–26.

The crucial portion of the section is vss. 8–11, which deal with the situation in Jerusalem where Levites, priests, and heads of families were appointed to handle cultic and civil cases. Of particular significance is the strong religious emphasis throughout, testifying once more to the principle of social solidarity governed by the cultic interests of the writer. The Jerusalem court was thus composed of priests, civil officials (occupying the position of the elders), and Levites. For the organization of the Jerusalem court and the Egyptian parallels, see the excellent study by Albright, AMJV, especially pp. 74–82. Amariah presided over cultic and Zebadiah over civil matters. Only once in Chronicles (II Chron xxxiv 9) is the late expression *kōhēn gādōl* (great priest) used. Frequently when the chief or head priest is referred to, the term *kōhēn hā-rō'š* (head priest) is used. This appears to have been an earlier designation than the former and may have had a different meaning, that is, that of the head of a priestly family. For a discussion of the problem of the high priesthood with biblical references, see J. Morgenstern, "A Chapter in the History of the High-Priesthood," AJSL 55 (1938), 1–24, 183–97, 360–77. The Levites were the court functionaries carrying out the decisions of the court. It had specific instructions on procedure (vs. 10) and all cases were to be judged on the principle of avoiding guilt before Yahweh so as to maintain the public welfare—that is, that the wrath of Yahweh may not "fall upon you and your brothers." The ostensible reason for the reform was to avert divine wrath, which could be interpreted as foreign invasion, or internal collapse and revolt.

The pattern followed at Jerusalem was apparently adhered to also in the district courts, the reference to which was due to their inclusion in the material the Chronicler was relaying (Albright, AMJV, p. 76). These local courts were in strategic centers, "in each of the fortified cities of Judah" (vs. 5), which replaced the administrative cities in the earlier and later arrangements. The Jerusalem court was probably a high court, as well as a local court, that dealt with cases referred to it by the district courts (cf. vs. 10 —"any case . . . involving any of your brothers living in their cities").

22. THE REIGN OF JEHOSHAPHAT (873–849 B.C.): JEHOSHAPHAT'S PIETY REWARDED (xx 1–37, xxi 1)†

Jehoshaphat's great victory

XX ¹ Later when the Moabites and the Ammonites, in company with the Meunites,ᵃ had come up to make war on Jehoshaphat, ² Jehoshaphat received the following message: "A great multitude from the other side of the sea, from Edom,ᵇ is coming against you and, see, they are already at Hazazon-tamar which is En-gedi." ³ Because he was afraid, Jehoshaphat turned his attention to seeking Yahweh and proclaimed a fast throughout all Judah. ⁴ So Judah came together to implore Yahweh [for assistance]—they came from all the cities of Judah to seek Yahweh. ⁵ Then Jehoshaphat stood up in the congregation of Judah and Jerusalem in the house of Yahweh in front of the new court ⁶ and said, "O Yahweh God of our fathers, are you not God in the heavens and the ruler of all the kingdoms of the nations? Power and might are in your hand so that none can prevail over you. ⁷ Have you not, our God, dispossessed the inhabitants of this land before your people Israel and given it to the seed of Abraham, your beloved, forever. ⁸ They have lived in it and have built for you there a sanctuary for your name, saying, ⁹ "If evil, sword, flood,ᶜ pestilence or famine come upon us and we stand before this house, before you—for your name is in this house—and cry to you because of our distress, you will listen and deliver [us]. ¹⁰ Look now, the Ammonites, the Moabites, and those from Mount Seir which you did not allow Israel to enter when

† II Chron xx 31–34 ‖ I Kings xxii 41–47; 35–37 ‖ I Kings xxii 48–50; II Chron xxi 1 ‖ I Kings xxii 51.

ᵃ Hebrew reads "Ammonite," which is impossible here. Cf. xxvi 7.
ᵇ So for Heb. "Aram," and as found in one manuscript.
ᶜ Transposition of consonants to *šṭp;* Hebrew has *špwṭ,* "to judge."

they came out of the land of Egypt—they went around them and did not destroy them—11 are repaying us by coming to drive us out from your possession which you have given us. 12 O our God, will you not judge them, for we do not have the strength to cope with this great multitude which has come against us and because we do not know what to do we are looking to you [for help]." 13 All Judah, including their *little children,* their wives, and their sons, were standing before Yahweh. 14 Then the spirit of Yahweh came upon Jahaziel, the son of Zechariah, the son of Benaiah, the son of Jeiel, the son of Mattaniah the Levite of the Asaph clan, in the midst of the congregation, 15 who replied, "Pay attention, all Judah, citizens of Jerusalem and King Jehoshaphat, thus has Yahweh said to you: Do not be afraid and do not tremble before this great multitude, for the war is not your affair but God's. 16 Tomorrow go down against them; look, they are coming up the ascent of Hassis*e* and you will meet them at the end of the wadi in the direction of the wilderness of Jeruel. 17 You will not have to fight in this [battle]; take your stand firmly and see the salvation of Yahweh for you, O Judah and Jerusalem. Do not be afraid and do not tremble; go out toward them tomorrow, for Yahweh is with you." 18 Then Jehoshaphat knelt down with his face to the ground and all Judah and the citizens of Jerusalem fell down before Yahweh, to worship Yahweh. 19 The Levites, both of the Kehathites and of the Korahites, rose to praise Yahweh God of Israel with an exceedingly loud voice. 20 So in the morning they prepared to go out to the wilderness of Tekoa. While they were going out Jehoshaphat stood up and said, "Listen to me, O Judah and citizens of Jerusalem, believe in Yahweh your God and you will be established, believe in his prophets and you will be successful." 21 After consulting with the people, he appointed singers for Yahweh who in holy attire were to go out ahead of the troops praising [him] with:

d–d Perhaps Hebrew here means "family," of which "wives and sons [children]" is an explanatory detail.
e LXX has "Asas," "Asae"; Vulg. "Sis." For location see Abel, *Géographie de la Palestine*, I, p. 403.

Praise Yahweh,
For his devotion is everlasting.

22 The moment they began with shouting and praise, Yahweh set ambushes against the Ammonites, the Moabites, and those from Mount Seir who had come against Judah and they were struck down. 23 In so doing, the Ammonites and Moabites opposed those from Mount Seir and wiped them out completely. When they had finished off the men of Seir, they destroyed each other. 24 When Judah came to the point overlooking the wilderness, in quest of the horde, lo they were corpses lying on the ground; not one had escaped. 25 When Jehoshaphat and his people came to claim the booty they found cattle ƒin abundance,ƒ equipment, garments,ᵍ and costly vessels beyond reckoning which they appropriated for themselves; so extensive was [the booty] that it took them three days to claim it. 26 On the fourth day they assembled in the valley of Beracah where they praised Yahweh; hence they called the name of that place the valley of Beracah as it is today. 27 Then all the men of Judah and Jerusalem returned with Jehoshaphat at their head; they returned to Jerusalem rejoicing because Yahweh had given them joy over their enemies. 28 They came to Jerusalem to the house of God with harps, zithers, and trumpets. 29 The fear of God came upon all the kingdoms of the lands when they heard that Yahweh had fought against the enemies of Israel. 30 Then the reign of Jehoshaphat was peaceful, for his God gave him rest on all sides.

Final observations on the reign of Jehoshaphat

31 And so Jehoshaphat was king over Judah. He was thirty-five years old when he became king and he was king in Jerusalem for twenty-five years; his mother's name was Azubah, the daughter of Shilhi. 32 He continued in the way of his father Asa, and did not deviate from it, doing right in the sight of Yahweh;

ƒ–ƒ So with LXX for Heb. "among them."
ᵍ With some manuscripts for MT "corpses."

33 only the high places did not cease because the people had not yet set their minds intently on the God of their fathers. 34 The remainder of the history of Jehoshaphat, from beginning to end, see it is written down in the records of Jehu the son of Hanani which are recorded in the chronicles of the kings of Israel.

Abortive maritime venture of Jehoshaphat

35 Afterward Jehoshaphat the king of Judah formed a partnership with Ahaziah the king of Israel, though he acted wickedly in so doing. 36 He joined him in constructing a fleet to go to Tarshish—they constructed the ships at Ezion-geber. 37 Then Eliezer the son of Dodavahu of Mareshah prophesied against Jehoshaphat as follows: "Because you became a partner with Ahaziah Yahweh has wrecked your work." So the ships were broken and could no longer go to Tarshish.

Death of Jehoshaphat

XXI   1 When Jehoshaphat slept with his fathers, he was buried with his fathers in the city of David and Jehoram his son became king in his place.

NOTES

xx 1. *Ammonites.* Shalmaneser III (858–824 B.C.) mentions an Ammonite king, Ba'sa son of Ruhubi, who contributed soldiers to an Aramaean confederacy (ANET, p. 279).

2. *Hazazon-tamar.* Location is uncertain but has been placed near the southern end of the Dead Sea (Abel, *Géographie de la Palestine*, II, pp. 344, 475; A. Alt, PJB 30 [1934], 20–24). M. Noth ("Eine palästinische Lokalüberlieferung in 2 Chr. 20," ZDPV 66 [1944], 50–56) locates it at el-ḥaṣāṣa, between En-gedi and Bethlehem.

5. *the new court.* The large court of iv 9. The king stood at the entrance to the priest's court while the people were assembled in the new court. The reference is to the postexilic temple.

7. Cf. Gen xviii 17–19; Isa xli 8; Prayer of Azariah xii; Jubilees xix 9.

16. *Jeruel.* Southeast of Tekoa, on the steep descent to En-gedi.

20. *they prepared. hškm* here means to get busy, active.

you will be established. Based on Isa vii 9, xxviii 16, etc.

23. In the confusion of the battle the enemy fought and killed each other (as in the Gideon story, Judg vii 22).

25. *beyond reckoning.* Literally "not burden," i.e., not capable of being carried away.

26. *Beracah.* "Blessing" or "praise." An etiological motive may underlie this verse; this is how the valley got its name. It may have been Wadi Berekut, between Tekoa and En-gedi.

33. *the high places did not cease.* Cf. xvii 6, where it is said that Jehoshaphat had removed the high places. This is clear indication of the stubbornness of the problem and the fact that the religious reformation was only temporarily successful.

35. *partnership.* I.e., in a trading syndicate. See W. F. Albright in *Studies Presented to David M. Robinson,* ed. G. E. Mylonas, I, 1951, p. 230. Verbal form is Aramaic.

36. The Kings parallel has "Tarshish fleet," i.e., refinery fleet, which is obviously correct. Cf. ix 21 and BASOR 83 (October 1941), 21.

37. *Dodavahu.* Perhaps to be read "Dodiyahu."

has wrecked. Prophetic perfect? As Jer xxviii 2, 4, shows, prophecy used both perfect and imperfect without clear distinction.

COMMENT

[Jehoshaphat's victory, xx 1–30]: This part of chapter xx represents another of the Chronicler's illustrations, from the history of the time, of Jehoshaphat's piety with its rewards. The essence of the story is not pure fabrication, although much of it is couched in terms drawn from the period in which the author was writing. Some older scholars (Wellhausen and Kautzsch) have seen in chapter xx a recasting of II Kings iii, a view now rejected by nearly all commentators. Benzinger refers to it as "a beautiful example of an historical midrash" (*Die Bücher der Chronik* [see Selected Bibliography, Commentaries], p. 107). Noth thinks it rests on a local tradition and not on an old historical source (ÜS, pp. 142f., n. 3; ZDPV 66 [1944], 45–71) which the writer employed to replace the story told in II Kings iii (ÜS, p. 159). Rudolph, p. 259, believes that external circumstances of the story rest on a good tradition. Certain features have been magnified (e.g., the great multitude of vs. 2) somewhat out of proportion but that can hardly be said to invalidate the true kernel of the story, which revolves around an invasion of Judah from the south.

The invaders were Moabites, Ammonites, and Meunites. Who the Meunites were is uncertain. They are mentioned in I Chron iv 41; II Chron xxvi 7; Ezra ii 50; Neh vii 52. For suggestions see Montgomery, *Arabia and the Bible,* pp. 182 f. In the passages noted, they appear with other groups on the southern borders of Judah and may have been equated with the Minaeans, who were the dominant South Arabian traders in the period of the Chronicler. Whether the undertaking of the invaders was a razzia or a more extensive military campaign cannot be determined; but whatever it was, the attack thoroughly alarmed the authorities at Jerusalem— perhaps because of the presence of invaders at a vital center before they were aware of it. News of the invasion came from the direction of En-gedi. There is some evidence for an Iron Age road from Hebron through Nahal Seelim to the shores of the Dead Sea and on to Moab which would have been threatened by the easterners. See IEJ 11 (1961), 16. The fortress cities of Rehoboam (xi 5–10) prevented their entrance from any other direction. Invaders sometimes took to the byways to reach their objectives (cf. Isa x 27 ff.).

The effect of the news of the invasion upon Jehoshaphat was stunning. He immediately proclaimed a fast in which every man, woman, and child participated (vs. 13; cf. Joel ii 15, 16). Before the assembled congregation the king offered a solemn prayer to Yahweh—as Asa had done when he was threatened by the Ethiopians (xiv 10 f.)—recalling the requests made by Solomon at the time of the dedication of the temple (vs. 9; cf. vi 14–42; on the prayer as a confession and declaration of faith, see O. Plöger, in *Festschrift für Gunther Dehn,* 1957, pp. 46 f.). The Chronicler's reference to "a great multitude" above and in vs. 12 is justification for the intervention of Yahweh; for Judah could not, of its own strength, cope with the invaders.

The oracle of Yahweh in answer to Jehoshaphat's prayer was given by Jahaziel, an Asaphite who was reckoned among the Levites. Asaph is referred to elsewhere (xxix 30, xxxv 15) as a seer, and Jahaziel was an inspired singer. As a member of the cult personnel, he delivered an oracle of salvation (the salvation of Yahweh, vs. 17), introduced and concluded by the old formula, "Do not be afraid" (vss. 15, 17) (cf. J. Begrich, "Das priestliche Heilsorakel," ZAW 52 [1934], 83, and A. R. Johnson, *The Cultic Prophet in Ancient Israel,* 1944, pp. 61 f.). Judah would not participate in the battle, for the battle was the Lord's (cf. Exod xiv 13–14; I Sam xvii 47; Ps xci 8 f.); but they would share in the victory. Jehoshaphat and the assembled citizens of Jerusalem and Judah responded to Jahaziel's oracle of salvation with worship and praise. The following morning the host was sent off with an exhortation by the king and a religious procession. Apparently the writer viewed the whole expedition as a holy war, since cultic personnel accompanied the army and played a major role in the campaign (see von Rad, *Der Heilige Krieg im alten Israel*, pp. 80 f., and COMMENT on Sec. 16, xiv 13). The victory celebration was marked by the claiming of the booty and a service of thanksgiving in the field. The whole celebration lasted four days. Another one, presumably involving all segments of the population, took place upon the return to Jerusalem of the victorious king and his army. One of the results of the spectacular triumph of Yahweh was to strike terror into Jehoshaphat's enemies so that he remained at peace afterward.

[Final observations on Jehoshaphat's reign, 31–34]: This summary represents an adaptation of I Kings xxii 41–47. The Chronicler omits the synchronism between the reigns of Jehoshaphat of Judah and Ahab of Israel but otherwise simply reproduces his source in vs. 31. In the following verse he modifies it somewhat, for example, "he continued in the way of his father Asa" for "he continued in all the way," etc. of I Kings xxii 43. The modification may be due to the maritime alliance with Ahaziah, condemned by Eliezer (vss. 35–37). Verse 33 is altered from "the people still sacrificed and burned incense upon the high places" of I Kings xxii 44 so that the blame seems to fall upon the people rather than upon the king, which does not harmonize with their response exhibited in the first portion of the chapter. The reference to the oracles of Jehu ben-Hanani said to contain other acts of Jehoshaphat is missing in Kings. "The chronicles of the kings of Israel" equals "the chronicles of the kings of Judah" in I Kings xxii 46; hence "kings of Israel" here is probably due to the Chronicler's view that Judah is really the true Israel. Rudolph's point, p. XI, that the oracles of the various prophets mentioned in Chronicles were a part of the chronicles of the kings appears to be confirmed by this verse.

[Jehoshaphat's abortive maritime venture, 35–37]: The position of this pericope again illustrates that the Chronicler followed the Deuteronomist closely, for it appears in exactly the same place in

I Kings xxii, though in different form. The Kings narrative says simply that Jehoshaphat built a Tarshish fleet for the purpose of bringing gold from Ophir. But it never sailed because it was smashed at Ezion-geber. There is some archaeological evidence that the second period of Ezion-geber was the work of Jehoshaphat (cf. BASOR 79 [October 1940], 8 f.). It dates from the ninth century. In any case, it did not remain under Judah for long, as we learn from xxi 8 ff. The Edomites remained in control until the time of Uzziah a century later (cf. BASOR 72 [December 1938], 7 f.).

After the destruction of the Tarshish fleet, Ahaziah volunteered to join Jehoshaphat but the latter refused the offer. The Chronicler has reinterpreted the story so as to make the maritime venture a joint enterprise with Ahaziah of Israel, thus contradicting the statement by the Deuteronomist. He may have been following an independent source here (cf. Rudolph, p. 265) that suggested a much closer relationship between the two kingdoms than is generally recognized. In any case, it gave him an excellent explanation of the cause for the disaster as the prophecy of Eliezer specifically indicates. There is no reference elsewhere to this prophet.

[The death of Jehoshaphat, xxi 1]: This verse belongs with the story of Jehoshaphat; it is the regular formula that concludes the story of nearly all of the kings.

23. THE REIGN OF JEHORAM (849–842 B.C.)
(xxi 2–20)†

Removal of possible opposition

XXI   2 His brothers, sons of Jehoshaphat, were Azariah, Jehiel, Zechariah, Azariah, Michael, and Shephatiah—all of them sons of Jehoshaphat the king of Israel.ª 3 Their father had presented to them rich gifts of silver, gold, and other valuables along with the fortified cities of Judah, but he gave the kingdom of Judah to Jehoram because he was the first-born son. 4 But when Jehoram had taken over the dominion of his father and established himself firmly, he put all of his brothers to the sword, along with some officials of Israel.

Character of his reign

5 Jehoram was thirty-two years old when he became king and remained king in Jerusalem for eight years. 6 He followed the path of the kings of Israel, just as the house of Ahab did—his wife was a daughter of Ahab—and did evil in the sight of Yahweh. 7 But Yahweh was unwilling to destroy the house of David because he had made a covenant with David in which he had promised to provide a light for him and his sons for all time. 8 In his time Edom rebelled against the rule of Judah and established their own monarchy. 9 Then Jehoram, with his captains and all his chariots, went over and at nightfall struck down the Edomites who had encircled him and his chariot captains. 10 The Edomites have continued their rebellion against the rule

† II Chron xxi 5–11 ‖ II Kings viii 17–22; **16–20** ‖ II Kings viii 23–24.

ª The Sebir, LXX, Syr., Vulg. read "Judah" here, but that may be a correction. It is more difficult to account for the presence of Israel because Jehoshaphat was the king of Judah.

of Judah to this day. Libnah also rebelled at that time against his rule because he had abandoned Yahweh God of his fathers. 11 He even made high places in the mountains of Judah, led the citizens of Jerusalem into apostasy and seduced Judah.

The Elijah document

12 Then a document of the prophet Elijah reached him with this message, "Thus has Yahweh God of your father David said, Because you have not followed the ways of Jehoshaphat your father and the ways of Asa the king of Judah 13 but have followed the way of the kings of Israel and led Judah and the citizens of Jerusalem to apostasy just as the house of Ahab led [Israel] to apostasy, and even slew your brothers, of your own father's house, who were better than you, 14 Yahweh is going to afflict your people, your sons, your wives and all your goods with a great plague, 15 and you yourself shall have a severe disease affecting your bowels so that your bowels will come out day after day because of the disease."

Last years of Jehoram

16 Then Yahweh stirred up the Philistines and the Arabs, who dwelt near the Ethiopians, against Jehoram. 17 They came up against Judah, forced their way into it, and carried away all the goods found in the king's house together with his sons and his wives so that not one of his sons was left except Jehoahaz, his youngest son. 18 After this Yahweh afflicted him in the bowels with an incurable disease. 19 In due time, at the end of about two years, his bowels protruded because of his disease and he died in severe pain. His people, however, did not provide for him a pyre like the pyre of his fathers. 20 He was thirty-two years old when he became king and reigned eight years in Jerusalem. He passed away unlamented and they buried him in the city of David, though not in the cemetery of the kings.

NOTES

xxi 4. *some officials of Israel*. May point to the presence of Israelite officials in Judah. That is quite possible considering the relationship between Judah and Israel at the time.

6. *his wife was a daughter of Ahab*. See J. Begrich, "Atalja, die Tochter Omris," ZAW 53 (1935), 78 f. and NOTE on xxii 2. Begrich thinks, on the basis of II Kings viii 26b (‖ II Chron xxii 2b), that Athaliah was the sister, not the daughter of Ahab. Cf. further H. J. Katzenstein, "Who Were the Parents of Athaliah," IEJ 5 (1955), 194–97, who holds that Athaliah was the daughter of Omri.

10. *Libnah*. Libnah has been identified with Tell es-Safi (Abel, *Géographie de la Palestine*, II, p. 85), some twenty miles southwest of Jerusalem, at the western edge of the Shephelah; and with Tell Bornaṭ (BASOR 15 [October 1924], 2–11; PJB 30 [1934], 58–63).

his . . . he . . . his. The pronoun refers to Jehoram, as the phrase "God of his fathers" shows. There is constant shifting back and forth between Judah and Jehoram in the preceding verses.

19. *a pyre like the pyre*. Literally "a burning like the burning."

COMMENT

[Removal of possible opposition, xxi 2–4]: This informative piece is found only in Chronicles and was doubtless taken from the historical records from which the writer drew his material. The matter-of-fact way in which the story is transmitted points to its basic authenticity. Jehoshaphat apparently followed the precedent established by Rehoboam (xi 23) in placing his sons in the fortified cities of Judah where he provided for them lavishly. The throne, however, was given to Jehoram, the oldest son—a rule generally, though not always, followed. As soon as Jehoram had matters well in hand, he proceeded to root out possible claimants to the throne (cf. Judg ix 5; II Kings xi 1 ‖ II Chron xxii 10), as well as the Jerusalem officials who stood in his way.

[The character of his reign, 5–11]: The writer's inclusion of the story just noted has broken the formula generally employed to introduce the reign of a king. The eight years' rule of Jehoram was a sorry one from the Chronicler's point of view. It was almost as bad as that of the monarchs of the Northern Kingdom. The one redeeming feature was the maintenance of the Davidic line (vs. 7). Jehoram was the victim of a marriage alliance with the house of Ahab whose influence was felt in Judah for some time. The main divergence from II Kings viii occurs in vs. 7 where "the house of David" replaces "Judah" (II Kings viii 19a), and "because of David his servant" is expanded to read "because he had made a covenant with David," both illustrations of his regard for the Davidic line.

Edom's revolt may have come soon after the death of Jehoshaphat, perhaps inspired by the unsettled situation in both Israel and Judah. There is some archaeological evidence at Ramet Matred (some thirty miles south of Beer-sheba) for destruction in the Negeb during either the Shishak raid or the revolt of Edom; see IEJ 10 (1960), 110. Ezion-geber probably fell victim to this Edomite expansionist movement that led to its independence (BASOR 72 [1938], 7). The notice here is somewhat contradictory, due to the confused text of the source from which the Chronicler received his information (II Kings viii 21). Verse 8 tells us that Jehoram and his army were encircled by the Edomites but broke through the latter's lines during the night. That escape the writer turns into a victory, thus carrying the assertion of the Deuteronomist a step further. But vs. 10a presents the bitter truth. Libnah also revolted. The reason given for both uprisings is stated only by the Chronicler and is naturally attributed to Judah's defection from Yahweh. Instead of removing the idolatrous objects, as his ancestors had done (xiv 2–4, xvii 6), Jehoram set about making new ones and thus seduced Judah, as Jeroboam had done in Israel (cf. vss. 12–13, below).

[The Elijah document, 12–15]: II Kings i 17 reports the accession of Jehoram of Israel in the second year of Jehoram of Judah. The former succeeded Ahaziah, who died in accordance with a prophecy of Elijah delivered at the time. Hence, it is argued, Elijah was still alive and had at least enough time to observe the blood bath following the accession of Jehoram (of Judah). But, apart from the difficulties involved in the synchronism noted above, Chronicles nowhere else mentions any prophecies of either Elijah or Elisha. In view of the Deuteronomist's high regard for the prophets, particularly Elijah, it is difficult to understand his omission of an episode that involves his favorite prophet, as this one does, if there had been the slightest hint of its existence. The only conclusion possible is that it is apocryphal. For a discussion of the various theories see Rudolph, p. 267. In a number of instances the Chronicler has prophets predicting disaster for kings before the event, for example, Shemaiah for Rehoboam (xii 5 ff.), Hanani for Asa (xvi 7 ff.), Jehu for Jehoshaphat (xix 2 f.), Zechariah for Joash (xxiv 20 ff.) and Azariah the priest for Uzziah (xxvi 17 f.). The letter could possibly have some basis in fact. In that case, the attribution to Elijah would be a mistake not uncommon in that stories and words are often shifted from a less well-known to a better known name. An interesting point here is that Elijah does not prophesy in the name of Yahweh God of Israel, but in the name of "Yahweh God of your father David."

[The last years and death of Jehoram, 16–20]: The Elijah document was the prophetic prelude to the troubles that beset Jehoram and finally brought about his end (cf. vss. 14, 15). The revolt of Edom and Libnah was successful and while it may not have encouraged others directly to take that course, it does indicate the weakness of Judah at the time. This movement was probably no more than a series of forays into the land by Philistines and Arabs from the west and southwest, a reversal of the situation prevalent in the time of Jehoshaphat (xvii 11). The Ethiopians referred to here are apparently the settlers around Gerar from the time of Shishak (cf. COMMENT on Sec. 16, xiv 8–14). The king's wives and sons may have resided in royal cities in the outlying districts of Judah and so fell into the hands of the invaders. There is no evidence of an attack upon Jerusalem at the time. It is possible that the invaders were bought off, the price being the king's wives and sons (cf. I Kings xx 5). It appears more plausible, however, that there was some resistance against the intruders, during which they lost their lives. Only Jehoahaz escaped because he was too young to participate in the fray (cf. xxii 1). That was the affliction foretold for the people in the Elijah document. The king died of a painful abdominal disease which was just what had been predicted for him. In contrast to the description of his death and burial in II Kings viii 24, Chronicles says he was buried in the city of David but not in the cemetery of the kings. The refusal of the people to accord him the customary funeral honors is noted only by our author.

The whole story appears to have been composed of legendary material and historical data, though the latter cannot be determined with finality. Certainly the reference to the Philistines and Arabs who lived in the vicinity of the Ethiopians has all the earmarks of authenticity. It is possible that the Chronicler copied the story pretty much as it stood in his source, which was independent of the account in Kings he follows most often.

24. THE REIGN OF AHAZIAH (ca. 842 B.C.)
(xxii 1–9)†

XXII ¹ Then the citizens of Jerusalem made Ahaziah his youngest son king in his place, for the freebooters who came with the Arabs against the camp had slain all the older ones. Thus it was that Ahaziah the son of Jehoram king of Judah became king. ² Ahaziah was ᵃforty-two years oldᵃ when he became king and reigned one year in Jerusalem. His mother's name was Athaliah, the daughter of Omri. ³ He also followed the ways of the house of Ahab, for his mother was his adviser to bring him into condemnation. ⁴ He did evil in the sight of Yahweh just like the house of Ahab, for they were his advisers after the death of his father and brought on his destruction. ⁵ He followed their advice and went with Jehoram, the son of Ahab, the king of Israel to fight against Hazael the king of Aram at Ramoth-gilead. When the Aramaeans wounded Joram, ⁶ and he returned to Jezreel to recover from the wounds they had inflicted on him at Ramah in his battle with Hazael the king of Aram, Ahaziah,ᵇ the son of Jehoram, king of Judah went down to see Jehoram the son of Ahab at Jezreel where he lay sick. ⁷ Now the downfall of Ahaziah when he went to Joram was God's doing, for when he arrived he went out with Jehoram to Jehu the son of Nimshi whom Yahweh had anointed to cut down the house of Ahab. ⁸ When Jehu was carrying out the judgment on the house of Ahab and found the captains of Judah and the sons of Ahaziah's brothers attending Ahaziah, he killed them. ⁹ Then he had a search made for Ahaziah and when they took him—for he was

† **II Chron xxii 1–9** ‖ II Kings viii 24b–29, ix 21, 27–28.

ᵃ⁻ᵃ See NOTE.
ᵇ So with many manuscripts, LXX, Vulg. MT has "Azariah."

hiding in Samaria—they brought him to Jehu *who slew him.*
But they buried him because they said, "he is the son of Jehoshaphat who sought Yahweh with his whole mind." However, there was no one left of the house of Ahaziah powerful
enough to rule over the kingdom.

– So with LXX; MT "they slew him."

NOTES

xxii 2. *forty-two years old.* That makes him two years older than his
father (cf. xxi 20), which is manifestly impossible. II Kings viii 26 has
"22 years." The chief LXX witnesses have "20," while there is some
minor support for "22," which may be due to the influence of MT of
II Kings viii 26. The MT of Chronicles may represent the conflation
of two traditions and exhibits a striking example of the effort to preserve
two divergent traditions. Originally the numbers were kept separate, e.g.,
22 or 20, and only later added together.

Athaliah. See Begrich, ZAW 53 (1935), 78 f.

3. *condemnation.* This is a legal term signifying that X has been
adjudged guilty, declared to be in the wrong.

8. *the sons of Ahaziah's brothers.* Probably should be omitted since
they would have been too young for such a mission at that time. Perhaps
the phrase ought to be rendered "the relatives of Ahaziah."

9. *the son.* A descendant; he was a grandson of Jehoshaphat.

COMMENT

The Chronicler alone mentions that the citizens of Jerusalem put
Ahaziah on the throne, which may very well have been the case
since in times when the succession was in jeopardy the *'am hā-'āreṣ*
intervened to stabilize the situation (xxiii 20–21, xxvi 1, xxxiii 25b,
xxxvi 1). Though the phrase *'am hā-'āreṣ* does not appear here, the
yōš°bē y°rūšālaim ("the inhabitants of Jerusalem") doubtless has
the same significance. On the meaning of the former in the history
of Judah see E. Würthwein, *Der 'amm ha'arez im Alten Testament,*
1936. The breakthrough of the freebooters who killed the king's
sons, except for the youngest, and carried out marauding expedi-

tions was sufficient cause for the remaining authorities to act. This reference must have come from the writer's source—the same one used in the preceding chapter—because of the appearance of the Arabs here as there. He probably chose to follow that source in preference to Kings because it supported his theory of retribution.

The rest of the story follows Kings in the main. As might be expected, the Chronicler makes Athaliah much more of an *adjutrix diaboli* than does Kings. She was responsible for the evil life of Ahaziah and her retinue became his advisers; and he was apparently a ready disciple—points stressed by the writer. Ahaziah joined Jehoram of Israel in a campaign against the Aramaeans at Ramoth-gilead where Jehoram was wounded. While recuperating at Jezreel, he was visited by Ahaziah—whether he came from the battlefield or sometime later from Jerusalem is not certain. That visit, says the Chronicler, was Yahweh's doing to bring about his overthrow. To understand the situation it is necessary to read II Kings ix 1–21, for only the part of the story involving Ahaziah directly is given here. While Ahaziah was visiting Jehoram, Jehu ben Nimshi, anointed by Elisha to purge the house of Ahab, was on the way to Jezreel to carry out the first part of his task. Both Jehoram and Ahaziah drove out in their chariots to meet Jehu. Then our story diverges from Kings, which tells of Ahaziah's flight after the shooting of Jehoram; but Jehu pursued him and dealt him a fatal blow "at the ascent of Gur near Ibleam" (II Kings ix 27). According to the Chronicler, Jehu first learned of Ahaziah's presence when he came across his attendants, whom he lost no time in dispatching. Then he turned his attention to the king of Judah who had hidden in Samaria. Jehu's police soon discovered him and brought him to Jehu, who slew him. Because of his position, he was buried, presumably at Samaria. The Kings parallel, on the other hand, says he died, of the wounds inflicted by Jehu's followers, near Megiddo but was taken to Jerusalem and sepulchered in the royal cemetery (II Kings ix 28). Benzinger, pp. 110 f., is probably right in attributing these verses to another source which the writer found more to his liking. Because Ahaziah's sons were too young to rule and all his brothers had met their doom earlier, Athaliah took over.

25. THE REIGN OF ATHALIAH (ca. 842–837 B.C.)
(xxii 10–12, xxiii 1–21)†

The murder of the royal family

XXII ¹⁰ When Athaliah the mother of Ahaziah learned that her son was dead, ªshe immediately exterminatedª all the royal seed of the house of Judah. ¹¹ But Jehoshabeath the king's daughter took Joash, Ahaziah's son, stole him away from the midst of the king's sons who were to be slain and hid him with his nurse in the bedroom. So Jehoshabeath, the daughter of King Jehoram and the wife of Jehoiada the priest—she was the sister of Ahaziah—kept him hidden from Athaliah so that she could not kill him. ¹² He remained hidden with them in the house of God for six years while Athaliah reigned over the land.

The presentation of Joash

XXIII ¹ In the seventh year Jehoiada determined to make a pact with the commanders of the hundreds—with Azariah the son of Jeroham, Ishmael the son of Jehohanan, Azariah the son of Obed, Maaseiah the son of Adaiah, and Elishaphat the son of Zichri. ² They traveled through all Judah and summoned the Levites from all the cities of Judah and the Israelite family heads who then came to Jerusalem. ³ The whole congregation made a covenant with the king in the house of God. Heᵇ said

† II Chron xxii 10–12 ‖ II Kings xi 1–3; II Chron xxiii 1–11 ‖ II Kings xi 4–12; 12–21 ‖ II Kings xi 13–20.

ª⁻ª MT "she arose and spoke." II Kings xi 1 "she arose and destroyed." All the versions have "destroyed," "exterminated" here.
ᵇ I.e., Jehoiada. LXX adds "and he showed to them the son of the king." Cf. II Kings xi 4, from which the LXX addition probably came.

to them, "Behold the son of the king shall reign just as Yahweh spoke concerning the sons of David. 4 This is what you are to do now: a third of you priests and Levites who come on duty on the Sabbath shall be porters at the gates; 5 a third [shall guard] the house of the king, a third the foundation gate, while all the people [shall remain] in the courts of the house of Yahweh. 6 None must enter the house of Yahweh except the priests and the Levitical ministrants; they may enter because they are consecrated; but all the people must observe the regulations of Yahweh. 7 The Levites are to surround the king, each one with his weapons in his hand—anyone entering the house shall be put to death—and accompany the king when he enters and departs." 8 So the Levites, and all Judah, did everything Jehoiada the priest had commanded, and each one took charge of his men, those who came on as well as those who went off Sabbath duty, for Jehoiada the priest had not released [any] divisions from duty. 9 Then Jehoiada the priest delivered to the captains of the hundreds the spears, and the great and small shields of King David which were in the house of God. 10 He stationed all the people to guard the king, each with his weapon in his hand, from the south side of the house to the north side of the house and all around the altar and the house. 11 Then they brought out the son of the king, put the crown upon him, [delivered to him] the royal stipulations, and made him king. When Jehoiada and his sons had anointed him, they shouted, "Long live the king."

The reaction of Athaliah

12 When Athaliah heard the sound of the people running and praising the king, she joined the people in the house of Yahweh. 13 As she looked, behold the king was standing in his place at the entrance and the captains and trumpeters were near the king, with all the people of the land rejoicing and blowing the trumpets, and the singers with all their instruments of song giving the signals for praise. Then Athaliah tore her garments and shouted, "Treason, treason." 14 Then Jehoiada the priest brought out the captains of the hundreds who were in charge

of the army and said to them, "Bring her out from between[e] the ranks, and let whoever follows her be slain with the sword!" For the priest had declared, "Do not kill her in the house of Yahweh." 15 So [d]they made way for her[d] and when she came to the entrance of the horse gate of the king's house, they slew her there.

The reformation

16 Then Jehoiada made a covenant between himself, all the people, and the king to remain Yahweh's people. 17 All the people then went to the house of Baal, pulled it down, smashed its altars and its images, and killed Mattan the priest of Baal before the altars. 18 Jehoiada placed the care of Yahweh's house into the hands of [e]the priests and the Levites[e] whom David had appointed over the house of Yahweh to offer the burnt offerings of Yahweh as prescribed in the law of Moses, and with joy and song as directed by David. 19 He also appointed porters for the gates of the house of Yahweh so that no one who was unclean in any way might enter. 20 Then he took the captains of the hundreds, the nobles, the governors of the people, and all the people of the land, and brought down the king from the house of Yahweh: they entered the house of the king through the upper gate and placed the king upon the royal throne. 21 So all the people of the land rejoiced and the city was quiet although they had slain Athaliah with the sword.

[e] So with Syr.
[d-d] So with LXX; Vulg. "they seized her." See W. Rudolph, FAB, p. 475.
[e-e] MT here has "Levitical priests." LXX and Vulg. have "priests and Levites."

NOTES

xxii 10. *learned*. Literally "saw."
11. *the daughter . . . the priest*. Note the marriage and blood ties between the royal and high-priestly families.
xxiii 5. *the foundation gate*. Cf. II Kings xi 6 has "Sur," the name of a gate. Cf. Rudolph, FAB, pp. 474 f.; L. H. Vincent and A. M. Steve, *Jerusalem de l'Ancien Testament*, 1954–55, p. 599, n. 3.

8. *those who came . . . Sabbath duty.* Literally "going on the Sabbath and going off the Sabbath."

11. *the royal stipulations.* I.e., the rules governing his position in relation to Yahweh and the people. See I Chron xxix 19. The document would signify the terms of the kingship under which the monarch would rule. There is good evidence that the covenant between king and people involved obligations for the king as well as for the people (from David's time on), and this would agree with the formula for kingship in Deuteronomy, which may be late in wording but assuredly expresses a long-standing principle of the role and subordination of the king to the word of Yahweh. Cf. Rudolph, p. 270; von Rad, TLZ 72 (1947), cols. 211 ff. Some think the term refers to bracelets (R. de Vaux, *Les Livres des Rois,* 1949, p. 166; Montgomery and Gehman, *The Books of Kings,* pp. 421, 425).

they shouted. I.e., the people.

13. *"Treason, treason."* Literally "conspiracy," "plot," and thus sedition or treason.

14. *the ranks.* Meaning is uncertain, perhaps a part of the temple.

15. *horse gate.* A gate of the temple enclosure, not the horse gate of the city. See M. Burrows, AASOR 14 (1934), 119 f. Cf. diagram of Athaliah's movements in Vincent and Steve, *op. cit.,* p. 600, Fig. 182.

16. *covenant.* The covenant confirms the prior agreement of the king; here the stress falls on the obligations of the people to Yahweh and the king.

18. *David . . . Moses . . . David.* Note the juxtaposition of David and Moses who, for the Chronicler, represent the two great personalities for the life of "all Israel."

COMMENT

[The murder of the royal family, xxii 10–12]: The actual reign of Athaliah is disposed of in few words by both Deuteronomist and Chronicler, perhaps because both wanted to forget the whole affair. It could also be because apparently no queen ruled in her own name in either Israel or Judah, though at times as regent. While Athaliah doubtless thought she was ruling in her own name—because she believed all the royal male issue had been destroyed—that was not the official view. See D. N. Freedman's remarks in G. E. Wright, *The Bible and the Ancient Near East,* 1961, p. 227, n. 40.

The one event agreed upon by both the Deuteronomist and the

Chronicler is the ruthless extermination of her own children, with the exception of Joash who was hidden by his aunt Jehoshabeath, the wife of Jehoiada the priest—a detail supplied by the Chronicler here. This little pericope is nothing more than a brief setting for the following story of the priestly and popular revolt against the atrocities of Athaliah, the maintenance of the Davidic line, and the consequences of defection from Yahweh.

[The crowning of Joash, xxiii 1–11]: The Chronicler's dependence upon II Kings xi is quite evident. But there are significant additions and omissions, in harmony with the author's religious views. For one thing, there is his concern to avoid desecration of the temple by providing ecclesiastical officials and guards rather than purely military ones as in I Kings xi (vss. 4–8). Moreover the people are kept in their proper place (vs. 5) and all "the regulations of Yahweh" with respect to the temple must be observed (vs. 6). The writer's feeling for Jerusalem and the house of Yahweh is stressed by the summoning of the leaders of the hundreds to Jerusalem and the careful handling of all movements that centered about the temple. Another concern was the perpetuation of the Davidic line, emphasized in vs. 3. Thus the two main features of the Chronicler's work stand out conspicuously—the temple and David, together with the emphasis upon the cult personnel. The latter point is illustrated, not only by the place given to priests and Levites in the coup against Athaliah, but especially in the specific statement that Jehoiada and his sons anointed the king (vs. 11).

[The reaction of Athaliah, 12–15]: This part follows the source closely, though not without significant points of emphasis. Here the noise which brought Athaliah to the scene was not simply that of officials and people but that of the people "running and praising the king"; again the king holds the center of the stage. The singers with their musical instruments also played an active role in the proceedings. The sanctity of the temple appears in the strong prohibition, "Do not kill her in the house of Yahweh" as opposed to the simple appeal in the parallel passage (II Kings xi 15). That may have been the motive for Jehoiada's provision for the safe conduct of the queen from the sacred precincts.

[The reformation, 16–21]: The first step taken by Jehoiada to restore Judah to its earlier state was the renewal of the covenant which bound all parties to remain Yahweh's people. This revival of religious leadership in Judah necessitated the uprooting of all vestiges of the Baal cult brought in under Athaliah. On the positive side it meant a return to the torah of Moses and the orders established by David. Most significantly, the claim of the Levites to an equal share with the priests in the cultic services is reaffirmed and care is taken to guard against desecration of the temple. Then the king was conducted from the house of Yahweh and enthroned in the palace. The only violence to disturb the otherwise orderly procedure was the slaying of the queen mother.

26. THE REIGN OF JOASH (ca. 837–800 B.C.)
(xxiv 1–27)†

The family relationships of Joash

XXIV 1 Joash was seven years old when he became king and reigned forty years at Jerusalem. His mother's name was Zibiah from Beer-sheba. 2 Joash did what was right in the sight of Yahweh all the days of Jehoiada the priest. 3 Jehoiada had him marry two wives and he fathered sons and daughters.

Renovation of the temple

4 Afterward Joash decided to renovate the house of Yahweh. 5 So he summoned the priests and the Levites and said to them, "Go out to the cities of Judah and collect money annually from all Israel to repair the house of your God, and you must expedite the matter." But the Levites were in no hurry. 6 Then the king called Jehoiada the chief priest and said to him, "Why have you not required the Levites to bring in from Judah and Jerusalem the tax which Moses the servant of Yahweh and the congregation of Israel [imposed] for the tent of testimony?"—7 Athaliah, that wicked woman, and her sons*a* had neglected the house of God and even had given all the sacred objects of the house of Yahweh to Baal.—8 So at the order of the king they made a chest, placed it outside the gate of the house of Yahweh, 9 and issued a proclamation to Judah and Jerusalem to bring to Yahweh the tax which Moses the servant of God [imposed] upon Israel in the wilderness. 10 Then all the captains and all

† **II Chron xxiv 1–3** ‖ II Kings xii 1–4; **4–14** ‖ II Kings xii 5–16; **23–27** ‖ II Kings xii 18–22.

a Another pointing is "her builders." But MT is supported by LXX and Vulg. Her sons were Ahaziah's brothers, who may very well have been associated with her in the neglect of the temple.

the people rejoiced, brought in and deposited [their contribu-
tions] into the chest until it was full. 11 Whenever the chest was
brought by the Levites for royal inspection and found to contain
enough money, the royal scribe and the official of the chief priest
would come and empty the chest and then take it back again to
its place. They did so day after day and thus collected much
money. 12 The king and Jehoiada gave it to those[b] in charge of
the work on the house of Yahweh who in turn hired masons and
carpenters to renovate the house of Yahweh, as well as iron and
brass workers to repair the house of Yahweh. 13 The workmen
labored on—the repair work progressed in their hands—until they
had restored the house of God to its proper state and had put it
into good condition [again]. 14 When they had finished [it],
they returned to the king and Jehoiada the surplus money from
which they made vessels for the house of Yahweh: vessels for
the service and for the burnt offering, bowls and [other] gold
and silver vessels.

Reversal of the policy of Jehoiada

They offered burnt offerings continually in the house of
Yahweh throughout the lifetime of Jehoiada. 15 When Jehoiada
was old and well along in years he died; he was a hundred and
thirty years when he died. 16 They buried him with the kings
in the city of David because he had well served Israel and God
and his house. 17 After the death of Jehoiada the captains of
Judah came and did homage to the king. When the king yielded
to them 18 they abandoned the house of Yahweh God of their
fathers and served the Asherahs and the images so that wrath
came upon Judah and Jerusalem for this guilt of theirs. 19 So
he sent prophets among them to lead them back to Yahweh;
they threatened them but they would not listen. 20 Then the
spirit of God put on Zechariah the son of Jehoiada the priest
who stood before the people and said to them, "Thus has God
said, why have you transgressed the commandments of Yahweh
so that you cannot succeed; for if you abandon Yahweh, he will

[b] Plural with LXX. Cf. also II Kings xii 12.

abandon you." 21 But they conspired against him and, at the command of the king, stoned him in the court of the house of Yahweh. 22 Thus Joash the king did not remember the devotion which Jehoiada his father displayed on his behalf, but murdered his son. When he died, he cried, "May Yahweh observe and requite!"

The Aramaean invasion and death of Joash

23 At the turn of the year the Aramaean army came up against him. When they came to Judah and Jerusalem, they annihilated all the captains of the people from among the people and shipped all their booty to the king at Damascus. 24 Although the Aramaean army that came was a small body of men, Yahweh delivered a very large army into their hand, because they had abandoned Yahweh God of their fathers. Therefore they executed judgment against Joash. 25 When they departed from him—for they left him with many wounds—his servants conspired against him because of the blood of ᶜthe sonᶜ of Jehoiada the priest and killed him on his bed. After he was dead, they buried him in the city of David, though they did not bury him in the cemetery of the kings. 26 These were the ones who conspired against him: Zabad the son of Shimeath the Ammonitess and Jehozabad the son of Shimrith the Moabitess. 27 [The record] of his sons, of the many oracles against him, and of the renovationᵈ of the house of God is written down in the commentary on the chronicle of the kings. Amaziah his son then became king in his place.

ᶜ–ᶜ Singular with LXX and Vulg.
ᵈ Heb. "foundation."

NOTES

xxiv 3. *he fathered sons and daughters.* The language here is just like that in *P*'s genealogies (cf. Gen v). The influence of *P* on the present text of Chronicles is unmistakable. Whether it was edited into the text (A. C. Welch, *The Work of the Chronicler*, 1939, pp. 78–80) or whether Chronicles is a continuation of *P* cannot be determined at present.

6. *chief priest.* Add "priest" with vs. 11. On term "chief priest" see COMMENT on Sec. 21, xix 11.

the tax . . . testimony. Cf. Exod xxx 12 ff.

7. Athaliah was accused of murdering the king's sons (i.e., Ahaziah's), her grandchildren, with the exception of Joash (xxii 10). The reference to her wanton neglect of the temple occurs only here.

11. *for royal inspection.* Literally "for the inspection of the king."

13. *its proper state.* The import of the whole verse seems to be that the temple was made as secure on its foundations as it was before. In short they restored its structural soundness and solidity.

15. *a hundred and thirty years.* Apparently a symbolic figure; older than Moses (120 years) or Aaron (123 years).

17. *did homage.* In flattery.

18. *Asherahs.* Asherah was originally a sea-goddess, the consort of El in Ugaritic mythology. In the Bible she appears as wife of Baal. The *asherahs* then were probably images of some sort or cult objects symbolizing the goddess with her peculiar function, particularly detested by the prophets (Isa xvii 8, xxvii 9; Mic v 14).

20. *the spirit of God.* For this significant expression see Judg vi 34; I Chron xii 18; Job xxix 14. See discussion of the idea by A. R. Johnson, *The One and the Many in the Israelite Conception of God,* 1942, pp. 5, 15, 33.

21. Cf. Matt xxiii 35; Luke xi 51; Josephus *Wars* IV.v.4.

22. *which his father displayed.* I.e., the *ḥesed* which he had done, the acts of devotion (or kindness) which he had done.

23. *the turn of the year.* In the spring of the year. According to J. Begrich (*Die Chronologie der Könige von Israel und Juda,* 1929, pp. 79 ff., 156 ff.), this is in accord with the Chronicler's calendrical system.

27. *the commentary.* See Sec. 15, NOTE on xiii 22.

COMMENT

This represents an augmented theological interpretation of the reign of Joash, the chief source for which is II Kings xii or a parallel source with the same story in general, though with some significant variations as will appear below.

[The family relationships of Joash, xxiv 1–3]: There is of course no co-ordination of Joash's reign with that of Jehu as in II Kings xii 2. For theological reasons and in conformity with his plan, the Chronicler modifies somewhat the characterization of Joash. He affirms that Joash did what was right so long as Jehoiada lived and then fell into apostasy. His source speaks of the king having done right all his life because of the instruction of Jehoiada and hence says nothing about his defection after the latter's death. Jehoiada, acting as regent, married him to two wives, a sort of compromise between the practice of his predecessors (e.g., David, Solomon, Abijah) and the Deuteronomic injunction (xvii 17). The reference to his sons and daughters is partly an indication of Yahweh's blessing and partly an explanation of the record (vs. 27).

[The renovation of the temple, 4–14ab]: While there may be no disagreement between Kings and Chronicles in the over-all picture of the renovation of the temple, there are significant variations in detail that illustrate the viewpoint of the Chronicler. A characteristic feature of Chronicles, the magnification of the Levites, is carried through here. Thus the Levites were summoned by the king (vs. 5) to participate along with the priests in the collection of funds for the enterprise (on provisions for the temple and its repairs see K. Galling, "Königliche und nichtkönigliche Stifter beim Temple von Jerusalem," BBLA [1950], especially pp. 134–39); indeed they appear to have been placed in charge of the operation (vss. 6, 11)— a priest, scribe, and Levite were placed in charge of the temple's treasuries by Nehemiah (xiii 13). But the observation that at first they were somewhat dilatory in the performance of their duties does not seem to be quite in line with the Chronicler's theory. Yet this indicates that he was not so biased as is sometimes suggested and that he may have drawn from another source (cf. vs. 27 and Rudolph, p. 277) than Kings for his information. It should be observed that the priests are absolved from blame here (cf. II Kings xii 6–8). The Levites appear to have been barred altogether from the actual handling of funds (vss. 11, 12), which were under the jurisdiction of the royal scribe and a representative of the chief priest and dispensed by the king and Jehoiada.

According to the writer, a special campaign was to be conducted among the cities of Judah (vs. 5) for the repair project. The appeal was to be made on the basis of the head tax decreed by Moses (Exod xxx 12–16, xxxviii 25–28) for the furnishing of the tabernacle. The tax fell into disuse, since it is specifically said to have been renewed by Nehemiah (x 32) and applied in part to temple repairs (see W. Rudolph, *Esra und Nehemiah,* 1949, pp. 177–79). It may be that this method was resorted to when the campaign for voluntary offerings failed, or that the Chronicler read back into this situation the later method adopted by Nehemiah. At any rate, there was no lack of funds after the proclamation of the summons; characteristically, there was a surplus, which was used for other purposes (vs. 14). There is no reference to a surplus in II Kings xii.

It is interesting to note that according to II Kings xii 9 the chest was placed beside the altar and the offerings were placed therein by the priests. The Chronicler has it placed "outside the gate of the house of Yahweh" (vs. 8) where all groups deposited their own contributions (vs. 10)—thus preserving the sanctity of the sacred precincts and at the same time providing for direct personal participation of the people.

[A reversal of policy, 14c–22]: The happy state of affairs during the lifetime of Jehoiada is indicated by the uninterrupted sacrifices. Thus the reformation of the cult and the preservation of the Davidic line were the product of the efforts of the chief priest, whose character and honor the Chronicler celebrated by calling attention to his long life and the place of his burial. Jehoiada's symbolic age, 130 years (see NOTE to vs. 15), indicated that he was favored by Yahweh. That he was honored by the people—the nation—is shown by his burial in the royal cemetery.

When the guiding hand of the priest was no longer present, Joash was deflected from his course by the officials—possibly holdovers from the earlier regime—and reverted to former practices. To bring them back to the ways followed by Jehoiada, Yahweh sent prophets among them but without success. Finally Zechariah, the son of Jehoiada, was used by Yahweh to remind king and people of their transgression and that to abandon Yahweh meant failure for both. Instead of showing respect for him, they rewarded him by putting him to death in the very temple where a few years before his father had brought them deliverance from the machinations of Athaliah and her minions. The dying words of the prophet were soon to find fulfillment.

[The downfall of Joash, 23–27]: While II Kings also refers to an Aramaean campaign against Judah that threatened Jerusalem, the Chronicler was dependent upon another source, as may be seen from a close comparison between the stories. He speaks of an Aramaean army making a kind of foray into Judah during which those officials responsible for misleading Joash were rooted out, and booty taken and shipped to the king (Hazael) at Damascus. Kings, on the other hand, tells of an invasion of Judah during which Gath was captured and Jerusalem threatened by the Aramaean king and his army. To spare the capital, Joash stripped the temple and palace of the votive gifts accumulated during the preceding three reigns. Kings knows nothing of the wounding of Joash in the fray, because there was actually no attack upon Jerusalem according to the Deuteronomist. There is agreement on the conspiracy against Joash in which he was murdered and there is some evidence that even the names are the same (manuscript variation on the name "Zabad" can be found in II Kings xii 21, where MT has "Jozabad," but some manuscripts of LXX have "Jozakar"). According to Kings, Joash was buried "with his fathers," which the Chronicler denies—he was not buried in the cemetery of the kings.

The Chronicler's version of the episode was probably taken from the treatise (midrash) he mentions in vs. 27. Unless these materials are regarded as largely fictitious and fabricated, like the vast body of intertestamental pious literature (cf. also the "Words of Moses" and the "Psalms of Joshua" from the Qumran caves), then the Chronicler must have had at his disposal extensive sources in addition to canonical Samuel and Kings. The religious motives were uppermost in his mind and must have been more apparent in his source than in the Deuteronomic parallel. The officials who misled Joash were rooted out, the small Aramaean band overcame a much larger force because of their defection, and Joash himself was the victim of a conspiracy because of his guilt in the death of Zechariah.

27. THE REIGN OF AMAZIAH (ca. 800–783 B.C.)
(xxv 1–28)†

Accession of Amaziah

XXV 1 Amaziah was twenty-five years old when he became king and reigned twenty-nine years at Jerusalem. His mother's name was Jehoaddan from Jerusalem. 2 He did what was right in the sight of Yahweh, only not wholeheartedly. 3 When the kingdom was securely established under him, he slew his servants who had struck down the king, his father. 4 However he did not put their sons to death, because it is written in the law—in the book of Moses—which Yahweh commanded, saying, "The fathers shall not die for the sons nor shall the sons die for the fathers, but each one shall die for his own sin."

Campaign against Edom

5 Amaziah convoked Judah and classified all Judah and Benjamin, according to families, to captains of thousands and captains of hundreds. He also registered them from twenty years old and upward and found that there were three hundred thousand select men, ready for service and capable of wielding spear and shield. 6 Moreover he hired one hundred thousand warriors from Israel for a hundred talents of silver. 7 Then a man of God came to him, saying, "O king, let not the Israelite army go with you for Yahweh is not with Israel, or with any of the Ephraimites. 8 Though you might appear to gain support from them for war, God will overturn you before the enemy, for God has the power to help or to cast down." 9 Amaziah said to the man of God, "But what is to be done about the hundred talents I have

† II Chron xxv 1–4 ‖ II Kings xiv 2–6; **5–16** ‖ II Kings xiv 7; **17–28** ‖ II Kings xiv 8–20.

paid for the troops of Israel?" "God is able to give you more than that," said the man of God. 10 Then Amaziah released the troops that had come to him from Ephraim so they could go home again. They were very angry with Judah and returned home full of wrath. 11 However, Amaziah took courage, led out his people, went to the Valley of Salt, and struck down ten thousand men of Seir. 12 The men of Judah took ten thousand more alive, brought them to the top of the Rock and cast them down from the top of the Rock so that they were all dashed to pieces. 13 The troops whom Amaziah sent back from accompanying him to battle, plundered the cities of Judah from Samaria to Beth-horon, struck down three thousand of their people and took a large quantity of booty. 14 When Amaziah returned from the destruction of the Edomites, he brought along the gods of the men of Seir, set them up as his gods, bowed down before them, and burned incense to them. 15 The anger of Yahweh blazed against Amaziah and he sent a prophet to him who said to him, "Why do you inquire of the gods of the people who could not even deliver their own people from your hand?" 16 While he was still speaking to him, he said, "Have we made you a royal adviser? Stop, or you will be struck down!" So the prophet ceased with the retort, "I know that God has resolved to destroy you because you did this and did not listen to my advice."

War with Joash of Israel

17 Then Amaziah the king of Judah resolved to send the following message to Joash, the son of Jehoahaz, the son of Jehu the king of Israel: "Come, let us meet face to face!"*a* 18 Joash the king of Israel sent the following reply to Amaziah the king of Judah: "The briar of Lebanon sent the following message to the cedar of Lebanon: Give your daughter as a wife for my son, but a wild animal of Lebanon ran over and trampled down the briar. 19 You thought, 'Behold I have struck down Edom' and your ego has been inflated to seek even greater glory. Now, stay in your own place; why should you engage in disaster, since both

a LXX^B omits, by homoioteleuton, all of the verse except "Amaziah resolved."

you and Judah will perish?" 20 But Amaziah refused to listen, for it was an act of God to give them *b*into the hand of Joash*b* because he inquired of the gods of Edom. 21 So Joash the king of Israel came up and he and Amaziah the king of Judah met face to face at Beth-shemesh which belonged to Judah. 22 Judah was routed before Israel and each man fled to his tent. 23 But Joash the king of Israel seized Amaziah the king of Judah, the son of Joash the son of Ahaziah*c* at Beth-shemesh, brought him to Jerusalem, and then broke down four hundred cubits of the wall of Jerusalem between the gate of Ephraim and the corner gate. 24 He took along back to Samaria all the gold and silver, all the vessels found in the house of God in charge of Obed-edom, the treasures of the king's house, and the hostages. 25 Amaziah, the son of Joash, the king of Judah lived for fifteen years after the death of Joash, the son of Jehoahaz, the king of Israel. 26 The remainder of the history of Amaziah, from beginning to end, is it not recorded in the chronicle of the kings of Judah and Israel? 27 From the time that Amaziah defected from Yahweh, they raised a conspiracy against him in Jerusalem so that he fled to Lachish. But they sent to Lachish after him and killed him there. 28 Then they transported him on horses and buried him with his fathers in the city of Judah.

b–b MT "into a hand." Targ. "in his hand." Reading here is that of LXX*L*.
c So with II Kings xiv 13; MT "Jehoahaz."

Notes

xxv 1. *reigned . . . Jerusalem*. On the vexing problem of chronology see Albright, BASOR 100 (December 1945), p. 21, n. 21.

2. *wholeheartedly*. Literally "with his whole heart."

4. *"The fathers . . . own sin."* Law of Deut xxiv 16. Cf. M. Greenberg, who discusses the significance of this law and its observance in connection with the Ten Commandments and other indications of family punishment (*Yehezkel Kaufmann Jubilee Volume*, 1960, pp. 21 f.). The difference between individual and family punishment for transgressions would presumably be in the nature of the crime or sin; also the law, while doubtless old, was often disregarded by kings and usurpers for

whom it would be a matter of course to wipe out the family of those involved. Here the procedure was dictated on the one hand by practical considerations, and on the other (in the case of prophetically inspired purges) by the overriding will of God. As in the case of Achan, certain crimes merited punishment for the whole family. Divine judgment involved taint but human judgment was forbidden to extend beyond the guilty individual.

5. *three hundred thousand.* On the unit basis (*eleph*=one unit), there would be 300 (and 100 in vs. 6) units.

6. *a hundred talents of silver.* About 3¼ tons.

11. *the Valley of Salt.* Identified with Wadi el-milḫ, east of Beersheba, by Abel, *Géographie de la Palestine,* I, p. 407; with the Araba, south of the Dead Sea by Grollenberg and the older geographers.

12. *the Rock.* Play on the word Selaʿ of II Kings xiv 7; Selaʿ is now identified with Umm el Biyārah (AASOR 14 [1934], 77; AASOR 15 [1935], 49).

13. *Samaria.* Samaria is doubtful here because it is difficult to understand why the Ephraimites would have plundered their own territory, unless they began their raid from that point. It may be a mistake for some Judean town. Rudolph, pp. 278 f., suggests Migron (I Sam xiv 2; Isa x 28). Cf. G. Dalman, PJB 12 (1916), 44.

Beth-horon. Beth-horon was in the Valley of Aijalon, some ten miles west-northwest of Jerusalem, on the border between Ephraim and Benjamin. See COMMENT on Sec. 9, viii 5. Earlier it belonged to Ephraim (I Chron vii 24).

14. *the gods . . . Seir.* I.e., the gods were images.

16. *Stop, . . . down.* Literally "Cease, why should they strike you."

resolved. Implies that consultation had taken place, perhaps with advisers.

17. *"Come, . . . to face!"* An English equivalent might be, "Come, let us look each other in the eye."

21. *Beth-shemesh.* About fifteen miles southwest of Jerusalem, on the border between Judah and Dan (Josh xv 10).

23. *four hundred cubits.* About six hundred feet.

the gate of Ephraim and the corner gate. Cf. Vincent and Steve, *Jerusalem de l'Ancien Testament,* pp. 93 f.; M. Avi-yonah, *Sepher Yerushalayim,* I, 1956, opposite p. 160, Map 9, according to which the Ephraim gate was located at the northwest corner of the city and the corner gate (cf. Neh iii 31) at the northeast corner.

24. *He took.* With II Kings xiv 14.

in charge of Obed-edom. Cf. I Chron xxvi 15; i.e., those in that part of the house of God in his care.

hostages. Term and idea occur only here and in the parallel in II Kings xiv 14.

28. *Judah*. II Kings xiv 20 has "David." But the Chronicler's phrase is equally correct for his time, since Jerusalem is referred to in the Babylonian Chronicle as *al ia-a-ḫu-du* "city of Judah" (see D. J. Wiseman, *Chronicles of Chaldaean Kings* (626–556 BC) *in the British Museum*, 1956, p. 73).

COMMENT

[Accession of Amaziah, xxv 1–4]: The Chronicler omits any reference to the synchronism with the Northern Kingdom (II Kings xiv 1), confining himself to a simple statement as to Amaziah's age when he became king and the length of his reign. Defining his character, he says only that he did right, though not with his whole heart. There is no comparison with David and Joash his father as in II Kings xiv 3bc. The Deuteronomic law specified that only the guilty and not their families were to be put to death for crimes.

[The Edomite campaign, 5–16]: Only one verse is devoted to this episode in II Kings xiv 7; the Chronicler has a considerably expanded account which he obviously took from one of his other sources because of the religious interests involved. In preparation for the campaign, the army was reorganized and a military census, like the one undertaken by David (I Chron xxi), Asa (II Chron xiv 8), and Jehoshaphat (II Chron xvii 14–19), was taken to discover the available manpower (see Junge, *Der Wiederaufbau* . . . , pp. 41–42). Amaziah also enlisted a hundred thousand men from Israel to achieve the required strength. These men were free lances, enlisted privately from the border territory. In addition to the stipend given them by Amaziah, they were to share in the booty; when they were sent home on the advice of the prophet, they made up their loss by raiding Judean communities while the king and his army were in Edom (vs. 13).

One of the religious interests of the Chronicler is evident in his explanation of why the recruits from Israel were refused permission to assist in the campaign—because Yahweh was not with Israel, or any Ephraimite. To go through with Amaziah's original plan would therefore have meant defeat. Moreover, Yahweh was not

dependent upon numbers to achieve victory (cf. xiii 3–18). Thus
with prophetic assurance the campaign was undertaken and proved
successful. A large number of Edomites were slain—the numbers
here, as elsewhere in Chronicles, are greatly exaggerated—and an
equal number were thrown down from the Rock. As indicated in
the NOTE on vs. 12, this was probably Selaʻ in Petra itself. It was
accessible only by a very difficult trail (AASOR 15 [1935], 82;
the best description of the acropolis is that of W. H. Morton, BA 19
[1956], 27–28, and for a view see Grollenberg, *Atlas of the Bible,*
p. 111, Fig. 311). The success of the campaign was doubtless
Amaziah's reward for giving heed to the word of the prophet.

Of equal theological significance for the writer was the sequel to
the Edomite campaign, vss. 14–16. Amaziah acted like one of the
great oriental kings who frequently transported the gods of conquered people to their capitals for various reasons. But nowhere else
is a Hebrew king reported to have done so. Of course, the Chronicler's attempt to find a reason for Amaziah's defeat at the hands of
Joash of Israel provides the occasion for the story. Again a prophet
intervenes with the reminder of the impotence of the gods of Edom,
as the king's victory had just demonstrated. The silencing of the
prophet by the authorities led him to retort "God has resolved to
destroy you"; and for two reasons, (a) because he harbored and
paid homage to the gods of Edom and (b) because he rejected the
advice of the prophet.

[War with Joash of Israel, 17–28]: The Chronicler's account of
the war between Amaziah and Joash follows the parallel in II Kings
xiv 8–20 with only minor deviations. The boldness of the former was
inspired by his success in the campaign against Edom. In replying
to the presumptuous message of Amaziah, Joash reacted firmly,
though gentlemanly. But Amaziah was not to be deflected from his
purpose because, as the writer adds, "it was an act of God" to bring
punishment upon him for his invocation of the gods of Edom (vs.
20). The result was just as the prophet had predicted (vs. 16):
Amaziah was defeated, his army put to flight, the king humiliated
before his people in his own capital, the house of God and the
treasuries of the king stripped, hostages taken, and a portion of the
walls of the city broken down. Amaziah may have been personally
so shaken as to be ineffective as ruler. In any case, a conspiracy was
raised against him after some years and he fled to Lachish, where he

was slain. The Chronicler's observation that the conspiracy took place after his religious defection may refer only to the opposition of the religious authorities such as the prophet referred to in vss. 15–16, which was ultimately to issue in a full-blown rebellion.

28. THE REIGN OF UZZIAH (ca. 783–742 B.C.)
(xxvi 1–23)†

General observations

XXVI 1 Then all the people of Judah took Uzziah, who was sixteen years old, and made him king in the place of his father Amaziah. 2 He [re]built Eloth and restored it to Judah after the king slept with his fathers. 3 Uzziah was sixteen years old when he became king and reigned for fifty-two years at Jerusalem. His mother's name was Jecoliah from Jerusalem. 4 He did what was right in the sight of Yahweh, just as Amaziah his father had done. 5 He inquired of God so long as Zechariah, who instructed him *in the fear of God,*ᵃ lived, and so long as he inquired of Yahweh, God gave him success.

Campaigns

6 He went out and fought with the Philistines, breaking down the wall of Gath, the wall of Jabneh, and the wall of Ashdod. He also built cities [in the region of] Ashdod and in [the other territory of] the Philistines. 7 God assisted him against the Philistines, the Arabs who lived at Gur-baal, and the Meunites. 8 The Meunitesᵇ paid tribute to Uzziah and his fame extended as far as Egypt, for he grew increasingly stronger.

Internal developments

9 Uzziah erected towers in Jerusalem, at the corner gate, at the valley gate, and at the corner and fortified them. 10 He also erected towers in the wilderness and carved out many cisterns

† **II Chron xxvi 1–5** ‖ II Kings xiv 21–xv 4; **16–23** ‖ II Kings xv 5–7.

ᵃ⁻ᵃ So with LXX and a number of Hebrew manuscripts. MT "in seeing God."
ᵇ So for MT "Ammonites," with LXX.

because he had many cattle both in the Shephelah and in the plains, and farmers and vinedressers in the mountains and the fertile areas, for he loved the land. 11 Moreover Uzziah had an army ready for military service organized in companies according to the number of their complement by Jeiel the scribe and Maaseiah the officer and under the direction of Hananiah, one of the king's captains. 12 The entire register of family heads of the mighty men numbered twenty-six hundred. 13 Under them was an army of three hundred and seven thousand, five hundred men ready for war, a powerful enough force to support the king against the enemy. 14 Uzziah provided shields, spears, helmets, armor, bows, and slingstones for the entire army. 15 He also set up skillfully contrived devices on the towers and corners of Jerusalem [from which] to shoot arrows and [hurl] large stones. Hence his fame spread far and wide for he was miraculously assisted until he became strong.

Pride and downfall of Uzziah

16 But when he was strong, his arrogance was so great that it led to his downfall; he was disobedient toward Yahweh his God when he entered the temple of Yahweh to burn incense upon the incense altar. 17 Azariah the priest accompanied by eighty valiant priests of Yahweh went in after him; 18 They confronted Uzziah the king and said to him, "It is not permissible for you, Uzziah, to burn incense to Yahweh; only the Aaronite priests consecrated for the purpose may burn incense. Leave the sanctuary, for you have disobeyed and will have no honor from Yahweh God." 19 But Uzziah, who already had a censer in his hand to burn incense, became so angry that in the altercation with the priests a lesion broke out on the skin of his forehead before the priests in the house of Yahweh near the incense altar. 20 So when Azariah the chief priest and all the priests turned toward him, behold leprosy was on his forehead and they hurried him out of there; and he also was anxious to get out because Yahweh had afflicted him. 21 Uzziah the king was thus a leper to the day of his death and lived in house

of quarantine as a leper because he was excluded from the house of Yahweh. Jotham his son, who was in charge of the royal palace governed the people of the land. 22 The remainder of the history of Uzziah, from beginning to end, Isaiah the prophet, the son of Amoz has written down. 23 So Uzziah slept with his fathers and they buried him with his fathers in the field [beside] the cemetery of the kings because they said, "he is a leper." Then Jotham his son became king in his place.

NOTES

xxvi 1. *Uzziah*. Frequently referred to as "Azariah," which was apparently the personal name, "Uzziah" the throne name. (Cf. A. M. Honeyman, JBL 67 [1948], 20–22.) May have been avoided by the Chronicler because of the name of the high priest (vss. 17, 20).

sixteen years old. Cf. Albright, BASOR 100 (December 1945), 21. But see also H. Tadmor, *Scripta Hierosolymitana*, VIII: *Studies in the Bible*, 1961, p. 232, n. 1.

2. *Eloth*. The seaport constructed by Solomon at the head of the Gulf of Aqaba (viii 17, 18; I Kings ix 26–28), which Uzziah reactivated.

3. *reigned . . . Jerusalem*. See second NOTE on vs. 1.

5. *inquired of God*. A technical term meaning "to seek an oracle" or "to worship."

6. *Gath*. One of the Philistine cities, some twenty-five miles southwest of Jerusalem though it could have been Gittaim, a few miles north of Gezer. Cf. B. Mazar, "Gath and Gittaim," IEJ 4 (1954), 227–35, especially p. 231. But Gath was destroyed before the time of Amos (i 6–8, vi 2), possibly by Uzziah as indicated here. On the location, see S. Bülow and R. A. Mitchell, "An Iron Age II Fortress on Tell Nagila," IEJ 11 (1961), 101–10.

Jabneh. A city on the border of Judah (Josh xv 11), approximately 30 miles west of Jerusalem, later Jamnia (I Maccabees iv 15), present-day Yebna.

Ashdod. Near the coast twelve miles north of Gath.

7. *Gur-baal*. Unknown. "Gerar" may be meant. The consonantal text would then have been *bgrr* (*w*) *'l hm'wnym* "at Gerar (and) against the Meunites." But see A. Alt, JPOS 12 (1932), 135, n. 4, and Abel, *Géographie de la Palestine*, II, p. 340.

Meunites. See COMMENT on Sec. 22, xx 1–30.

9. *the corner gate . . . the valley gate . . . the corner*. For the loca-

tion of these points, see references listed in the second NOTE on xxv 23, Sec. 27, and especially the topographical map in Avi-yonah, *Sepher Yerushalayim*, I, opposite p. 160.

10. *farmers*. For an interpretation of the term see BASOR 167 (October 1962), 34.

12. *twenty-six hundred*. A slightly different pointing of *'lpm* as *'allūpīm* ("chiefs") would mean there were six hundred chiefs.

13. This figure, 307,500 men, looks like the sort that G. E. Mendenhall (JBL 77 [1958], 52–66) has successfully resolved. The 300 units (*'ªlāpīm*) consist of 7500 men, which would be a rather large army, though not impossible. The preceding verse (see NOTE) would indicate that there were 600 chiefs for the 7500 men in 300 units. The distribution does not quite fit the usual Israelite groupings of 10s, 50s, 100s, 1000s. But the general scope of the numbers is reasonable for the official standing army, including those on active duty and the ready reserves.

14. *helmets*. For a discussion of the term see E. A. Speiser, JAOS 70 (1950), 47–49.

15. *skillfully contrived devices*. On the defensive character of these devices, see Y. Sukenik, "Engines Invented by Cunning Men," BJPES 13 (1946/47), 19–24. Catapulting devices were unknown then; the defenses of Lachish illustrate the nature of the constructions of Uzziah (ANEP, pp. 130–31). They were thus protective or shielding devices from which the defenders could shoot arrows and hurl stones at the attackers. For the possibility of the Assyrians having catapults, see B. Meissner, *Babylonien und Assyrien*, I, 1920, p. 110; Galling, BRL, col. 95; E. Unger, "Belagerungsmaschinen," *Reallexikon der Assyriologie*, I, pp. 471 f.

18. *only . . . incense*. For the priestly regulations see Exod xxx 7–10; Num xviii 1–7. Cf. M. Haran, "The Uses of Incense in the Ancient Israelite Ritual," VT 10 (1960), 113–29.

20. *the chief priest*. Note the use of *kōhēn hā-rō'š* here for the more widely used *hak-kōhēn* in vs. 17. See COMMENT on Sec. 21, xix 4–11.

leprosy. In the biblical sense a generic term under which were included all kinds of skin ailments. Only one group of these would correspond to modern leprosy. Actually, we don't know what Uzziah had but it must have been a loathsome disease. Unless it had happened under extraordinary circumstances, or was especially disabling, it is hard to see why he withdrew from active service. Naaman, who had a similar disease, apparently continued as commander in chief. Uzziah must have retired for cultic reasons (Jotham took over official duties while Uzziah apparently continued in charge of foreign policy) or else he must have been very ill indeed.

21. *house of quarantine. Bēt haḥopšīt.* Term occurs in Ugaritic texts as *bthptt* "the house of pollution." Cf. Gray, *The Legacy of Canaan,* p. 46, n. 1.

who . . . palace. For significance of the phrase see H. J. Katzenstein, IEJ 10 (1960), 149–54, especially p. 152.

COMMENT

[Summary observations on the reign of Uzziah, xxvi 1–5]: With a few variations due to the special interests of the writer, this summation corresponds with the Deuteronomic account in II Kings xiv 21–xv 4. The chief differences are: (a) the Chronicler's omission of the reference to Uzziah's failure to remove the high places (II Kings xv 4) and (b) his statement that the king sought the Lord so long as his religious mentor lived (cf. the situation of Joash [xxiv 2, 17–22]). In line with his theology, he notes that so long as Uzziah "inquired of Yahweh" he was successful. At the same time, he prepares for the subsequent story of the king's downfall. One of Uzziah's significant contributions was the reconquest of Ezion-geber (Elath), lost to Judah in the reign of Jehoram (xxi 8–10) and the reconstruction of the city. The excavations of Nelson Glueck reflect three periods in the history of Ezion-geber before the Judean exile. The first period was that covering the activity of Solomon, the second that of Jehoshaphat, and the third that of Uzziah (BA 3 [1940], 54). The third period belongs to the eighth century B.C. (BASOR 79 [October 1940], 12 f.). The city remained in the hands of the kings of Judah until ca. 735 when it was retaken by the Edomites. The famous seal of Jotham (BASOR 79 [October 1940], 13 ff., Figs. 8, 9, and note by Albright, p. 15), which was used in official transactions, indicates that Ezion-geber was an important center in the time of Uzziah and Jotham.

[Conquests, 6–8]: The writer, relying upon another source of information, refers to significant conquests of Uzziah directed against the Philistines and the Arabs residing on the southwestern borders of Judah. For pertinent remarks on the conquests of Azariah, notably that of the Philistine cities, see G. Rinaldi, "Quelques remarques sur la politique d'Azarias (Ozias) de Juda en Philistie (2 Chron. 26:6 ss)," in SVT: *Congress Volume* (Bonn, 1962), pp.

225–35. Following the conquests, Uzziah lost no time in strengthening his hold upon the territory in question. He constructed cities (probably fortresses) in the conquered territory. The fortress at Tell Mor near Ashdod may have been the work of Uzziah (cf. IEJ 9 [1959], 271 f.; 10 [1960], 124; RB 67 [1960], 397). Tadmor argues strongly for an expansionist movement under Uzziah after the death of Jeroboam II (see *Scripta Hierosolymitana*, VIII, pp. 232–71). Since there was no possibility of extending his rule northward, where Jeroboam II was in undisputed control, he could only move toward the west and south. It was noted above that Uzziah turned his attention to Elath; he also moved westward from there (see COMMENT on Sec. 16, xiv 8–14) and subdued the Meunites associated with Edom and the Arabs around Gerar both of whom doubtless had taken advantage of the unsettled conditions in Judah prevailing since the time of Ahaziah.

[Internal developments, 9–15]: Archaeological explorations confirm the building and agricultural activity here attributed to Uzziah. It was a period of progress in many directions. Apart from the fortifications of Jerusalem, there is additional clear evidence of the hand of the great king, as our author maintains (vs. 10). For example, the *migdal* (tower) IIIB at Gibeah may date from this period (AASOR 4 [1924], 52 f.); so may the prosperous stratum at Tell Abu Selimeh (C. C. McCown, *The Ladder of Progress in Palestine,* 1943, p. 131). Father de Vaux also points out the evidences for early buildings and cisterns at Qumran and Ain Feshkha in the time of Uzziah (RB 63 [1956], 535–38, 575; note especially the cistern at Qumran). There are evidences of activity in this period also in the Nahal Seelim area—at Hasron and two locations above the north branch of Nahal Hardof (see IEJ 11 [1961], 15–16). But perhaps the most striking confirmation of the Chronicler's report is found in the recent discoveries in the Negeb of Judah around Beersheba, where fortifications, cisterns, farms, etc., have been located, as for instance, at Khirbet al-Gharra and Hurvat Uzzah (cf. IEJ 8 [1958], 33–38; Glueck, *Rivers in the Desert,* pp. 174–79) and other sites in the vicinity. See also the article by R. L. Schiffer, "The Farms of King Uzziah," *The Reporter,* September 1, 1960, pp. 34–38, which describes the excavation of a farmhouse in the Negeb, dated by Aharoni and Evenari in Iron Age II (ninth-eighth centuries B.C.); also nearby were cisterns and well-developed drainage channels. This is an excellent illustration of the Chronicler's remark that Uzziah loved agriculture (the land). The importance of Uzziah in his time may be seen from the fact that important persons identified themselves as his servants (cf. seals of Abiyau servant of Uzziah and Shebanyau servant of Uzziah [D. Diringer, *Le iscrizioni antico-ebraiche Palestinesi,* 1934, pp. 221 f., 223 f.; M. Lidzbarski, *Altsemitische Texte,* 1907, pp. 10 f.] and also the Uzziah or Azariah seal found in a cistern at Tell Beit Mirsim [AASOR 21–22 (1943), 63 f., 73]).

The conquests of Uzziah naturally demanded a strong, well-organized army under the leadership of a single head. Apparently each company had some 116+ men, though the numbers themselves are probably exaggerated; the ratio of officers to men is doubtless fairly accurate. It is interesting to note that no longer did the soldiers supply their own arms but were armed by the king. The latest equipment was evidently kept in the local fortress ready for immediate use in case of attack. The respect in which Uzziah's army was held is indicated by the part it took in a coalition against Assyria in the time of Tilgath-pileser III (see ANET, p. 282. For a discussion of the reference see Thiele, *The Mysterious Numbers of the Hebrew Kings,* pp. 78–98; Albright, BASOR 100 [December 1945], 18, n. 8, and JBL 71 [1952], 251). The great strength and prosperity of Uzziah was attributed by the Chronicler to Yahweh, because he did right in his sight.

[The downfall of Uzziah, 16–23]: Too much prosperity was Uzziah's undoing, according to the Chronicler, because it made him proud and led him to overstep his bounds as a layman. (Note the use of the unqualified "Uzziah" by Azariah the priest in addressing the king in vs. 18.) The misfortune that befell the king—his leprosy and consequent isolation—was due directly to a violation of the priestly prerogatives set up by the *P* code (on the sin of Uzziah, see J. Morgenstern, HUCA 21–22 [1937–38], 1 ff.; for later speculation on its effect see Josephus *Antiquities* IX.x). The Deuteronomist (II Kings xv 5) speaks of Yahweh's afflicting Uzziah with leprosy but naturally does not go into the reason for it. It was earlier recognized as legitimate for the king to officiate at the altar (cf. David and Solomon); nor was Ahaz condemned by him for offering sacrifice upon his new altar (II Kings xvi 12–13). Nevertheless, the Chronicler credits the king with speedy recognition of his situation and co-operation with the priests in getting away from the house of Yahweh. Jotham then assumed control of affairs as regent for his father, who was living in quarantine. How long the coregency lasted is not certain; Albright (BASOR 100 [December 1945]) thinks it was about eight years, from 750–742 B.C.

The final observations by the writer, that his source also contained the record of Isaiah, who was a younger contemporary of the king, and that he was interred in the field beside the cemetery of the kings, are doubtless based on factual materials. Both Amos (i 1) and Zechariah (xiv 5) refer to the earthquake in the reign of Uzziah. Isaiah (vi 1) received his call the year Uzziah died. The Uzziah tomb inscription from the first century B.C. appears to confirm the burial of the king outside the royal burial ground (cf. Galling, BRL, col. 405).

29. THE REIGN OF JOTHAM (ca. 750–735 B.C.)
(xxvii 1–9)†

XXVII 1 Jotham was twenty-five years old when he became king and reigned sixteen years at Jerusalem. His mother's name was Jerushah the daughter of Zadok. 2 He did what was right in the sight of Yahweh just as Uzziah his father had done, only he did not come to the temple of Yahweh. But the people continued to do wrong. 3 He built the upper gate of the house of Yahweh and greatly extended the wall of the Ophel. 4 He also built cities in the highland of Judah and in the wooded areas he constructed fortified places and towers. 5 He fought against the king of the Ammonites and prevailed over them so that the Ammonites gave him a hundred talents of silver, ten thousand kors of wheat, and ten thousand kors of barley that year. This amount the Ammonites delivered to him the second and third years. 6 Jotham became strong because he continued unflinchingly in his ways before Yahweh his God. 7 The remainder of the history of Jotham, together with all his wars and exploits, behold they are recorded in the chronicle of the kings of Israel and Judah. 8 He was twenty-five years old when he became king and reigned for sixteen years at Jerusalem. 9 Then Jotham slept with his fathers and they buried him in the city of David while Ahaz his son became king in his place.

† II Chron xxvii 1–9 ‖ II Kings xv 32–38.

NOTES

xxvii 3. *the upper gate.* Located at the north entrance to the temple enclosure (see Avi-yonah, *Sepher Yerushalayim*, I, map opposite p. 160).
the Ophel. For the location of Ophel see map *ibid.* and sketches of other views on p. 160.
5. *a hundred talents of silver.* About 3¼ tons.
ten thousand kors of wheat. About sixty-five thousand bushels.

COMMENT

[General observations, xxvii 1–2]: As might be expected, Jotham continued the attitude and policies of his father, for which he received the commendation of the writer. The discovery of the seal of Jotham at Ezion-geber reflects the continuity of administrative activity at the Aqabah seaport (BASOR 79 [October 1940], 13 ff.; BASOR 163 [October 1961], 18–22). Yadin thinks it was a signet ring used by Jotham, not as king but as minister, since the bellows on it indicates "a limited and specific authority" rather than that of a sovereign. Jotham's only caveat, if it be such, was that he did not enter the temple of Yahweh. For what reason we do not know. This remark may actually be an expression of approval on the part of the Chronicler indicating that Joham observed his status as a layman and did not violate the sacred precincts as his father had done. However, the introductory word in Hebrew (*raq*) appears to indicate an exception (cf. II Kings xv 35). If that is the case, some other reason must have dictated the action of the king in this respect. We can only guess at what it may have been. Cf. remarks by Cazelles, p. 202, n. d. The writer summarizes the observation of the Deuteronomist (II Kings xv 35ab) by saying that the people continued to do wrong.

[Building activity, 3–4]: Nothing is said of Uzziah's local building activity in Jerusalem, except in connection with the defense devices made for the towers and corners of the city (xxvi 15). That Uzziah made the necessary repairs after the fiasco of Amaziah may be taken for granted. Jotham built the upper gate of the house of Yahweh and extended the walls of Ophel. His efforts to continue the progressive program of his father did not stop there; he constructed cities in the highlands of Judah probably as lines of defense to fall back upon in case of invasion. He erected towers and fortifications in the wooded areas; hidden in this word may be another of Uzziah's activities, that is, a program of reforestation (cf. Akk. *ḫarāšu* "to plant trees"). Jotham had learned much from his experience as coregent.

[Campaign against the Ammonites, 5–6]: Verses 3b–6 were taken from a source other than Kings where there is no mention of the achievements involved. But, as in the case of Uzziah's progressive undertakings, there is no reason to doubt the substantial accuracy of these reports. It has been affirmed that there could have been no war between Judah and Ammon since their borders were not contiguous at the time. But Israel was rapidly losing prestige and power after the death of Jeroboam II, in the wake of which the border peoples spilled over, as they always did, into the territory where the power vacuum existed. Moreover the Syro-Ephraimitic wars, which would have offered ample opportunity for Ammonite expansion, may already have been in progress. It was doubtless such a movement that brought Jotham into conflict with them (cf. Noth, ÜS, p. 142, n. 2). The enormous amount of tribute is probably an exaggeration. The king's success is attributed to his loyalty to the ways of Yahweh.

[Obituary, 7–9]: Verse 8 repeats the first half of vs. 1. The other two verses (7, 9) refer to the achievements of Jotham, the annals where they are recorded, the death and burial of the king, and the succession to the throne of his son Ahaz.

30. THE REIGN OF AHAZ (735–715 B.C.)
(xxviii 1–27)†

Character of Ahaz

XXVIII 1 Ahaz was twenty years old when he became king and reigned sixteen years at Jerusalem. He did not do what was right in the sight of Yahweh as David his father had done. 2 He followed the ways of the kings of Israel and even made molten images for Baal. 3 He burned incense in the valley of Ben-hinnom and burned his sons in the fire in accordance with the abominations of the nations whom Yahweh expelled before the Israelites, 4 and he sacrificed and burned incense on the high places, on the hills, and under every green tree.

Syro-Ephraimitic war

5 So Yahweh his God delivered him into the hand of the king of Aram; they defeated him and took a large number of them as captives whom they brought to Damascus. He also delivered him into the hand of the king of Israel who inflicted a great slaughter upon him. 6 Pekah the son of Remaliah killed one hundred and twenty thousand in Judah in a single day, all of them prominent men, because they abandoned Yahweh God of their fathers. 7 Zichri, an Ephraimite hero, slew Maaseiah the king's son, Azrikam the chief of the house, and Elkanah the second to the king. 8 The Israelites took captive two hundred thousand women, sons, and daughters of their brothers; they also took from them a large quantity of booty which they carried to Samaria.

† II Chron xxviii 1–4 ‖ II Kings xvi 1–4; **5–8** ‖ II Kings xvi 5; **16–21** ‖ II Kings xvi 7–9.

Prophecy of Oded

9 Now there was at that place a prophet of Yahweh by the name of Oded who appeared before the army when it entered Samaria and said to them, "Behold, because Yahweh God of your fathers was angry with Judah, he delivered them into your hand, but you slew them in a rage that reaches to heaven, 10 and now you plan to subjugate the Judeans and Jerusalemites as your male and female slaves—have you not yourselves committed sins against Yahweh your God? 11 Listen to me now and return the captives you took from your brothers, otherwise the violent wrath of God will fall upon you." 12 Then some of the chiefs of the Ephraimites—Azariah the son of Jehohanan, Berechiah the son of Meshillemoth, Jehizkiah the son of Shallum, and Amasa the son of Hadlai—rose up against those of the army who had returned 13 and said to them, "You must not bring the captives here, for we have already sinned against Yahweh and you propose to multiply our sin and our guilt although our guilt is now sufficient to bring violent wrath upon Israel." 14 So the soldiers left the captives and the booty before the captains and the whole congregation. 15 Then the men who were designated by name took the captives and clothed all the naked with the booty; they clothed them, put sandals on them, fed them, gave them drink, poured oil upon them, transported on donkeys all the weak and brought them to Jericho, the city of palms, to their brothers; then they returned to Samaria.

Appeal of Ahaz to Assyria

16 At that time King Ahaz had sent to the king of Assyria for assistance for himself 17 because the Edomites had come again, beaten Judah and taken captives; 18 at the same time the Philistines raided the cities of the Shephelah and the Negeb of Judah, captured Beth-shemesh, Aijalon, Gederoth, Soco, and its dependencies, Timnah and its dependencies, and Gimzo and its dependencies, and settled down there. 19 For Yahweh

had humbled Judah because of Ahaz the king of Israel[a] who had exercised no restraint in Judah and greatly wronged Yahweh. 20 But Tilgath-pilneser the king of Assyria came up against him and oppressed him; he did not support him. 21 Although Ahaz robbed the house of Yahweh, the house of the king and the captains and gave [the proceeds] to the king of Assyria, he received no support from him.

Apostasy and death of Ahaz

22 Thus at the very time he was oppressed, he continued to wrong Yahweh; that was King Ahaz! 23 He offered sacrifice to the gods of Damascus who had beaten him for he thought, "Because the gods of the kings of Aram supported them I will offer sacrifice to them, perhaps they will help me too." But they served only to ruin him and all Israel. 24 Then Ahaz collected all the equipment of the house of God, cut up in fragments the equipment of the house of God, sealed up the doors of the house of Yahweh and made altars for himself in every corner of Jerusalem. 25 In every city of Judah he made high places to burn incense to other gods and thus provoked to anger Yahweh God of his fathers. 26 The remainder of his history and all his acts, from beginning to end, behold they are recorded in the chronicle of the kings of Judah and Israel. 27 When Ahaz slept with his fathers, they buried him in the city of Jerusalem but they did not bring him to the cemetery of the kings of Israel. Hezekiah[b] his son became king in his place.

[a] Some manuscripts and Vrs. read "Judah," obviously a correction. May be due to source or a tendentious reference to Ahaz, who acted like a king of Israel, depending on man rather than on God.
[b] Hebrew reads "Jehizkiah," but context indicates that "Hezekiah" is meant.

NOTES

xxviii 2. *Baal*. Cf. second NOTE on xvii 3, Sec. 19.

3. *the valley of Ben-hinnom*. On the south side of Jerusalem, joining the Kidron Valley at the southeast corner of the city. In Jeremiah's day there was a *tōpet* there (vii 31–32) where children were sacrificed

(cf. II Kings xxiii 10). Later the *gē-ben-hinnōm* "valley of the son of Hinnom" was corrupted to *gē-hinnōm* "Gehenna."

abominations . . . expelled. The spelling of these words is significant. Neither of them indicate the contracted diphthong (aw>ô) by the *waw*. Here we have *ktʻbwt,* "abominations" for *ktwʻbwt* and *hryš,* "expelled" for *hwryš.* The Chronicler normally has very full spelling; here he may have copied directly from an early (Northern?) source. The Kings parallel supplies the *waw* in *hwryš,* in accordance with typical Judahite orthography, while preserving the defective spelling in the other word.

7. *second to the king.* Phrase occurs only here and Esther x 3.

15. *the men . . . designated by name.* Not those named in vs. 12 (since four would hardly have been sufficient for the task) but men appointed by the assembly to act for it.

16. *At that time.* Refers to the events related in vs. 5.

18. *the cities . . . Gimzo and its dependencies.* All cities to the west of Jerusalem, on the border of the hill country; Gimzo was in the territory of Israel.

20. *Tilgath-pilneser.* Tiglath-pileser III (ca. 744–727 B.C.).

24. *the equipment.* Includes furnishings of all kinds—vessels, utensils, tools, etc.

27. *the cemetery . . . Israel.* Kings of Judah, since no monarchs of the Northern Kingdom were buried in Jerusalem. This is probably another of the writer's predilections for the Davidic line as the legitimate one in "Israel." But see Rudolph, p. 293. Ahaz, because of his apostasy, was unworthy to occupy a place in the cemetery of the ancestors.

COMMENT

[Characterization of Ahaz, xxviii 1–4]: The name of Ahaz is surrounded by infamy as may be seen from this evaluation but even more clearly from the references to him by Isaiah (Isa vii). It is striking that the name of his mother is not given. The Chronicler has taken his cue from the Kings story with a few additions, some of which may have been drawn from Isaiah; for example, the reference to images (cf. Isa ii 8–13, 20) and the illicit worship in the valley of Hinnom which may be simply a conjecture based on the following statement regarding the sacrifice by Ahaz of his sons but which was severely condemned by the prophets (Mic vi 7; Jer vii 31). The worst epithet that could be applied to a king of Judah, from the viewpoint of both the Deuteronomist and the Chronicler, was that "he followed the ways of the kings of Israel."

The name of Ahaz occurs on a seal in the Newell collection. The inscription reads: *l'šn' 'bd 'hz* "to Ušna the servant of Ahaz" (cf. BASOR 79 [October 1940], 27 f.; BASOR 82 [April 1941], 16 f.; BASOR 84 [December 1941], 17).

[The Syro-Ephraimitic war, 5–8]: The background for this story is II Kings xv 37, xvi 5; Isa vii; Hos v 8–vi 6 (see article by Alt, KS, II, pp. 163–87). The Chronicler was probably drawing upon a different source than Kings from which he derived his assessment of the character of Ahaz (Rudolph, p. 289, suggests that the source used by the writer contained separate accounts of the loss inflicted upon Judah by each member of the coalition). His objective must be kept in mind: it was to set forth the divine judgment upon the defection of Ahaz. Only vs. 5 reveals the true situation: that the invasion of Judah was due to the alliance between Pekah and Rezin, who were jointly responsible for it. According to II Kings xvi 5, Judah was invaded and Jerusalem attacked but without success. However, it is not stated here that Jerusalem was breached or even attacked; only the loss sustained at the hands of Israel is recounted, possibly as an introduction to the episode centering about the prophecy of Oded. The figures are grossly exaggerated, but that there was something to the invasion can hardly be doubted as the names of the important persons slain indicate. While nothing is known of these persons beyond what is said here, the names are common in postexilic times, though Elkanah and Maaseiah and possibly Zichri occur earlier.

[The prophecy of Oded, 9–15]: Injected into the account of Ahaz's troubles with Ephraim-Syria and the ensuing revolts all around is the sequel to the story of Judah's defeat at the hands of Israel. This is, in many respects, a remarkable passage whose essentials the writer found in his sources, because it runs counter to his otherwise strong emphasis on the separation of the two kingdoms, only one of which was legitimate. The prophet Oded is mentioned nowhere else but, like Elijah and Hosea, he was a Northerner. He does not question the execution of judgment upon Judah by Israel— it was the doing of Yahweh—but sternly rebukes Israel for venting its own wrath upon brethren. Israel was simply the instrument in the hands of Yahweh. Of special import is the Chronicler's allowing the word "brothers" to stand. They had gone too far. The Ephraimite chiefs were impressed by the prophet and appealed to the army to relent. The reaction of these men from Ephraim (vs. 15) illustrates the effectiveness of prophecy and the working of the mercy of Yahweh, even in judgment.

[Appeal to Assyria, 16–21]: The Syro-Ephraimite invasion was fraught with dire consequences for Judah. Despite the advice of Isaiah (see Isa vii), Ahaz appealed to Assyria for help—to man rather than to God. How serious the situation was is clear from vss. 17–18. According to II Kings xvi 6, Elath was taken from Judah never to be regained; the Philistines reclaimed what had been lost to them by the movements of Uzziah and even spilled over into the Negeb. It now appears that Ahaz's appeal for help was against Edom and Philistia rather than against Aram and Israel (cf. J. Gray, "The Period and Office of the Prophet Isaiah in the Light of a New Assyrian Tablet," *The Expository Times,* vol. 63, June 1952, pp. 263–65; and D. J. Wiseman, *Iraq* 13 [1951], 21–24). The new tablet records Tiglath-pileser's campaign against Philistia in the course of which his victory stele was set up at *Naḫalmuṣir,* the river of Egypt; and an Assyrian province (Du'ru) might also have been established at that time. Cf. Alt, "Tiglathpilesers III. erster Feldzug nach Palästina," KS, II, pp. 150–62. A Nimrud letter reflects this unrest in Palestine at the time (H. W. F. Saggs, *Iraq* 17 [1955], 131 f., 149–53) and indicates that the Chronicler utilized other sources besides Kings. In any case, Tiglath-pileser did come to the west and overran the Philistine territory as shown by the Nimrud fragment. But, as the Chronicler says, "He did not support him," for later in his reign the Assyrian king records tribute received from Ahaz (ANET, p. 282, where the full name of the Judean king appears *ia-u-ḫa-zi ia-u-da-a-a* "Jehoahaz of Judah"), just as from the Philistine states, Edom, Ammon and Moab. What the writer means is that though the rebellions were put down, the states involved were not returned to Judah but organized into Assyrian provinces. The tribute referred to in the inscriptions was in all probability ransom money. The resources of Judah were depleted to no avail. All this was due to the wrongdoing of Ahaz (vs. 19), according to our author, and not to the conspiracy of world politics at the time.

[Apostasy and death of Ahaz, 22–27]: The political situation forced upon Ahaz recognition of Assyrian hegemony in religious matters also, though he may not have been too reluctant in so doing. To judge from the complaints of Isaiah (vii–ix), the Chronicler may not be too far wrong in his assessment of the king's religious activities. The Kings narrative speaks only of an altar pattern imported from Damascus; this importation becomes for our author a worship of the gods of Aram because of their apparent superiority over the God of Israel. The removal of the furniture of the temple that was offensive to the king of Assyria (II Kings xvi 18) has been reinterpreted, probably under the influence of its destruction by the Babylonians, into a wholesale iconoclasm and padlocking of the temple itself. Thus Ahaz was guilty of apostatizing to the Baal of Israel and now to the gods of Aram. The whole land was made into a hotbed of foreign cultic practices. While he did not meet a violent death as punishment for his defection, he was, according to the Chronicler, buried outside the cemetery of the kings (cf., however, II Kings xvi 20).

31. THE REIGN OF HEZEKIAH (ca. 715–687 B.C.): REHABILITATION OF THE TEMPLE (xxix 1–36)†

Introductory observations

XXIX [1] Hezekiah[a] became king when he was twenty-five years old and remained king at Jerusalem for twenty-nine years. The name of his mother was Abijah[b] the daughter of Zechariah. [2] He did what was right in the sight of Yahweh just as David his father had done.

Cleansing of the temple

[3] In the first month of the first year of his reign he opened the doors of the house of Yahweh, having repaired them. [4] He brought the priests and the Levites together on the east plaza [5] and said to them, "Listen to me, O Levites: now consecrate yourselves and consecrate the house of Yahweh God of your fathers and remove the impurities from the sanctuary. [6] For our fathers were untrue and did evil in the sight of Yahweh our God, since they abandoned him, turned their faces away from the dwelling place of Yahweh and turned their back [on him]. [7] They even closed the doors of the portico, extinguished the lamps, failed to burn incense and offer burnt offerings in the sanctuary to the God of Israel. [8] Therefore the wrath of Yahweh fell upon Judah and Jerusalem and he made them a terror, a horror, and a mockery as you can see with your own eyes. [9] Behold, our fathers fell by the sword and our sons, our daughters, and our wives were taken captives because of it. [10] Now I firmly intend to make a covenant with Yahweh God of Israel that his violent anger may turn away from us. [11] My sons, now do not

† **II Chron xxix 1–2:** cf. II Kings xviii 1–3.

[a] Hebrew reads "Jehizkiah," but context indicates that "Hezekiah" is meant.
[b] II Kings xviii 1 "Abi." LXX "Abba" here and "Abou" in II Kings.

be remiss, for Yahweh has chosen you to stand before him in order to serve him as his ministers and incense burners." 12 Then the Levites arose—Mahath the son of Amasai and Joel the son of Azariah, from the Kehathites; Kish the son of Abdi and Azariah the son of Jehallelel, from the Merarites; Joah the son of Zimmah and Eden the son of Joah, from the Gershunnites; 13 Shimri and Jeuel, of the sons of Elizaphan; Zechariah and Mattaniah, of the sons of Asaph; 14 Jehiel and Shimei, of the sons of Heman; Shemaiah and Uzziel, of the sons of Jeduthun —15 and assembled their brothers and consecrated themselves and came to cleanse the house of Yahweh in accordance with the command of the king in harmony with the words of Yahweh. 16 So the priests entered the innermost part of the house of Yahweh to cleanse it and brought out all the unclean things they found in the temple of Yahweh to the court of the house of Yahweh where the Levites received it to remove it outside to the Kidron Valley. 17 They began the consecration on the first day of the first month and by the eighth day of the month they had reached the portico of Yahweh, so that in eight days they had consecrated the house of Yahweh and by the sixteenth day of the first month they had finished [the work].

Rededication of the temple

18 Then they went in to Hezekiah the king and said, "We have cleansed the whole house of Yahweh together with the altar of burnt offering with all its vessels and the table of layer bread with all its vessels. 19 We have also prepared and consecrated all the vessels which King Ahaz during his reign had removed in his defection. Behold they are before the altar of Yahweh." 20 So Hezekiah* the king went to work and assembled the chiefs of the city and went up to the house of Yahweh. 21 They brought seven bulls, seven rams, seven lambs, and seven he-goats as a sin offering for *the royal house,* for the

c–c So with Rudolph, p. 296, since Judah is mentioned later. MT reads h-mmlkh (usually meaning "kingdom"), which here means the royal family. Cf. Phoen., mmlkt.

sanctuary, and for Judah, and he told the Aaronite priests to offer them on the altar of Yahweh. 22 So they slaughtered the bulls and the priests took the blood and sprinkled it toward the altar; they slaughtered the rams and sprinkled the blood toward the altar, and they slaughtered the lambs and sprinkled the blood toward the altar. 23 Then they brought the goats for the sin offering before the king and the congregation and laid their hands upon them. 24 The priests slaughtered them and made a sin offering with their blood at the altar to atone for all Israel because the king had ordered a burnt offering and a sin offering for all Israel. 25 He stationed the Levites in the house of Yahweh with cymbals, harps, and zithers in accordance with the order of David, Gad the king's seer, and Nathan the prophet, for such was the command of Yahweh through his prophets. 26 The Levites stood there with the [musical] instruments of David, while the priests had the trumpets. 27 Then Hezekiah ordered the burnt offering to be offered on the altar and at the same time the burnt offering began, the song of Yahweh and the trumpets also began, to the accompaniment of the instruments of David the king of Israel 28 while the whole congregation worshiped. So the singers sang and the trumpeters sounded the trumpets, all continuing until the completion of the burnt offering. 29 When the sacrifice was completed, the king and all who were present with him knelt down and worshiped. 30 Then Hezekiah[a] the king and the chiefs ordered the Levites to praise Yahweh with the words of David and Asaph the seer; so they sang their praises with joy and knelt in worship.

Offerings brought for the occasion

31 Hezekiah[a] replied, "Now that you have consecrated yourselves to Yahweh, draw near and bring sacrifices for thank offerings to the house of Yahweh." Then the congregation brought sacrifices for thank offerings and those with generous spirits [brought] burnt offerings. 32 The number of burnt offerings which the congregation brought was as follows: seventy bulls, a hundred rams, and two hundred lambs; all these were for burnt

offerings for Yahweh. 33 The consecrated gifts amounted to six hundred bulls and three thousand sheep. 34 But unfortunately there were not enough priests; they were unable to slaughter all the burnt offerings so their brothers, the Levites, helped them until the work was finished or until [other] priests had consecrated themselves; for the Levites were more conscientious in consecrating themselves than the priests. 35 In addition to the abundance of burnt offerings, there were also the choice pieces for the peace offerings and the libations for the burnt offerings. Thus the service of the house of Yahweh was reinstituted. 36 Then Hezekiah[a] and all the people rejoiced over what God had provided for the people because the thing had been carried out so quickly.

NOTES

xxix 1. Exactly the same figures are given for Amaziah (xxv 1 and II Kings xiv) as Hezekiah, both as to age and length of life. Hezekiah's appears to be about right; Amaziah's reign of twenty-nine years is difficult to fit into the scheme of history: it is too long. (Cf. Albright, BASOR 100 [December 1945].)

3. *having repaired.* The use of the verb *ḥzq,* "strengthen," "repair," may be a play on the name of Hezekiah.

4. *the east plaza.* Hardly the plaza of the temple (Ezra x 9) because it was still unclean, but rather an assembly place like the one referred to in Neh viii 1, 3 (cf. Rudolph, p. 292).

6. *our fathers were untrue.* Cf. *ma'al 'ᵃbōtay* "the unfaithfulness of my fathers" in 1QH 4:34.

20. *went to work.* See first NOTE on xx 20, Sec. 22.

21. *the Aaronite priests.* Cf. xxxi 19; Josh xxi 19; 1QSa 1:15 f., 2:13.

23. See Lev iv for atonement offering ritual.

24. *all Israel.* "All Israel" is meant to include every group and stands for the whole nation as the Chronicler understood it (cf. Ezra vi 17, viii 35).

25. *his prophets.* David is not meant to be included among the prophets. The command of Yahweh was delivered by his prophets to David, who issued the order. Nathan and Gad are mentioned only here in this connection.

26. *[musical] instruments of David.* Cf. Amos vi 5.

27. *the song of Yahweh.* Technical expression for the anthem or hymn.

the instruments of David. Cf. Brockelmann, *Hebräische Syntax,* Sec. 110 i.

30. *to praise . . . Asaph.* Points to the use of a hymnal or psalter, perhaps somewhat like the canonical book of Psalms.

31. *Now . . . yourselves.* Literally "you have filled your hand," a technical term for consecration of the priests. Thus Hezekiah was addressing the priests, exhorting them to carry on their functions now that the temple was dedicated.

sacrifices for. Hebrew has "sacrifices and thank offerings" but the *w* ("and") before *tōdōt* ("thank offerings") is here taken as epexegetical.

COMMENT

The Hezekiah material must be evaluated in the light of the Chronicler's theology, since he departs rather widely from the presentation in II Kings. For a brief discussion see Introduction. The real question is the degree to which the Chronicler may be more correct in his portrait of Hezekiah than the author of Kings, who was also biased, though in a different direction. For the Deuteronomist (Kings), Josiah is the Davidic king par excellence, and he may be responsible for the only notable *vaticinium ex eventu* in the whole complex of his work, that is, the Josiah prophecy in I Kings xiii 2. Kings was written under the spell of the Deuteronomic reform set in motion by Josiah, and the writer was charmed by his early achievements. The Chronicler, on the other hand, was under no historical illusions about any of the Davidic kings. While there were many good kings, some of whom he might want to glorify in a special way, his great concern was for the present and how its problems could be met. His aim is predominantly to present the religious situation with a view toward the orientation of the nation in his own day. Hence he severely limits the historicopolitical details and stresses the points appropriate to his purpose. The historical data bearing on the religious situation are presented in homiletic fashion.

[Introduction, xxix 1–2]: Only the barest facts on the accession of Hezekiah are given—his age upon assuming the throne, the length of his reign, and his mother's name. On the important matter of dates see Albright, BASOR 100 (December 1945), 22. Hezekiah became king in 715 B.C. and died in 687. The date of accession is certain since it can be controlled by other sources; the date of his death is almost as sure (cf. H. H. Rowley, BJRL 44 [1961/62], 409 ff.). It was a welcome task to observe the well-doing of this king after the record of events that transpired under his father.

[The cleansing of the temple, 3–17]: According to the Chronicler, Ahaz had closed the temple (xxviii 24), perhaps only temporarily, and on some excuse. The first official move of Hezekiah in inaugurating his reformation was to restore the temple service. On the matter of official date of the beginning of his reign—whether postdating or antedating applied—see Albright, BASOR 100 (December 1945), 22, n. 29.

No time is lost or effort spared in placing the blame for the politico-religious conditions. The fathers had been untrue to Yahweh as shown by their evil deeds—abandoning Yahweh, closing the entrance to the temple, putting out the lamps, and failing to have formal services in the temple. No one could deny the calamities; they were apparent to everyone with eyes to see. Hezekiah wanted to return to the good old days. The nation's relationship to Yahweh was sustained by the covenant and that is precisely what Hezekiah determined to renew. Part of that renewal, the reinstitution of proper formal services in the temple could be done only after a thorough cleansing of the sacred precincts, which in turn required that the religious officials—the Levites—respond and fulfill their obligations as determined by David. This they did by first consecrating themselves and then performing the task of cleansing the polluted house of Yahweh. The work was completed in record time.

M. Buttenwieser (*The Psalms*, 1938, pp. 135–38) connects Psalm lxxviii with the cultic reformation of Hezekiah, which he thinks took place after Sennacherib's withdrawal from Jerusalem in 701 B.C. It was then that the religious leaders saw that God had destroyed Samaria and Ephraim by the Assyrian armies, but that he saved Jerusalem and Judah.

Note the full complement of Levitical officials (vss. 12–14), though not in the same order as earlier. The following lists are interesting:

I Chron vi 1–15	I Chron vi 16–32	Here
Gershon	Kehath	Kehath
Kehath	Gershon	Merari
Merari	Merari	Gershon

The Aaronites are included here with the Levites, in accordance with the Chronicler's high regard for the latter. While he has drawn upon materials included earlier, the situation appears somewhat confused (cf. K. Möhlenbrink, ZAW 52 [1934], 213). The expansion of the list by the addition of Elizaphan (cf. I Chron xv 8) indicates the incorporation of secondary elements and the fluid character of the situation. The inclusion of the Levitical singers is perfectly good tradition.

[Rededication of the temple, 18–30]: The fulfillment of the covenant proceeded in three steps. The first was the cleansing of the temple—its reconsecration which itself began through a reconsecration of officials. The second was the rededication of the reconsecrated house. The ceremony was inaugurated by a notification to the king that his order for reconsecration had been carried out according to plan and in all essentials. Hezekiah and the officials went to the sanctuary the next day. They brought the proper offerings for the atonement of the royal house, the sanctuary and the nation. All these stood in special need of it. The slaughtering was done properly and the blood handled according to prescription (Lev xvii 6; Num xviii 17). The Levites played their instruments (I Chron xxiii 5, xxv 1–7) and the priests the trumpets (I Chron xv 24, xvi 6; Ezra iii 10). The congregational act of worship (prostration before Yahweh) took place at the beginning and at the end of the offering—doubtless the procedure was characteristic of the writer's own time. At the direction of the king and officials, there was a concluding service at the end of the formal offering during which praises were sung and further worship ensued.

[Congregational offerings, 31–36]: When the dedicatory ceremonies were completed and the temple ready for use, Hezekiah called upon the people to present their offerings. The response was enthusiastic, as may be seen from the numbers of animals involved. While burnt offerings were presented in connection with the rededication, the people now offered some of their own—this may account for the smaller number here. For the law for burnt offerings, see Lev i. Nothing of this offering was for human consumption; it designated a particular zeal for Yahweh on the part of the worshiper. But along with the burnt offerings were the peace offerings—the thanksgiving offerings were types of peace offerings (cf. Lev vii 11 ff.). Portions of this offering were consumed on the altar and the remainder by the worshiper (cf. Lev iii). There were also libations for the burnt offering (Exod xxix 40; Num xv 1–10). The proceedings were somewhat marred by the shortage of priests. The circumstance was used by the writer to observe that the Levites were more conscientious than the priests and that on certain occasions the former could perform priestly functions. This could be a reflection of the Chronicler's own time when the priests were not so conscientious as the Levites and perhaps a certain cleavage between them existed. On the other hand, the rivalry may have been present in his sources. With these offerings, the temple cult was functioning again.

32. THE REIGN OF HEZEKIAH (ca. 715–687 B.C.): THE PASSOVER (xxx 1–27)

Preparations

XXX 1 Then Hezekiah[a] sent to all Israel and Judah and also wrote letters to Ephraim and Manasseh [inviting them] to come to the house of Yahweh at Jerusalem to celebrate the passover to Yahweh God of Israel, 2 for the king, his officials and the whole congregation at Jerusalem had agreed to celebrate the passover in the second month. 3 They had been unable to celebrate it at the proper time because the priests had not consecrated themselves in sufficient numbers and the people were not assembled at Jerusalem. 4 Therefore, since the plan pleased the king and the people, 5 they resolved to issue an invitation to all Israel from Beer-sheba to Dan to come to celebrate a passover at Jerusalem to Yahweh God of Israel, for they had not celebrated [it] en masse as prescribed. 6 Then, by order of the king, couriers delivered letters from the king and the officials throughout all Israel and Judah with the following message, "O Israelites return to Yahweh God of Abraham, Isaac and Israel and [b]he will return to your remnant[b] that has escaped from the hand of the kings of Assyria. 7 Do not be like your fathers and your brothers who wronged Yahweh God of their fathers; he brought them to desolation as you can see. 8 Do not be as obstinate as your fathers were, [c]submit to Yahweh,[c] come to his sanctuary which he has consecrated forever and serve Yahweh your God that his violent anger may depart from you. 9 If you

[a] Hebrew reads "Jehizkiah," but context indicates that "Hezekiah" is meant.
[b-b] There is some LXX support for "he will restore the remnant . . . ." But cf. Zech i 3.
[c-c] LXX "give glory to Yahweh God." See NOTE.

return to Yahweh, your brothers and your sons will be dealt
with mercifully by their captors and permitted to return to this
land, for Yahweh your God is gracious and merciful and he
will not turn his face from you, if you return unto him." 10 So
the couriers went from city to city in the land of Ephraim and
Manasseh as far as Zebulun, but they laughed at them and ridiculed them. 11 Nonetheless some from Asher, Manasseh, and
Zebulun humbled themselves and came to Jerusalem. 12 The
hand of God was also at work in Judah to give them a common
mind to obey the command of the king and the officials, consistent with the word of Yahweh.

Celebration

13 A huge crowd of people assembled at Jerusalem to celebrate the festival of unleavened bread in the second month—it
was a very numerous congregation. 14 So they arose and removed
the altars that were in Jerusalem; they also removed the incense altars and cast them into the Kidron Valley. 15 They
slaughtered the passover [lambs] on the fourteenth day of the
second month. Meanwhile the priests and the Levites had become ashamed of themselves and consecrated themselves and
brought burnt offerings to the house of Yahweh. 16 So they now
stood at their stations according to their custom prescribed in
the law of Moses the man of God; the priests sprinkled the
blood which they received from the hand of the Levites. 17 Because many of the congregation had not consecrated themselves,
the Levites took care of the slaughter of the passover lambs so
as to consecrate [them] to Yahweh for all who were not clean.
18 There were many people, especially from Ephraim, Manasseh, Issachar, and Zebulun, who had not purified themselves, for
they did not eat the passover as prescribed. But Hezekiah*
prayed for them as follows: "May the good Yahweh pardon
19 everyone whose heart is ready to seek God, Yahweh God of
his fathers, though [he is not cleansed] according to the [cere-
monial] purification of the sanctuary." 20 Yahweh listened to
Hezekiah* and healed the people. 21 The Israelites present in

Jerusalem celebrated the festival of unleavened bread for seven
days with great joy; the Levites and the priests praised Yahweh
day after day with the mighty instruments of Yahweh. 22 Then
Hezekiah*ª* congratulated the Levites who had exhibited such excellent skill [in the conduct of the service] of Yahweh.

The second seven days

*ª*After they had concluded*ª* the seven-day festival during
which they sacrificed peace offerings and praised Yahweh God
of their fathers, 23 the whole congregation resolved to celebrate
for another seven days. So they celebrated [another] seven days
with joy, 24 for Hezekiah the king of Judah contributed a thousand bulls and seven thousand sheep for the congregation and
the officials contributed a thousand bulls and ten thousand
sheep for the congregation; a large number of priests consecrated
themselves. 25 So the whole congregation of Judah, the priests
and the Levites, the whole congregation that came from Israel,
and the resident aliens who came from the land of Israel as
well as those who lived in Judah rejoiced. 26 There was great
joy in Jerusalem; nothing like this had taken place in Jerusalem
since the days of Solomon the son of David, the king of Israel.
27 Then the priests and the Levites arose and blessed the people
and Yahweh*ᵉ* listened to their cry and their prayer came to his
holy dwelling place, to the heavens.

ᵈ⁻ᵈ LXX. Heb. "After they had eaten."
ᵉ Insert with Syr. because of suffix in next clause.

NOTES

xxx 3. *at the proper time.* I.e., at the time when the ceremonies
recorded in the preceding chapter took place.

8. *submit to Yahweh.* Literally "give the hand to the Lord," a cov-
enantal expression. (Cf. R. Kraetzchmar, *Die Bundesvorstellung im Alten
Testament,* 1896, p. 47; and for the giving of the hand in oaths see J.
Wellhausen, *Reste arabischen Heidentums,* 1897, p. 186.)

14. *the altars . . . Jerusalem.* Cf. xxviii 24 f.

incense altars. A hapax legomenon but to be explained on the basis of xxviii 25.

18. *the good Yahweh.* Phrase occurs only here in the Bible.

21. *praised Yahweh . . . Yahweh.* M. Buttenwieser (JBL 45 [1926], 156–58) thinks *biklê* means "song" and *'ōz la'ᵃdōnai* are the initial words of the song.

27. *the priests and the Levites.* May be Levitical priests here because the giving of the blessing was a priestly function (cf. Lev ix 22; Num vi 22).

COMMENT

[Preparations for the passover, xxx 1–12]: That some sort of religious celebration, apart from the rededication of the temple, took place soon after the accession of Hezekiah is extremely likely, especially in view of the character and ambitions of the king (cf. II Kings xviii 4–6). It is usually held that the Chronicler transferred to Hezekiah some of the religious celebrations of Josiah, notably this one. See the commentaries on Kings and Chronicles for details. It must not be forgotten that the Josiah story is Deuteronomic. On the case for a reform in the time of Hezekiah see BJRL 44 (1961/62), 425–31. While the Chronicler may have used some of the language and ideas employed by the Deuteronomist (particularly in vss. 6–9), there is no reason to believe that he invented the story itself. There is good reason to believe that Josiah followed, at least to some extent, the policies of Hezekiah. The political and religious exigencies demanded resolute action. The Northern Kingdom had fallen, the heavy hand of Assyria was laid to the throat of the west, and only Yahweh could deliver Judah, as Isaiah had indicated. Ahaz had tried co-operation and failed. With his death the stage was set for religious reformation, which was prosecuted with vigor (II Kings xviii 4 ff.) and an attempt made to reclaim some of the territory won by Uzziah and lost under Ahaz (II Kings xviii 8). Thus Hezekiah had political ambitions that could be realized only with the help of the religious officials, who apparently had the upper hand at the time. The debacle at Samaria strengthened the hand of the reform groups who naturally supported the king, but perhaps for different reasons. Indeed it appears that the reform activities of Hezekiah and their partial success formed the pattern upon which the Deuteronomic movement later proceeded with the same purpose—to save the nation. (Cf. BP, p. 42.) In short, Deuteronomy's legislation may have been based, in part, on a Hezekian precedent, in which case the *D* code may have been formulated in connection with Hezekiah's attempt to unify the nation in the worship of Jerusalem; and it is possible that *D* was to some extent discovered in the temple, having been lost during the reaction under Manasseh. Hezekiah plausibly appropriated the northern traditions of both *E* and *D* partly to further his objective. See also Elmslie (Selected Bibliography, Commentaries), pp. 524, 541.

It must be remembered that this is a sermon for the time of the Chronicler but based squarely on broad historical precedents and therefore later details may easily have intruded themselves as the preacher made his point. The fact that the initiative was taken so early in the reign of Hezekiah indicates that the advisers of the king had thought through their plans pretty well. Of course not all elements were sympathetic, at least not wholly so as is demonstrated by the dilatoriness of the priests (vs. 3).

The national significance of the passover lent itself admirably to the purposes of king and officials. Refugees from the north had doubtless found their way to Judah in the wake of the Assyrian conquest of Samaria. Bethel had been refurbished as a center of religion (II Kings xvii 28) and syncretism was rampant (II Kings xvii 29–34) throughout the Assyrian province of Samaria. Now was the time to appeal to the true followers of Yahweh in Israel. The language of the decision to issue the invitation and its wording are couched in the writer's own ideas and were quite obviously meant to apply also to his own situation, but the underlying framework is historical. How else is one to account for the fact that the wives of Manasseh and Josiah came from Galilee (cf. W. F. Albright's review of Abel's *Géographie de la Palestine* in JBL 58 [1939], 185; but see H. L. Ginsberg, in AMJV, pp. 350 f.). A further indication of Hezekiah's interest in the north is that he named his heir after a Northern tribe and eponymous hero. Politically the situation in the early years of Hezekiah's reign was quite opportune for such a religious appeal. Sargon II was occupied with northern and eastern areas from the sixth to the tenth years of his reign (ca.

716–712 b.c.) as we know from his annals (cf. ARAB, II, pp. 4–13).

A mission was sent throughout the territory of the old Northern Kingdom with a strong appeal to the people to rejoin their brethren at Jerusalem. There was some response from the Galilean area and Manasseh but none from Ephraim, possibly because the true followers of Yahweh had already withdrawn to Judah while the remainder cared little about the matter or because the people there were afraid to go because of the political implications involved— and the Assyrian officials probably kept close watch over Ephraim for any sign of rebellion.

[Celebration of the passover, 13–22a]: As already remarked, certain Deuteronomic prescriptions were woven into the Chronicler's narrative (vss. 5, 12) but that does not necessarily mean that he invented the whole story. At least some of the details have no meaning apart from the time of Hezekiah. It is important to observe that there were two deviations from general practice in this celebration of the passover: (a) the time of its celebration (on the fourteenth day of the second month), and (b) the exemption of Israelites from ritual prescriptions. Verses 18–19 are exceedingly illuminating since they portray the writer as no thoroughgoing ritualist. In cases of necessity, ritual could be set aside in favor of the worship of the broken and contrite heart. His belief in the efficacy of prayer should not be overlooked. On the matter of date of passover see H. J. Kraus, *Evangelische Theologie* 18 (1958), 47–67; S. Talmon, VT 8 (1958), 48–74. The shift in calendar reflects Hezekiah's desire to accommodate the Northerners who had been celebrating this feast a month later (to correspond with their autumn festival held in the eighth month). Observe the difference in approach between Hezekiah and Josiah (II Kings xxiii 15 f.), who destroyed the altar at Bethel.

Of course the writer's enthusiasm is evident through his reference to the very large congregation. A further reformation took place, this time in the city from which all foreign accouterments of worship were removed and cast into the refuse place in the Kidron Valley. The response of the people inspired the priests and Levites to consecrate themselves so that they occupied their stations for the service. Hence they could also step in to slay the passover lambs for those who could not meet ritual prescriptions. (This was probably a misunderstanding, as Rudolph, p. 301, thinks, as according to the law [Exod xii 6; Deut xvi 6] the family heads were to slay the lambs. The Levites probably did act for those from Israel who were not ritually capable of doing so.) The whole combination of festivities—festival of unleavened bread, passover, and peace offerings—continued for a full seven days after which the Levites were congratulated by the king—another indication of the esteem in which they were held by the Chronicler. The story probably had some homiletic application for the writer.

[A second period of festival, 22b–27]: Hezekiah appears like a second Solomon, who celebrated two weeks when the temple was dedicated (vii 8–9). The king and his officials contributed the sacrificial animals. The priests too had caught the spirit of joy and consecrated themselves. The festivities were shared by Judah, the Israelites who had come as pilgrims or refugees, the resident aliens, and the priests and Levites. No celebration like this (it is not referred to as any special feast) had taken place since the days of Solomon. It was concluded by the priestly blessing (cf. Num vi 22–27).

33. THE REIGN OF HEZEKIAH (ca. 715–687 B.C.): REFORM ACTIVITIES (xxxi 1–21)†

Cleansing of the land

XXXI 1 After all this was over, all Israel present went out to the cities of Judah, broke the pillars, cut to pieces the Asherahs, and wrecked completely the high places and the altars from all Judah, Benjamin, Ephraim, and Manasseh. Then all the Israelites returned to their cities, each one to his property.

Assignments of priests and Levites

2 Hezekiah*a* assigned the divisions of the priests and Levites according to their divisions, each one of the priests and Levites for his service, to offer burnt offerings and peace offerings, to minister and to give thanks and praise *b*in the gates of Yahweh's camp.*b*

Assignment for offerings

3 [He also assigned] the king's portion from his possessions for the burnt offering, the [regular] morning and evening burnt offerings and the burnt offerings for the Sabbaths, the new moons, and the festivals as prescribed in the law of Yahweh.

Provision for support of religious officials

4 Moreover, he requested the people who lived in Jerusalem to present the portion of the priests and Levites *c*that they might occupy themselves [unreservedly] with the law of Yahweh.*c*

† **II Chron xxxi 1:** cf. II Kings xviii 4.

a Hebrew reads "Jehizkiah," but context indicates that "Hezekiah" is meant.
b–b MT "camps." Vulg. follows MT. LXX "in the courts of the house of the Lord"; Syr. omits "house." See NOTE.
c–c LXX "that they excel in the service of the house of the Lord."

5 As soon as the order was proclaimed, the Israelites provided the first fruits of grain, must, oil, honey, and all the produce of the field in abundance; they brought in the tithe of everything in great quantities. 6 The Israelites and Judeans who lived in the cities of Judah also brought in the *ᵈtithe of cattle,*ᵈ sheep, and the sacred gifts consecrated to Yahweh their God and placed them on piles. 7 They began to accumulate the piles in the third month and by the seventh month had finished [them]. 8 When Hezekiah*ᵃ* and the chiefs came and saw the piles they praised Yahweh and his people Israel. 9 When Hezekiah*ᵃ* consulted with the priests and Levites about the piles, 10 Azariah the chief priest of the house of Zadok answered him as follows: "Since they began to bring the contributions to the house of Yahweh there has been enough to eat and an enormous surplus, for Yahweh has blessed his people, and so we have this great quantity." 11 Then Hezekiah*ᵃ* ordered [them] to prepare storerooms in the house of Yahweh and, when they had prepared [them], 12 they conscientiously brought in the contributions, the tithes, and consecrated gifts and they placed Conaniah the Levite in charge of them with Shimei his brother as assistant; 13 Jehiel, Azaziah, Nahath, Asahel, Jerimoth, Jozabad, Eliel, Ismachiah, Mahath, and Benaiah were overseers under Conaniah and Shimei his brother in accordance with the order of Hezekiah*ᵃ* the king and Azariah the chief of the house of God. 14 Kore the son of Imnah the Levite and porter of the east [gate] was in charge of the freewill offerings of God and the distribution of the contributions of Yahweh and the consecrated gifts. 15 Supporting him loyally in the priestly cities were Eden, Minjamin, Jeshua, Shemaiah, Amariah, and Shecaniah who distributed to their brothers according to their divisions, whether old or young, 16 irrespective of their official genealogy, to the males from thirty*ᵉ* years old and upward—to every one [of them] who entered the house of Yahweh to fulfill his daily obligations—for

ᵈ⁻ᵈ LXX "tithes of goats."
ᵉ So for Heb. *šlwš* ("three"). Vulg. *tribus,* "third," or "tribe." See NOTE.

their work in their ministrations according to their divisions:
17 both the officially registered priests according to their families
and the Levites from twenty years old and upward according
to their services in their divisions. 18 And the official genealogy
included all their small children, their wives, their sons, and
their daughters, for the whole congregation, because they kept
dedicating themselves in their devotion. 19 The Aaronites, the
priests who lived on the pasture lands belonging to their cities,
had men of renown in every city ready to distribute portions to
every male among the priests and to everyone included in the
official genealogy of the Levites.

Characterization of Hezekiah

20 Hezekiah*a* did so throughout all Judah; he did what was
good, right, and true before Yahweh his God. 21 Every work
which he undertook, whether in the service of the house of God
or in the law or in the commandments, he carried out with
utter devotion in the worship of his God, and so succeeded.

NOTES

xxxi 2. *in the gates of Yahweh's camp.* Cf. I Chron ix 18, 19, where
the camps (plural) of the Levites are mentioned in connection with
their service at the tent as their fathers had served the camp (singular)
of Yahweh. The writer was doubtless influenced by *P*'s wilderness tradition. There is probably no relation to an eschatological conception found
later in 1QM 4:9.

5. *the Israelites.* Refers to the dwellers in Jerusalem, not North Israelites.

honey. Honey could not be used with the burnt offering (Lev ii 11),
though it may have been acceptable as a cereal offering.

6. *The Israelites.* The refugees from Israel living in the cities of
Judah.

the tithe of cattle . . . sacred gifts. This does not appear in the law
of Moses (but cf. Neh x 38).

13. *the chief. nāgīd* (cf. I Chron ix 11; Neh xi 11).

16. *thirty years old.* MT "three." Must be "thirty" because they came
to work (cf. I Chron xxiii 3).

COMMENT

[Cleansing of the land, xxxi 1]: The compression of reform
activity into two chapters (xxx and xxxi) represents a schematization of the reforms characteristic of the whole reign of Hezekiah,
which was influenced greatly by the preaching of Micah and Isaiah
(cf. Bright, *A History of Israel,* pp. 261–67).

Just as Jerusalem had been cleansed (xxx 14) before the festival
of unleavened bread and passover, the whole land was swept clean
of impurities left over from the days of Ahaz. The two verses belong
together and are an expansion of II Kings xviii 4, except that nothing
is said here about the destruction of the bronze serpent. No specific
extent of the reformation is recorded in II Kings, but it probably per-
tained to Judah. How far it went beyond that is uncertain, though
there may have been some such activities in local situations conducted by those who had participated in the Jerusalem festivities.

[Priestly and Levitical assignments, 2]: The background for this
verse is viii 14 which itself refers to I Chron xxiii 26. Hezekiah
reaffirmed the old order established by Solomon in accordance with
the command of David. The priests were in charge of the offerings
and the Levites supervised and carried out their functions of music
at the established posts and time.

[Provision for offerings, 3]: According to viii 12–13, Solomon
provided burnt offerings regularly for the temple services. Hezekiah
followed the precedent of Solomon—the Chronicler looks upon him
as a kind of second Solomon (cf. ii 4). The provisions for these
offerings are enumerated in Num xxviii–xxix.

[Provision for the religious personnel, 4–19]: The zeal for the
reformation can be judged by the popular and royal provision for
temple services. When the royal decree was issued for provision
for religious personnel, the response was overwhelming, both from
Jerusalem and from the cities of Judah—much to the surprise of the
king. The contributions consisted of the best gifts (*rēʼšīt*) and the
tithe. According to Num xviii, the gifts were for the priests (vs. 12)
and the tithe for the Levites (vs. 21). In his colloquy with the
religious leaders, the chief priest Azariah informed him that the
huge stock piles were due to the generosity of the people and the

blessing of Yahweh. At the command of the king storage rooms were readied in the temple for the tithes (cf. I Chron ix 26, xxvi 20–28, xxviii 12). Twelve Levites were placed in charge of the collections (cf. I Chron xxvi 26–28). As in the case of Joash and Jehoiada (xxiv 12), Hezekiah and Azariah co-operated closely in this project. Kore, the Levitical porter of the east gate, had charge of the voluntary offerings and the distribution of contributions and gifts, a very important function. To assist him in the proper discharge of his duties was a corps of priests in the various cities of Judah, so that proper care was taken of the families of those religious officials who were performing their duties. The register of priests was according to families, that of Levites according to functon (divisions); (cf. the organization of David, I Chron xxiii–xxvi). The landed priests too were included in the scheme of service and were thus eligible to share in the contributions. Much of this material doubtless reflects the practice obtaining in the time of the writer, though there may have been such an order carried out under the reformation of the period of Hezekiah.

[Evaluation of Hezekiah, 20–21]: This little pericope is based on II Kings xviii 5–7a and emphasizes his activity for his entire kingdom, his utter devotion to Yahweh in all he undertook and hence his success. But the Chronicler, despite his obvious bias for Hezekiah, does not go so far as the Deuteronomist in declaring him to have been the best king ever (II Kings xviii 5).

34. THE REIGN OF HEZEKIAH (ca. 715–687 B.C.):
THE ASSYRIAN INVASION
(xxxii 1–23)†

XXXII 1 After these faithful acts, Sennacherib the king of Assyria came and invaded Judah, and laid siege to the fortified cities with the thought of conquering them. 2 When Hezekiah*a* saw that Sennacherib had come with the main purpose of making war on Jerusalem, 3 he consulted with his chiefs and warriors about closing up the water courses outside the city; they supported him. 4 A large number of people were brought together to stop up all the springs and the brook that ran *b*through the midst of the land,*b* saying, "Why should the kings of Assyria find abundant water when they come." 5 He also went to work with determination and repaired every section of the wall that was damaged, erected towers upon it, [constructed] another wall on the outside, strengthened the Millo of the city of David, and made a large quantity of spears and shields. 6 He placed military officers in charge of the people, summoned them to himself on the plaza at the city gate, and spoke directly to them as follows: 7 "Be strong and courageous, do not be afraid or tremble before the king of Assyria and all the multitude accompanying him, for those with us are more than those with him. 8 He has only *c*human power*c* but we have Yahweh our God to help us and to fight our battle." The people were encouraged by the words of Hezekiah*a* the king of Judah. 9 After this, while he and all his command were at Lachish, Sennacherib sent his servants to Jerusalem, to Hezekiah*a* and all Judah at

† II Chron xxxii 1–23 ‖ II Kings xviii 13–37, xix 14–19, 35–37, Isa xxxvi 1–22, xxxvii 14–19, 36–38.

a Hebrew reads "Jehizkiah," but context indicates that "Hezekiah" is meant.
b–b LXX "through the city." See NOTE.
c–c MT "arm of flesh." For expression, see Jer xvii 5; cf. also Isa xxxi 3.

Jerusalem with the following message: 10 "Thus has Sennacherib the king of Assyria said: In what do you put your confidence, you who sit in the fortress of Jerusalem? 11 Is not Hezekiah*a* deluding you in order to deliver you to death by famine and thirst when he says, 'Yahweh our God will save us from the hand of the king of Assyria'? 12 Is Hezekiah*a* not the one who removed his high places and his altars and said to Judah and Jerusalem, 'Before one altar you must worship and upon it burn incense'? 13 Don't you know what I and my fathers did to all the peoples of the lands? Were the gods of the nations of the lands able at all to deliver their land from my hand? 14 Who among all the gods of these nations whom my fathers devoted to destruction was able to deliver his people from my hand, that your God should be able to deliver you from my hand? 15 Now, do not let Hezekiah*a* mislead you; do not let him delude you like this; do not believe him. No god of any nation or kingdom was able to deliver his people from my hand or the hand of my fathers, how much less can your God deliver you from my hand?" 16 His servants spoke still further against Yahweh God and Hezekiah*a* his servant. 17 He also wrote letters to insult Yahweh God of Israel and spoke against him, saying, "As the gods of the nations of the lands could not deliver their people from my hand, so the God of Hezekiah*a* cannot deliver his people from my hand." 18 Then they shouted with a loud voice in the Jewish language to the people of Jerusalem who stood on the wall to frighten and terrify them, hoping to capture the city. 19 They spoke against*d* the God of Jerusalem as [they had] against the gods of the peoples of the earth which were the product of men's hands. 20 Then Hezekiah*a* the king and Isaiah the prophet, the son of Amoz, prayed about this and cried to the heavens. 21 Then Yahweh sent a messenger who destroyed every mighty man, leader and captain in the camp of the king of Assyria; so he had to return to his country shamefacedly and when he entered the house of his god his own offspring there struck him down with the sword. 22 So Yahweh

d So for Heb. "to."

saved Hezekiah[a] and the citizens of Jerusalem from the hand of Sennacherib the king of Assyria and from the hand of all [others] and [e]gave them peace[e] on every side. 23 Then many brought gifts to Yahweh at Jerusalem and costly presents to Hezekiah[a] the king of Judah; from then on he was exalted in the estimation of all the nations.

[e–e] So with LXX and Vulg. for Heb. "and he led them." Cf. also Josh xxi 42; II Chron xiv 6, xv 15, xx 30.

NOTES

xxxii 1. On the campaigns of Sennacherib in Palestine see Bright, *A History of Israel*, pp. 282–87, and the references there listed.

3. *the water courses.* I.e., the springs, wells, and conduits.

4. *all the springs.* Thought to have been Gihon and En-rogel. Rudolph, p. 311, thinks the Dragon's fountain may also have been involved.

the brook . . . land. May refer to open conduits that carried the water to a pool within the city (Isa vii 3). See Vincent and Steve, *Jerusalem de l'Ancien Testament*, Pt. i, pp. 280, 289–97. Hezekiah later replaced these open water channels with the Siloam tunnel; see xxxii 30, next section.

5. *another wall on the outside.* On the location of the second wall see Avi-yonah, *Sepher Yerushalayim*, I, pp. 157 f., and map opposite p. 160; Galling, BRL, 301–4; Vincent and Steve, *op. cit.*, Pt. iii, p. 647.

6. *and spoke directly.* Specifically and directly, to encourage them.

7. *Be strong . . . tremble.* Cf. Deut xxxi 6; Josh x 25.

those with us . . . him. Cf. II Kings vi 16, words of Elisha to his servant. There may be some connection with Isa vii 14 here (Immanuel= God with us), just as in Isaiah there is a connection between Immanuel and Hezekiah, which was accepted by the Chronicler. While this is explicit only later in Rabbinic sources, it has a long history, going back at least to the Chronicler, if not to Isaiah himself. The royal prophecies belong to the early period of the prophet and refer originally and essentially to the hopes in the royal house, and presumably to Hezekiah. The latter's boldness, and his close association with the prophet, could be understood in this light, even though neither Hezekiah nor any other king could completely fulfill the hopes of the poet-prophet.

12. The play on the resentment of the people about the highhanded reform reflects the writer's view that Hezekiah carried out a Deuteronomic reform.

13. *Don't you know . . . the peoples of the lands?* Cf. 1QH 4:26.

19. *the God of Jerusalem.* Phrase found scratched on the wall of a cave near Lachish. *Land of the Bible: Newsletter,* Vol. 3, No 26 (April/May 1962), 1.

21. *struck . . . sword.* For discussions on the problem of the strange death of Sennacherib, see references in ANET, p. 288.

COMMENT

Comparison with II Kings xviii–xx shows that the Chronicler reversed the emphasis: he stressed the religious activities of Hezekiah to which he devoted two chapters. The Deuteronomist dismissed the reformation with only four verses (II Kings xviii 3–6). But the Chronicler did not deal so curtly with the political events as his predecessor had done with Hezekiah's reformation. However, the political involvements of the period as presented by the writer are so telescoped that they cannot be understood without the records of Kings, the references in Isaiah, and the Assyrian inscriptions.

[Countermeasures of Hezekiah, xxxii 1–8]: According to II Kings xviii 13 (cf. Isa xxxvi 1), Sennacherib invaded Judah in the fourteenth year of Hezekiah (ca. 701 B.C.). The Chronicler tells only of the Assyrian king's *thought* of conquering the fortified cities of Judah; he does not say that they were actually taken. According to the Taylor Prism, Sennacherib took forty-six cities and a huge number of prisoners, gave some of Hezekiah's territory to the neighboring kings of Ashdod, Ekron, and Gaza, and laid a heavy tribute upon him (ANET, pp. 287 f.). For results of excavations of Lachish and Tell Beit Mirsim reflecting this period see Wright, *Biblical Archaeology,* pp. 164–72. Hezekiah took three measures in preparation for meeting the invaders—all with reference not to the outlying areas of Judah which were probably already as good as lost but to Jerusalem, where the last stand was to be made. The first had to do with the water problem, which was tackled from both a defensive and offensive point of view. The springs and wells outside the city were stopped up to prevent the enemy from using them—a powerfully offensive weapon in a water-famished region. Steps were taken at the same time to use the available supply for the defenders of the city. The second was the strengthening of the fortifications of the city: repairing the weak spots in the wall, erection of towers, construction of an outside wall, and building up the Millo (cf. Isa xxii 9–10; for the Millo, see my *I Chronicles,* COMMENT on Sec. 15). Finally, Hezekiah reorganized the army, placed the nation on a wartime footing, and supplied his forces with weapons of war (cf. Isa xxii 8b).

The Chronicler attempts to clear Hezekiah of failure to consult Yahweh, as charged by Isaiah (xxii 11), by having him exhort the military and people to trust in Yahweh who will fight their battle. With him on their side there is no need to fear or tremble before an arm of flesh.

[Sennacherib's message, 9–19]: During the siege of Lachish, Sennacherib sent envoys to Jerusalem with a message for Hezekiah and the people of Jerusalem with the hope of throwing them into panic (see ANET; for a reproduction of the Assyrian relief showing the siege and capture of Lachish see ANEP, pp. 372–73). There is no mention of the army sent with the envoys (II Kings xviii 17). The message spoken of here is composed of the communication of Sennacherib (II Kings xix 10–13) and the speech of the Rabshakeh (II Kings xviii 19–35); more precisely, the sources of the verses here are: vs. 10 ‖ II Kings xviii 19, 20b; vs. 11 ‖ II Kings xviii 32b; vs. 12 ‖ II Kings xviii 22b; vs. 13 ‖ II Kings xix 11 and xviii 33; vs. 14 ‖ II Kings xviii 35; and vs. 15 ‖ II Kings xviii 29. The Chronicler has composed Sennacherib's message in accordance with his own views, choosing to omit the well-known references by the writer of II Kings to the strength of Hezekiah and the Egyptian alliance (xviii 19–25). He takes up the religious argument propounded by the Rabshakeh in II Kings xviii 28–35 which follows quite logically after Hezekiah's address to his people to inspire them with confidence. Verse 18 refers to the speech of the Rabshakeh.

[Hezekiah's deliverance, 20–23]: For a fuller description of Hezekiah's reaction to the appeal of the Assyrian commander see II Kings xix. Here he is said to have been joined in prayer by Isaiah, probably on the basis of II Kings xix 20. Both the prayer of Hezekiah and the response of Yahweh through the prophet are omitted by the Chronicler (cf. II Kings xix 15–19, 21–34) because he is more concerned about the reward of faithfulness and doing right (cf. James v 16). Our author and the Deuteronomist are agreed on the deliverance of Hezekiah and Jerusalem, though it was not without a tremendous price (see ANET, p. 287) and after Jerusalem was actually laid under siege (cf. II Kings xviii 17, xix 35). Not only was Jerusalem spared but Hezekiah's stature rose tremendously, and countless offerings were brought to Yahweh as thank offerings for his goodness and mercy. On the whole matter of Sennacherib's campaigns to the west, see NOTE on vs. 1 and Rowley, BJRL 44 (1961/62), 395 ff.

35. THE REIGN OF HEZEKIAH (ca. 715–687 B.C.): THE LATER YEARS
(xxxii 24–33)†

Hezekiah's illness

XXXII 24 At that time Hezekiah^a became mortally sick and when he prayed to Yahweh, he responded and gave him a token.

The pride of Hezekiah

25 But Hezekiah^a did not repay the benefit received by him; rather he became proud so that wrath would fall upon him and upon Judah and Jerusalem. 26 However, when Hezekiah^a, with the citizens of Jerusalem, humbled himself in respect to his pride, the wrath of Yahweh did not come upon them in the time of Hezekiah.^a

Wealth and honor of Hezekiah

27 Hezekiah^a became very rich and respected; he provided for himself treasure houses for his silver, gold, precious stones, spices, shields, and all kinds of desirable articles, 28 as well as storage places for the produce of grain, must, and oil, and stalls for all kinds of cattle and pens for the flocks. 29 He also provided cities for himself, in addition to an abundance of wealth in the form of sheep and cattle, because God gave him a very great abundance of wealth. 30 Hezekiah^a also was the one who closed the upper outlet of the waters of Gihon and channeled them straight down on the west side of the city of David. Hezekiah^a was successful in all his undertakings. 31 But when the

† **II Chron xxxii 24** ‖ II Kings xx 1–3, Isa xxxviii 1–3; **25–26** ‖ II Kings xx 12–19, Isa xxxix 1–8; **32–33** ‖ II Kings xx 20–21.

^a Hebrew reads "Jehizkiah," but context indicates that "Hezekiah" is meant.

representatives of the chiefs of Babylon were sent to him to inquire about the sign that was done in the land, God left him alone to test him so that he might know his mind fully.

Conclusion

32 The remainder of the history of Hezekiah[a] and his devoted acts, behold they are written down in the vision of Isaiah, the son of Amoz, the prophet in the chronicle of the kings of Judah and Israel. 33 When Hezekiah[a] slept with his fathers, they buried him in the upper section of the graves of the sons of David; so all Judah and Jerusalem honored him at his death. Manasseh his son then became king in his place.

NOTES

xxxii 27. *shields.* May have been ornamental shields.

33. *the upper section.* Cf., however, A. B. Ehrlich, *Randglossen zur hebräischen Bibel,* VII, 1914, p. 381, and Rudolph, *in loco,* who suggest "prominent or honored place."

COMMENT

[Hezekiah's illness, xxxii 24]: A simple statement of the fact without details illustrates the writer's method of utilizing well-known episodes to strengthen his argument in a given case. His audience required no more. The token refers to the sundial (II Kings xx 8–11).

[The pride of Hezekiah, 25–26]: These verses must manifestly be interpreted in the light of the story of the visit of the representatives of Merodach-baladan (II Kings xx 12–19; Isa xxxix 1–8) during which Hezekiah proudly displayed *his* treasures. His pride was bound to lead to disaster, as the prophet Isaiah declared. Though only the royal house stood under judgment, the Chronicler brings Judah and Jerusalem into the picture because he was aware of the wider consequences of such action—the deeds of leaders always involve those they lead. The response of Hezekiah to the rebuke of

Isaiah averted trouble for the time being (cf. II Kings xx 19).

[Wealth and honor of Hezekiah, 27–31]: This catalogue of achievements is meant to demonstrate the blessings of God upon the king who did good in his sight (cf. vs. 29b). While the list is too indefinite for purposes of specific comparison, certain archaeological discoveries tend to support the over-all features of a rather prosperous reign. A seal found at Tell Beit Mirsim with Hezekiah's name dates from around 700 B.C. (*l-ḥzq* [*yw*]; cf. AASOR 12 [1932], 78). The *l-mlk* jar-handle stamps may have originated in the period of Hezekiah (Albright dates class 1 to this period [AASOR 21–22 (1943), 73–75]; cf. also D. Diringer's study in BA 12 [1949], 70–86, especially pp. 84–86). The famous Siloam inscription appears to come from the same age. For the history of the discovery, illustrations, and translation of the inscription, cf. Wright, *Biblical Archaeology,* pp. 169–72. Another interesting and significant item is the Great Shaft uncovered at Lachish; Hezekiah may have had something to do with its construction (see Tufnell, *Lachish III: The Iron Age,* pp. 158–63). For a study of the water courses in the period of Ahaz and Hezekiah, see M. Burrows, "The Conduit of the Upper Pool," ZAW 70 (1958), 221–27.

According to the Chronicler the Babylonian officials came to Jerusalem to study "the sign that was done in the land," that is, the token of the sundial (II Kings xx 9–11). The Babylonians had developed astrological interests long before this time.

While it seems clear that behind the writer's story of the visit of the delegation from Babylon lies that of the mission of the representatives of Merodach-baladan reported in Kings, Chronicles says nothing about Hezekiah's display of his treasures to the Babylonians. The Chronicler chooses rather to connect the mission with an inquiry about the sign of the sundial. The coming of the delegation was nevertheless interpreted by him as a test for the king and in which he was left to himself. Traditionally, in time of testing, God was thought to have abandoned the one being tested (cf. Abraham, Job, and, in part, Israel in the wilderness). The purpose of the test was to establish Hezekiah's devotion to Yahweh, demonstrated in part by his prayer (vs. 24) but rendered uncertain by his subsequent pride (vs. 25). He had indeed repented after experiencing the divine displeasure but this test was to show if his devotion was now wholehearted.

[Conclusion, 32–33]: Follows the general pattern but lays special stress on "his devoted acts" and the source in "the vision of Isaiah" recorded in the history of the kings of Judah and Israel. It should not be overlooked that other activities may have taken place in the time of Hezekiah, notably that of wise men (Prov xxv–xxix). See O. Eissfeldt, *Einleitung in das Alte Testament,* 3d ed., 1964, pp. 641 ff.

36. THE REIGN OF MANASSEH (687–642 B.C.) (xxxiii 1–20)†

Relapse

XXXIII 1 Manasseh was twelve years old when he became king and remained king at Jerusalem for fifty-five years. 2 He did evil in the sight of Yahweh, following the abominations of the nations whom Yahweh dispossessed before the Israelites. 3 He rebuilt the high places which Hezekiah*a* his father had smashed, he erected altars for Baal, made Asherahs, and worshiped all the host of the heavens and served them. 4 He built altars in the house of Yahweh of which Yahweh himself had said, "My name shall remain in Jerusalem forever." 5 He built altars for all the host of the heavens in both courts of the house of Yahweh. 6 He made his sons to pass through the fire in the valley of Ben-hinnom, practiced soothsaying, divination, and sorcery, and dealt in necromancy and familiar spirits; he did so much evil in the sight of Yahweh, inciting him to anger. 7 He also set up the slab-image which he had made, in the house of God of which God had said to David and to Solomon his son, "I will put my name forever in this house and in Jerusalem which I selected from all the tribes of Israel. 8 I will not again remove the foot of Israel from the ground upon which I permitted your fathers to stand so long as they are careful to observe all that I commanded them with respect to all the law, the statutes and the judgments [given] through Moses." 9 But Manasseh misled Judah and the citizens of Jerusalem into doing

† II Chron xxxiii 1–10 ‖ II Kings xxi 1–10; **18–20** ‖ II Kings xxi 17–18.

a Hebrew reads "Jehizkiah," but context indicates that "Hezekiah" is meant.

greater evil than the nations whom Yahweh destroyed before the Israelites. 10 When Yahweh spoke to Manasseh and his people, they paid no attention [to him].

Conversion of Manasseh

11 Then Yahweh brought against them the captains of the army of the king of Assyria who captured Manasseh with hooks, bound him with bronze chains, and took him to Babylon. 12 When he was in distress, he placated Yahweh his God and humbled himself greatly before the God of his fathers. 13 When he prayed to him, he was moved by his entreaties, listened to supplication for favor, and brought him back to Jerusalem to his kingdom. Then Manasseh knew that Yahweh is God. 14 Afterwards Manasseh built the outer wall of the city of David on the west side of Gihon, in the valley, to the fish gate and around the Ophel and made it very much higher. Then he stationed army captains in all the fortified cities of Judah. 15 He also removed the foreign gods and the idol from the house of Yahweh as well as all the altars he had erected on the mountain of the house of Yahweh and in Jerusalem and threw them outside the city. 16 He repaired*b* the altar of Yahweh, sacrificed peace offerings and thank offerings upon it, and commanded Judah to serve Yahweh God of Israel. 17 Nevertheless, the people continued to sacrifice at the high places, only to Yahweh their God.

Concluding observations

18 The remainder of the history of Manasseh, his prayer to his God and the oracles of the seers who spoke to him in the name of Yahweh God of Israel—they are in the records of the kings of Israel. 19 His prayer, [how God] was moved by his entreaties, all his sins, his wrongdoing, the locations where he built high places, his setting up of Asherahs and images before he humbled himself are written down in the records of his seers.

b So with LXX and Vulg., for Heb. "prepared."

20 When Manasseh slept with his fathers, they buried him °in his house°. Amon his son became king in his place.

°–° LXX "garden of his house," following the parallel in II Kings xxi 18, where it is further defined as the garden of Uzza, not otherwise identified except as the burial place of Amon (II Kings xxi 26).

NOTES

xxxiii 1. *fifty-five years.* For chronology see Albright, BASOR 100 (December 1945), 22. He reduces the length of Manasseh's reign to forty-five years.

3. *the host of the heavens.* Astral cults pointing to subservience to Assyria.

6. *the valley of Ben-hinnom.* See NOTE on xxviii 3 in Sec. 30.

soothsaying . . . spirits. Assyria was deeply involved in the occult at the time. (Cf. F. M. Th. de Liagre Böhl, *Opera Minora,* 1953, pp. 384–422.) None of the terms used here are very clear. They cover the whole field of magic and divination.

7. *slab-image.* This meaning of *semel* is Albright's (ARI, p. 221, n. 121). According to II Kings xxi 7, it was an image of Ashera which would have been particularly offensive to Yahwists.

19. *his seers.* So instead of "my seers." The *w* of the third person masculine singular suffix of the plural noun was omitted by haplography.

COMMENT

The Chronicler devotes one more verse than the Deuteronomist to Manasseh, but the evaluation of his reign is vastly different.

[Relapse under Manasseh, xxxiii 1–10]: The first passage is almost identical with its parallel and source (II Kings xxi 1–10). For one thing, our writer curiously omits the name of the king's mother, a practice he generally follows elsewhere, with the exceptions of Joram and Ahaz earlier, and does not name the kings' mothers again in Chronicles. It is not difficult to understand why he does not refer to Ahab, king of Israel in comparison with Manasseh—no king of Judah could be that bad, for all of them were of the Davidic line. There are also a few additions such as "in the valley of Ben-hinnom" (6), "the statutes and the judgments" (8) interpreting the content of the law of Moses, and "Judah and the citizens of Jerusalem" (9), a characteristic expression, which spells out more clearly the objects of Manasseh's seduction.

The relapse under Manasseh was, no doubt, due to the conditions which prevailed in his day, as in the time of Ahaz. The climax of Assyrian intervention in the west came in this period, for the most part because of the protracted crises in Egypt which occupied much of the time of Esarhaddon (680–669). Manasseh's name occurs in the list of twenty-two kings of Hatti, the seashore and the islands, who were summoned to Nineveh (ANET, p. 291). The inscriptions of both Esarhaddon and Asshurbanipal are full of references to Egypt and the Palestinian states, indicative of their activity in these regions. As Ahaz before him, Manasseh was doubtless caught in the stream of world politics and had perforce to become subservient to Assyria. That meant, in part, the adoption of Assyrian religion which in turn compelled the nullification of the achievements of his father and earned for the king the enmity and violent opposition of prophets and religious officials, many of whom worked underground. Manasseh was, in all probability, not an unwilling tool —though certainly not at first—in the hands of the Assyrian kings. Prophecy was not altogether quiescent, as can be inferred from vs. 10 (cf. II Kings xxi 10), but its message availed little and was even met with violence (II Kings xxi 16).

[Conversion of Manasseh, 11–17]: That Manasseh found himself in the presence of the Assyrian king is quite probable in view of the vassal-treaties of Esarhaddon (see D. J. Wiseman, "The Vassal-Treaties of Esarhaddon," *Iraq* 20 [1958], 1–99). These treaties are dated in the year 672 and center around the ceremony of induction of the crown prince Asshurbanipal. Representatives of all the lands under Assyrian hegemony were gathered at the royal palace, where in special ceremony they were bound with fearful oaths to support the crown prince after the death of his father. Among other things, they were sworn not to arouse the ire of the gods or goddesses against him (line 265) and to serve Ashur as their own god (line 409). The interest and activity of both Esarhaddon and Asshurbanipal in the west could well have forced compliance with their demands in Judah, though undoubtedly opportunities were not missed to deviate from them or even to rebel. Possibilities for rebellion existed in connection with the activities of Psammeticus I and perhaps at the time of difficulty with Shamash-shum-ukin (see Bright, *A History of Israel,* pp. 291–93). The occurrence of the name of Manasseh in the inscriptions of both points in that direction. It may be taken for granted that the vassal kings were allowed to return to their countries after having been placed under the threat of divine retribution with its fearful consequences. However, if such was the case, the Chronicler interprets it as due to a change of heart on the part of Manasseh, who prayed to Yahweh who brought him back to Jerusalem. The ensuing reformation does not coincide with the Kings sources or with Jeremiah (xv 4), all of which agree that the sin of Manasseh remained. It is possible that the long life of the king, on the theory of the Chronicler, was the ultimate source for the story, which continued to grow as may be seen from the apocryphal prayer of Manasseh based on vs. 13 (see E. J. Goodspeed, *The Apocrypha,* 1938, pp. 369–72). At any rate, the writer himself says that Amon followed in the footsteps of his father (vs. 22) and that the abominations were removed by Josiah. There may be a historical kernel in vs. 14; if so, the fortification of Jerusalem would not have been against Assyria but against the renascent power of Egypt under Psammeticus I, Judah figuring as a buffer state between Egypt and the Palestinian provinces of Assyria (cf. Rudolph, p. 317, but see A. Malamat, "The Last Wars of the Kingdom of Judah," JNES 9 [1950], 226, n. 30).

[Conclusion, 18–20]: This is simply a summary of the supposed activities of Manasseh by way of indicating the sources where they have been recorded. It is interesting to note the mention of the oracles of his seers!

37. THE REIGN OF AMON (642–640 B.C.)
(xxxiii 21–25)†

XXXIII 21 Amon was twenty-two years old when he became king and reigned at Jerusalem for two years. 22 He did evil in the sight of Yahweh as Manasseh his father had done; Amon sacrificed to the images which Manasseh had made and served them. 23 He did not humble himself before Yahweh as Manasseh his father had humbled himself; but he, [that one] Amon, rather increased his guilt. 24 Finally his servants conspired against him and killed him in his own house. 25 Then the people of the land slew those who conspired against King Amon, and the people of the land made Josiah his son king in his place.

† II Chron xxxiii 21–25 ‖ II Kings xxi 19–24.

COMMENT

The short reign of Amon is a repetition of that of Manasseh with its evils and apostasy. The story here follows closely that in II Kings xxi, with the addition of vs. 23 based on the story of the conversion of Manasseh. The palace revolt issuing in the death of Amon was put down by the *'am hā-'āreṣ*, "people of the land," the free landholders of Judah who always acted decisively in times of crises to see that the Davidic dynasty was perpetuated (see Würthwein, *Der 'amm* . . . , especially pp. 30 ff.). A. Malamat ("The Historical Background of the Assassination of Amon, King of Judah," IEJ 3 [1953], 26–29) thinks Amon was slain by anti-Assyrian opponents of his foreign policy who were, in turn, ousted by the *'am hā-'āreṣ* to avoid a direct collision with Assyria. Nothing is said of his burial (cf. II Kings xxi 26).

38. THE REIGN OF JOSIAH (640–609 B.C.):
DISCOVERY OF THE LAWBOOK OF MOSES
(xxxiv 1–33)†

Introductory statement

XXXIV 1 Josiah was eight years old when he became king and reigned at Jerusalem for thirty-one years. 2 He did what was right in the sight of Yahweh, following the ways of David his father and turning neither to the right nor to the left.

First steps in reformation

3 During the eighth year of his reign, while he was still a youth, he began to seek the God of David his father and in the twelfth year he began to purge from Judah and Jerusalem the high places, the Asherahs, and the carved and molten images. 4 He smashed the altars of Baal in his presence, cut to pieces the incense altars that were above them, broke up and pulverized the Asherahs and the carved and molten images, and strewed [the dust] before the graves of those who sacrificed to them. 5 He burned the bones of their priests upon their altars and thus cleansed Judah and Jerusalem. 6 And in the cities of Manasseh, Ephraim, and Simeon, as far as Naphtali, and around their plazas, 7 he smashed the altars and the Asherahs, reduced to dust the carved images, and cut to pieces all the incense altars in all the land of Israel. Then he returned to Jerusalem.

Repairs for the temple

8 In the eighteenth year of his reign, after purging the land and the temple, he sent Shaphan the son of Azaliah, Maaseiah the mayor of the city, and Joah, the son of Jehoahaz, the

† **II Chron xxxiv 1–2** ‖ II Kings xxii 1–2; **8–13** ‖ II Kings xxii 3–7; **14–21** ‖ II Kings xxii 8–13; **22–28** ‖ II Kings xxii 14=20; **29–33** ‖ II Kings xxiii 1–3.

speaker to refurbish the house of Yahweh his God. 9 When they came to Hilkiah the high priest, they delivered the money brought to the house of God and collected by the Levitical porters from Manasseh and Ephraim, from all the remainder of Israel, from all Judah and Benjamin, and from *the citizens* of Jerusalem. 10 They delivered [it] to the workmen, who were commissioned, for the house of Yahweh and the workmen delivered it to those who worked on the house of Yahweh for repairing and refurbishing the temple—11 they delivered it to the craftsmen and builders for the purchase of hewn stones and lumber for beams to undergird the buildings which the kings of Judah had allowed to decay. 12 The men did the work faithfully; their foremen were Jahath and Obadiah, the Levites of the Merarite line and Zechariah and Meshullam, of the Kehathite line, who exercised supervision. The Levites—all of whom were expert with musical instruments—13 had charge of the burden-bearers and supervised all the workmen from job to job. Some of the Levites also served as scribes, officials, and porters.

Discovery of the lawbook

14 In the course of bringing out the money that had been contributed for the house of Yahweh, Hilkiah the priest found the book of the law of Yahweh given by Moses. 15 Hilkiah spoke as follows to Shaphan the scribe, "I have found the book of the law in the house of Yahweh"; then Hilkiah gave the book to Shaphan, 16 and Shaphan brought the book to the king and also gave him the further report: "Everything that has been entrusted to your servants they have done. 17 They have poured out the money that was found in the house of Yahweh and placed it in the hands of the supervisors and in the hands of the workmen." 18 Shaphan also told the king, "Hilkiah the priest gave me a book." Shaphan then read from it in the presence of the king. 19 When the king heard the words of the law, he tore his garments. 20 Then the king gave the following order

a–a MT, Qere "and they returned"; Kethib "citizens"; so also LXX and Vulg.

to Hilkiah, Ahikam the son of Shaphan, Abdon the son of Micah, Shaphan the scribe, and Asaiah the king's minister: 21 "Go and inquire of Yahweh on my behalf and on behalf of the remnant of Israel and of Judah about the words of the book that has been discovered; for great is the wrath of Yahweh which has been poured out upon us because our fathers did not observe the word of Yahweh by acting in harmony with everything prescribed in this book."

Prophecy of Huldah

22 So Hilkiah and those whom the king *ʰhad designatedʰ* went to Huldah the prophetess, the wife of Shallum, the son of Tokhath, the son of Hasrah the keeper of the wardrobe, who lived in the second quarter of Jerusalem and spoke to her about this. 23 She replied to them, "Thus has Yahweh God of Israel said: Tell the man who sent you to me, 24 Thus has Yahweh said: Behold I am going to bring evil upon this place and all its citizens, all the curses recorded in the book which they have read in the presence of the king of Judah; 25 because they have abandoned me and burnt incense to other gods so as to provoke me to anger by all the works of their hands, my wrath shall be poured out on this place and it cannot be quenched. 26 And as for the king of Judah who sent you to inquire of Yahweh, thus shall you say to him: Thus has Yahweh God of Israel said, As for the words which you heard—27 because your heart has become tender and you humbled yourself before God when you heard his words concerning this place and its citizens, and you humbled yourself before me, tore your garments and wept before me, I have taken cognizance: the oracle of Yahweh. 28 Behold when I gather you to your fathers, you shall be gathered to your grave in peace so that your eyes shall not look upon all the evil which I am going to bring upon this place and its citizens." Then they brought back the report to the king.

ᵇ–ᵇ Add with LXX.

Response of king and people

29 So the king called together all the elders of Judah and Jerusalem. 30 Then the king, together with all the men of Judah, the citizens of Jerusalem, the priests, the Levites, and all the [other] people, great and small, went up to the house of Yahweh where he read in their hearing all the words of the book of the covenant discovered in the house of Yahweh. 31 The king standing in his place then entered into the covenant before Yahweh to follow Yahweh, to observe his commandments, testimonies and statutes with all his mind and soul and to carry out the terms of the covenant as prescribed in this book. 32 He made all those present at Jerusalem, and Benjamin, stand [by it]; the citizens of Jerusalem acted in accordance with the covenant of God, the God of their fathers. 33 Josiah removed all the abominations from all the territories belonging to the Israelites and required all present in Israel to serve Yahweh their God; throughout his life they did not deviate from following Yahweh God of their fathers.

NOTES

xxxiv 3. *in the twelfth year*. Ca. 628 B.C.

6. *their plazas*. Reading *birḥōbōtēhem* for *beḥar bōtēhem*.

8. *the mayor*. Literally "captain of the city."

the speaker. See my *I Chronicles*, Sec. 20, NOTE on xviii 15 f.

9. *delivered*. Rudolph reads "poured out," as in vs. 17.

10. *the workmen*. I.e., the building committee.

14–15. For examples of the book of the law, see ANET, p. 495a.

20. *Abdon the son of Micah*. II Kings xxii 12 reads "Achbor son of Micaiah."

21. *the remnant*. The situation in the time of the Chronicler. See parallel in II Kings xxii 13.

22. *Tokhath, the son of Hasrah*. II Kings xxii 14 reads "Tikvah son of Ḥarḥas" (perhaps a non-Semitic name). Chronicles is to be preferred here. Cf. Noth, IPN, p. 260.

the second quarter. Usually regarded as the northern extension of the city. See M. Burrows, JBL 54 (1935), 37 f. for possible connection with y^{e}šānāh gate of Neh iii 6.

31. *in his place.* Cf. xxiii 13—the cultic place of the king in the temple.

32. *and Benjamin.* Rudolph reads "by the covenant" for Benjamin, but without any textual evidence in either MT or the versions. The idea of "standing" has a double significance—to stand in their cultic position (cf. xxxv 5) and to stand by the covenant.

COMMENT

[Introductory statement, xxxiv 1–2]: With the exception of the omission of Josiah's mother's name, this passage follows almost exactly the parallel in II Kings xxii 1–2.

[Removal of offenses, 3–7]: This important pericope has hitherto been viewed with unwarranted skepticism, partly because there is no reference to it elsewhere and partly because it appears to follow the regular pattern of reform movements taking place in the earlier reigns of Asa (xv 8–15) and Hezekiah (xxix). While there is some schematization here, there is no reason to suspect the basic elements involved. Since the writer was concerned primarily with religious matters, he naturally stresses the removal of foreign cult objects and the institution of regular, authentic rites—all of which took some time, though they tend to be telescoped. The chronological data is so reasonable in itself that it is difficult to see how the episode can be seriously questioned. During the early years of Josiah, the kingdom was under a regency, which must have been characterized by moderation, to judge from the action of the people of the land after the death of Amon. If the preaching of Zephaniah is connected with events dating between 630–625 B.C., Josiah's early piety (at the age of sixteen) is quite credible (Eissfeldt, *Einleitung in das Alte Testament,* p. 572; C. Kuhl, *The Prophets of Israel* [1960], p. 95; cf. Bright, *A History of Israel,* pp. 297–300, for an excellent description of the situation). The first overt move began four years later (ca. 628 B.C.) when there was a noticeable decline in the fortunes of Assyria during the last years of Asshurbanipal. For a discussion of the political conditions, see F. M. Cross, Jr., and D. N. Freedman, "Josiah's Revolt against Assyria," JNES 12 (1953),

11

56–58. The chronology needs some revision, but the basic arguments remain. Asshurbanipal died in 627/26 B.C. See C. J. Gadd in *Anatolian Studies,* VIII, 1958, pp. 70 f. There was probably no immediate effort to extend his purge of the high places beyond Judah, that is, before the death of Asshurbanipal. But soon after that event, Josiah apparently assumed the obligation of caretaker of the territory of Israel, perhaps at first as a vassal for Assyria. As a loyal and patriotic son of Israel his ambition was to claim his people for Yahweh, and perhaps to be a second David. Hezekiah had interested himself in the religion of the people of the north; Josiah followed in his footsteps but with far more propitious times in his favor. (On Josiah's Northern reformation with its political overtones, see *Studies in Old Testament Prophecy,* ed. H. H. Rowley, 1950, p. 165.) The first steps toward restoration of the land to Yahweh were taken in Judah and Jerusalem, where Josiah was in complete control. This is a sure indication that there was no effective reformation under Manasseh, as the Chronicler asserts. Then he extended his command into the territory of the former Northern Kingdom—as far as Naphtali, that is, to the northern border of the land. The Hebrew inscriptions found near Yavneh-yam, dating from the seventh century B.C., point to Judean control in the area at the time and help to substantiate the biblical witness to Josiah's political activities. (See J. Naveh, "A Hebrew Letter from the Seventh Century B.C.," IEJ 10 [1960], 129–39.) The destruction of the Bethel cult, long a rival of Jerusalem, must have been one of the aims of the young king (II Kings xxiii 15).

[Temple repairs, 8–13]: Six years later Josiah undertook a temple reconstruction program, necessary according to the Chronicler because it had fallen upon lean times under Manasseh and Amon. A similar program followed the reign of Ahaz (xxix 3). The king took the initiative in the temple work, as David had done in the plans for the original building; he sent the three top officials to negotiate with the religious authorities and to deliver the funds for the enterprise. Compare the view of the Deuteronomist in II Kings xxii 4 ff. The royal officials were sent to supervise the emptying of the offering chest (cf. II Kings xii 11; II Chron xxiv 11). According to II Kings xxii 3 Shaphan was the royal secretary. II Kings xxiii 8 speaks of a Jehoshua as the mayor of the city. However, in the II Kings parallel passage only Shaphan is mentioned. For a discussion of the functions of these officials, see NOTE on I Chron xviii 15 f. and R. de Vaux, *Les Institutions de l'Ancien Testament,* I, 1958, pp. 201–3, 211 f.

Since the kings of Judah had permitted the deterioration of the temple (vs. 11), Josiah now took the necessary steps to repair the damage. II Kings xxii 4 asserts that the money had been collected by the porters at the temple's gates. The Chronicler, on the other hand, speaks of the Levites collecting the funds from Manasseh, Ephraim, all the rest of Israel, Judah, and Benjamin and the citizens of Jerusalem. Perhaps he thinks of them as accompanying Josiah on his mission of purification and collecting as they proceeded. It may be that he is sermonizing here, stressing his favorite theme of all Israel having a share in the temple as the true center of worship for the entire nation. The whole project, as the organization shows, was well planned in advance. The Levites were the chief functionaries, though only two classes appear here, the Merarites and Kehathites. The Gershunnites are not mentioned. (For the reasons, see Möhlenbrink, ZAW 52 [1934], 213, and Rudolph, pp. 322 f. For references to musical accompaniment in building, see Rudolph, p. 323.)

[Discovery of the lawbook, 14–21]: More nearly in line with the story of II Kings, the Chronicler now connects the discovery of the lawbook with the emptying of the money chests. From vss. 15–33 he follows the Deuteronomist closely. Verse 18 says that Shaphan read from only part of a larger book (see Goettsberger, p. 376), whereas II Kings xxii 10 apparently reflects a more accurate view: the whole book was read to the king. Verse 21 reflects the period of the writer rather than that of Josiah.

[Prophecy of Huldah, 22–28]: For the names of those who accompanied Hilkiah see II Kings xxii 14. The prophecy delivered by Huldah was an uncomfortable one as may be seen from the substitution of "all the curses" for "all the words"; this may be a more specific application of Deut xxvii, xxix 20. The prophecy concerning the peaceful end of Josiah was not fulfilled (xxxv 23 f.). Yet the Chronicler did not revise the prophecy. There were, however, two aspects to it, and one was realized: that he would not see the destruction of the city and nation. It is rather remarkable that prophecies were faithfully preserved intact regardless of conformity in detail to what was known to have happened.

[Response of king and people, 29–33]: The response of the

king was to summon the elders of Judah and Jerusalem for consultation, the outcome of which was the decision to renew the covenant. The Chronicler here follows quite closely the Deuteronomic source, which limits the participants, with the officials, to the men of Judah and Jerusalem. Only one significant variant occurs—in vs. 30 when the Levites replace the prophets of II Kings xxiii 2. A. R. Johnson thinks this reflects the time of the writer when the cult prophets were the singers who in turn were merged with the Levites (*The Cultic Prophet in Ancient Israel,* pp. 60 f., and note on p. 64). The ceremony of covenant renewal was cultic in character and consisted of a procession to the temple, the reading of the terms of the covenant and the solemn oath taken by the king in the presence of the people. Following the king's covenanting, the people were pledged also to stand by it. Cazelles, p. 234, n. b., points out the cultic aspects involved in this statement, that is, the liturgical position (standing in their place as the king stood in his) of the people. The last part of vs. 32 and all of vs. 33 is a typical expansion of the writer in which he particularly makes the covenant apply to all Israel.

39. THE REIGN OF JOSIAH (640–609 B.C.): THE PASSOVER
(xxxv 1–19)†

XXXV ¹ Then Josiah celebrated a passover to Yahweh at Jerusalem. They slaughtered the passover on the fourteenth day of the first month. ² He assigned the priests to their posts and encouraged them in the service of the house of Yahweh. ³ He also said to the Levites who were the instructors of all Israel [and] were dedicated to Yahweh: "Put the sacred ark in the house which Solomon, the son of David, the king of Israel constructed; you need no longer carry it around on your shoulders. Now serve Yahweh your God and his people Israel! ⁴ Prepare yourselves by families in accordance with your divisions and in harmony with the decree of David the king of Israel and the decree of Solomon his son. ⁵ Stand in the sanctuary according to the family divisions of your brothers, the laity, ᵃso that for each family division there may be Levites.ᵃ ⁶ Slaughter the passover, consecrate yourselves and prepare [it] so that your brothers may observe it in accordance with the word of Yahweh through Moses." ⁷ Josiah contributed for the laity sheep, lambs, and young goats—everything for the passover for those present—to the number of thirty thousand, together with three thousand head of cattle; these came from the king's property. ⁸ His officials also contributed voluntarily for the people, the priests and the Levites; and Hilkiah, Zechariah, and Jehiel, the chiefs of the house of God, gave two thousand six hundred [lambs] and three hundred head of cattle to the priests for the passover offerings. ⁹ Conaniah, Shemaiah, Nethanel his brother, Hashabiah, Jeiel, and Jozabad, the Levitical chiefs, contributed five thou-

† II Chron xxxv 1–19 ‖ II Kings xxiii 21–23.

ᵃ⁻ᵃ MT is difficult, but this appears to be the meaning.

sand [lambs] and five hundred head of cattle to the Levites for the passover offerings. 10 So the service was prepared and the priests took their place and the Levites [occupied] their divisions in accordance with the command of the king. 11 Then they slaughtered the passover and while the priests sprinkled some of the blood[b] received from them, the Levites did the skinning. 12 Next they put aside the burnt offering for presentation to the family divisions of the laity that they might offer it to Yahweh in accordance with the prescription of the book of Moses; they did the same with the cattle. 13 They roasted the passover on fire in accordance with the regulation and boiled the consecrated offerings in pots, kettles,[c] and pans and brought them speedily to all the laity. 14 Afterwards they provided for themselves and the priests, for the Aaronite priests were engaged in offering burnt offerings and fat until night; thus did the Levites provide for themselves and for the Aaronite priests. 15 The Asaphite singers occupied their place according to the command of David and Asaph, Heman and Jeduthun, the king's seer; so did the porters at each gate; because they could not leave their duties, their brothers the Levites provided for them. 16 So all the service of Yahweh was prepared that day for the celebration of the passover and the offering of the burnt offering on the altar of Yahweh as King Josiah had commanded. 17 At that time the Israelites who were present celebrated the passover and the festival of unleavened bread for seven days. 18 There was not celebrated a passover like it in Israel since the days of Samuel the prophet, nor did any of the kings celebrate such a passover as Josiah, the priests, the Levites, all Judah and Israel who were present, and the citizens of Jerusalem celebrated. 19 This passover was celebrated in the eighteenth year of Josiah's reign.[d]

[b] Added with LXX.
[c] Heb. *dwd*—see PEQ (1939), 80 f.
[d] LXX inserts here II Kings xxiii 24–27. Cf. also I Esdras i 23–24. For discussion see Rudolph, pp. 329–31.

NOTES

xxxv 1. I Esdras begins its history with Josiah's passover. See Rudolph, *Esra und Nehemia*, p. xiv.

3. *you . . . shoulders.* The meaning is that since the ark had been deposited in the temple (I Chron xxiii 25 f.) the Levites no longer functioned as gatekeepers (I Chron xv 15, xxiii 28 f.) but as assistants to the priests with regularly assigned duties. For rendering, see Rudolph, Galling (*Die Bucher der Chronik, Esra, Nehemia* [see Selected Bibliography, Commentaries]), Rehm, and Ehrlich (*Randglossen zur hebräischen Bibel*, VII)—"Since the sacred ark has been placed . . . you need no longer. . . . Now therefore. . . ."

8. *Hilkiah, . . . God.* Three persons share the title *nāgīd*, "chief" of the house of God. Cf. I Chron ix 11; II Chron xxxi 13; Neh xi 11, where only one person bears it.

9. The names "Conaniah" and "Jozabad" occur also in xxxi 12–13, though not of the same persons.

11. *they.* I.e., the Levites.

13. *roasted.* Literally "boil in the fire." A conflation of Exod xii 8 f., which requires roasting, and Deut xvi 7, which requires boiling.

COMMENT

Verse 1 is based on the tradition transmitted in II Kings xxiii 21, though it is rewritten. Here the king acts for the nation, whereas in Kings he gives the command to his officials and the people. The Chronicler specifies the proper time (Lev xxiii 5), rather than the exceptions made by Hezekiah (xxx 2 f.). Like the latter's celebration, the passover was held at Jerusalem in accordance with the general interpretation of Deuteronomy (xvi 5 f.). No reference is made to "the book of this covenant" (II Kings xxiii 21) because the Chronicler regards Josiah's passover as following the pattern established by Hezekiah and hence is nothing new.

Verses 2–19, absent in Kings, offer a description of this great event (cf. II Kings xxiii 22). As in the case of Hezekiah, appointment and encouragement of religious officials precedes the actual ceremony. The priests were assigned to their posts (i.e., their cultic

positions) and exhorted specially to carry out their service in connection with the temple. The priests required special urging, as noted
elsewhere (xxix 34, xxx 3); for the Chronicler, who is not very well
inclined toward them, this was an important point.

The Levites, too, were assigned their functions. But, as the text
now stands, they went about their job of instructing the people—
for the Chronicler, one of the duties of the Levites was to teach
the people (cf. xvii 8; Neh viii 7 f.) out of the torah, a function
earlier devolving upon the priests (cf. Hos iv 6; Jer v 31, xviii 18)
—and were dedicated (I Esdras i 3 has the imperative here); this
is another illustration of the Chronicler's favoritism. But the Levites
had other duties since the time of David (I Chron xvi 4, 41, vi 16 f.
[vi 31 E f.]; xxiii 4 ff.). Their obligations are then enumerated:
they are to arrange themselves by families into appointed divisions
according to the decrees of David and Solomon (cf. viii 14) and be
ready in the court of the temple to render their service to the laity
as the situation required. Their service was to kill the passover lamb
and prepare it for the people while the priests took care of the blood.
Rudolph, p. 325, is doubtless correct in saying that the emergency
functions carried out by the Levites in the time of Hezekiah (xxx
17) were now normalized. The Levitical regulations here set forth
obtained beyond the Josiah passover (see Goettsberger, p. 381, as
opposed to von Rad, *Gesammelte Studien* . . . , pp. 248 f.). In
any case, the Chronicler's conception of the Levitical service was
not a degradation as in Ezek xliv 10–14.

An important phase in the preparation for the passover was the
provision of sacrificial animals. The enormous number (highly exaggerated) is intended to suggest the liberality of the providers and
possibly the great concourse of people participating in the ceremonies. For the figures, see references in Rudolph, pp. 326 f. The
fact that sheep, lambs, goats, and cattle were provided seems to
indicate that provision was made for both passover and peace offerings. The proportion of small cattle to large cattle is interesting—
ten to one, except for the animals provided by the chiefs of the
house of God.

The preparation began with the priests and Levites occupying
their stations—the former at the altar, the latter in the court at the
service of the families participating in the passover. The Levites
slaughtered the passover animals and then passed the blood to the

priests who sprinkled it upon the altar. The blood could no longer be disposed of in the customary way (Exod xii 7), since the Deuteronomic centralization law required the passover to be eaten at the sanctuary. Meanwhile the Levites did the skinning and the separation of the portions (of the cattle) for the burnt offering (vs. 14). Apparently both the paschal animals and the cattle were slaughtered at the same time (cf. vs. 16; the sprinkling of the blood and the burning of the fat pieces is characteristic of the burnt offering). While the passover was roasting, the consecrated offerings were boiled; the Levites seem to have been active in that task. The priests were occupied with the burnt offerings; hence the provision for both priests and Levites was set aside until their tasks were completed. Moreover, the musicians and porters were occupied at their respective posts so that the Levites had to provide for them too. All in all, there can be no doubt about the writer's feeling for the Levites—they were present everywhere and played a significant role in every phase of the celebration. This really is the new emphasis the Chronicler brings to the celebration. Another noticeable feature is the combination of the passover with the burnt offering.

Verse 18 is a somewhat altered version of II Kings xxiii 22, with additions, and the substitution of Samuel for the judges. The writer may have had in mind Josh v 10 after which the passover remained a family rite, until this time. Evidently the meaning of the verse is that precedents antedate the foundation of the kingdom. De Vaux (*Les Institutions de l'Ancien Testament,* II, 1960, p. 388) thinks there may have been such celebrations at a central cult shrine in premonarchial times. Certain features of the Chronicler's treatment stand out: (a) the command of the king (vss. 10, 16); (b) the decrees of David and Solomon; (c) reference to Moses (twice). He has combined the commands of Moses dealing with the passover and burnt offering and the Davidic and Solomonic decrees relating to the Levites. For further discussion see Rudolph, p. 329.

The final verse of the section parallels II Kings xxiii 23, though a portion of the latter, "in Jerusalem," was transferred to vs. 1.

40. THE REIGN OF JOSIAH (640–609 B.C.):
THE LATER YEARS
(xxxv 20–27)†

XXXV 20 After all this, when Josiah had provided for the
house, Neco the king of Egypt came up to fight at Carchemish
on the Euphrates and Josiah went out to engage him. 21 But
he sent messengers to him, saying, "What have we to do with
each other, O king of Judah; *I am not coming* against you
today but against the house with which I am carrying on war.
God has commanded me to move quickly, so forbear for your
own sake from interfering with God who is on my side, lest he
destroy you." 22 However, Josiah did not turn away but determined[b] to fight him; so he would not listen to the words of
Neco which issued from the mouth of God but went to fight
on the plain of Megiddo. 23 The archers shot King Josiah.
Then the king said to his servants, "Take me away for I am
seriously wounded." 24 So his servants took him out of his chariot and laid him on a second chariot which he had and brought
him to Jerusalem where he died and was buried in the cemetery
of his fathers. All Judah and Jerusalem held mourning rites
for Josiah. 25 Jeremiah composed a lamentation for Josiah, and
all the male and female singers lament for Josiah in their dirges
to this day and chant[c] them according to established custom
throughout Israel; they are recorded in the Lamentations. 26 The
remainder of the history of Josiah and his acts of devotion as

† **II Chron xxxv 20–27** ǁ II Kings xxiii 28–30.

a–a Reading *'anī 'ōteh*, with LXX, Vulg.
b MT "he disguised himself." LXX "he was determined"; I Esdras i 26 "he
attacked him"; Vulg. "he had prepared for war against him."
c The root here is *tnh* (piel=*yetannūm*), not *ntn* as MT. Cf. Judg xi 40; Ps
viii 2 (Ps viii 1E).

recorded in the law of Yahweh, 27 along with his acts from beginning to end, are recorded in the chronicle of the kings of Israel and Judah.

NOTES

xxxv 20. *the house.* I.e., the temple.

Neco . . . Euphrates. The parallel passage in Kings is not clear; "Carchemish" is omitted (but cf. Jer xlvi 2, dated in the reign of Jehoia-kim). Carchemish was the main military base of the Egyptians during the period of control over Syria-Palestine. See also Josephus *Antiquities* X.v.1. Cf. M. Noth, "Die Einnahme von Jerusalem im Jahre 597 v. Chr.," ZDPV 74 (1958), 143 f. Verses 20–24 appear more reliable than II Kings xxiii 28–30—Malamat, JNES 9 (1950), 220, n. 14.

21. *the house.* Bēt milḥamtī has never been satisfactorily explained. I Esdras i 25 has *Perath,* "Euphrates." J. Lewy ("Forschungen zur alten Geschichte Vorderasiens," MVAG 29 [1925], 21) thinks it refers to the permanent encampment of the pharaoh in Syria, or his front line position. B. Alfrink ("Die Schlacht bei Megiddo und der Tod Josias," *Biblica* 15 [1934]) renders "Kriegsstadt, Garnisonsstadt, Festungsstadt."

24. *a second chariot.* Doubtless a chariot carrying supplies.

COMMENT

We know next to nothing about Josiah's movements between the reformation and the time of his death. It seems fairly certain that he organized and strengthened the administration, to judge from the extensive use of the scroll-type stamps. Cf. Diringer, BA 12 (1949), 74–76; Tufnell, *Lachish III: The Iron Age,* tables on pp. 346 f.— 161 out of a total of 492 of these stamps belong to this type, to which must be added the 68 from el-Jib (*Hebrew Inscriptions and Stamps from Gibeon,* ed. J. B. Pritchard, 1959, pp. 18 ff.). The battle at Megiddo in which he was mortally wounded took place in 609 B.C. (cf. W. F. Albright, BASOR 143 [1956], 31 f.). That a battle took place as implied by the Chronicler seems to be indicated by the excavations at Megiddo where stratum II suffered some destruction (Lamon and Shipton, *Megiddo,* I, p. 87; W. F. Albright, *The Archaeology of Palestine* [Penguin Books, revised and reprinted, 1960], p. 130). Cf. D. N. Freedman, BA 19 (1956), 53, n. 10. For date see also H. Tadmor, JNES 15 (1956), 228.

According to the Chronicler, Pharaoh Neco was on an urgent mission to assist the Assyrians, whose forces were poised to recross the Euphrates in an attempt to retake Harran (Wiseman, *Chronicles of Chaldaean Kings,* p. 19; cf. A. Dupont-Sommer, *Semitica* 1 [1948], 55 ff.). There was an Egyptian garrison at Carchemish which withstood the Babylonians until 605 B.C. Neco was thus going to Carchemish (the Chronicler has correctly transmitted the course of events) to reinforce his garrison and assist the Assyrians. Josiah was apparently an ally of the Babylonians and thus attempted to impede the march of Neco and he may have succeeded better than he knew, for the Assyro-Egyptian forces were thwarted in their endeavor to retake Harran (Wiseman, *loc. cit.,* and p. 63).

Neco was on a divine mission, that is, of his god, for he certainly did not recognize Yahweh (Rudolph, pp. 331 f.; B. Couroyer, RB 55 [1948], 388 ff.). However, the Chronicler probably understands the meaning to be Yahweh (as I Esdras i 27 f.). If an Egyptian deity was involved, Josiah rightly refused to listen, but Yahweh sometimes used foreign rulers to carry out his plans (cf. Isa xlv 1; Jer xxvii 6) and the author of I Esdras i 28 interprets the warning as coming from Jeremiah. Verse 22 is quite definite —the words of Neco issued from the mouth of God, that is, Yahweh. Josiah failed to heed the warning and thus lost his life. His death evoked profound sorrow throughout the nation and was the occasion for an extended period of mourning. The lamentation said to have been composed by Jeremiah is no longer extant. The mention of Lamentations in vs. 25b in all probability is meant to suggest that it was included in our Book of Lamentations, which may indeed have been part of a collection of such dirges. But that work does not now have it nor is it to be found in the Book of Jeremiah. According to I Esdras i 33 it was preserved in the official history of the kings of Judah. The death of Josiah is said to have been celebrated regularly in a memorial service.

41. THE REIGNS OF JEHOAHAZ (609 B.C.), JEHOIAKIM (609–598 B.C.), AND JEHOIACHIN (598 B.C.) (xxxvi 1–10)†

The reign of Jehoahaz

XXXVI 1 Then the people of the land took Jehoahaz the son of Josiah and made him king at Jerusalem in place of his father. 2 Jehoahaz was twenty-three years old when he became king and he reigned three months at Jerusalem.ᵃ 3 The king of Egypt deposed him at Jerusalem and laid the land under [tribute to the extent of] a hundred talents of silver and a talent of gold.

The reign of Jehoiakim

4 The king of Egypt then made Eliakim his brother king over Judah and Jerusalem and changed his name to Jehoiakim; but Neco took along Jehoahaz his brother and brought him to Egypt.ᵇ 5 Jehoiakim was twenty-five years old when he became king and reigned eleven years at Jerusalem. He did what was evil in the sight of Yahweh his God. 6 Nebuchadnezzar the king of Babylon came up against him and bound him in bronze chains to bring him to Babylon. 7 Nebuchadnezzar also brought some of the articles of the house of Yahweh to Babylon and put them in his palace at Babylon. 8 The remainder of the history of Jehoiakim, the abominations of which he was guilty, and what happened to him [because of them] are recorded in the chronicle of the kings of Israel and Judah. Jehoiachin his son became king in his place.

† **II Chron xxxvi 1–3** ‖ II Kings xxiii 30b–33; **4–8** ‖ II Kings xxiii 34–xxiv 7; **9–10** ‖ II Kings xxiv 8–17.

ᵃ LXX inserts II Kings xxiii 31b–33a here.
ᵇ LXX, on the basis of the Kings parallel, adds "and he died there." Between verses 4 and 5 it inserts a version of II Kings xxiii 35.

The reign of Jehoiachin

9 Jehoiachin was eight years* old when he became king and reigned for three months and ten days at Jerusalem. He also did what was evil in the sight of Yahweh. 10 At the turn of the year King Nebuchadnezzar sent and brought him to Babylon together with the costly articles of the house of Yahweh, and made Zedekiah his brother king over Judah and Jerusalem.

*LXX and II Kings xxiv 8 read "eighteen years," obviously correct. See NOTE.

NOTES

xxxvi 3. *a hundred talents of silver*. About 3¾ tons.

a talent of gold. About 75½ lbs.

4. *changed his name to Jehoiakim*. On double name, see NOTE on xxvi 1, Sec. 28.

6. This must be the episode referred to in Dan i 1 f. The Chronicler's reference is independent and certainly much older than Daniel. Perhaps there is some historical foundation to the story after all. Neither story is clear about what actually happened to Jehoiakim. Both distinctly indicate that the temple vessels were brought to Babylon, but they do not say explicitly that Jehoiakim was taken to Babylon. He may only have been threatened by Nebuchadnezzar and frightened into submission by being put into chains. See Rudolph, p. 335.

8. *what . . . him*. Literally "what was found against him."

9. *eight years old*. See textual note *. Jehoiachin already had five sons in 592 B.C. (E. Weidner, *Mélanges Syriens offert à Monsieur René Dussaud*, II, pp. 925 f.) which means that at least one of them was born in Jerusalem before 597 B.C., unless he had more than one wife (cf. W. F. Albright, "King Jehoiachin in Exile," BA 5 [1942], 53; and II Kings xxiv 15).

10. *At . . . year*. II Kings xxiv 10 reads "at that time," a much less definite phrase.

brother. II Kings xxiv 17, "uncle," is correct (cf. Jer xxxvii 1). He was perhaps chosen because Jehoiachin had no available sons at the time (cf. II Kings xxiv 15; Jer xxii 30).

COMMENT

[The reign of Jehoahaz, xxxvi 1–3]: After the untimely death of Josiah, the 'am hā-'āreṣ (see Würthwein, *Der 'amm* . . . , pp. 33–36) acted quickly to fill the vacancy by putting Jehoahaz on the throne. The Chronicler does not give the name of his mother nor any characterization of him. There is no reference to his being put in chains at Riblah, though there is to his exile in Egypt (vs. 4b). The heavy tribute laid upon the land is mentioned but not the method by which it was collected or from whom (cf. II Kings xxiii 35). It should be noted that Jehoahaz was the last king of Judah invested by the people. Henceforth Egypt and Babylon appointed the kings, though the Davidic line remained intact until after the final siege of Jerusalem. Jehoiakim was probably regarded as regent for the captive king until his death.

[The reign of Jehoiakim, 4–8]: Josiah, like Hezekiah before him, was beholden to the Babylonians. Jehoiakim began as an Egyptian vassal and remained so until after the battle of Carchemish in 605 B.C. (for an idea of conditions in Judah in the interim, see Jer xxiii 13–19). A year later Nebuchadnezzar's army appeared at Ashkelon, where a severe engagement took place that resulted in the devastation of the city (Wiseman, *Chronicles of Chaldaean Kings,* p. 69) and the deportation of its inhabitants. Cf. an Aramaic letter to the pharaoh, which may have come from the king of Ashkelon (H. L. Ginsberg, BASOR 111 [October 1948], 24–27; Dupont-Sommer, *Semitica* 1 [1948], 43–68). Possibly in connection with that invasion, Jehoiakim shifted his allegiance to Babylon. Whether Nebuchadnezzar actually invaded Judah is uncertain; perhaps the news of his treatment of Ashkelon was enough (cf. Jer xlvi, but see Albright, BASOR 143 [1956], 31). Wiseman (*Chronicles of Chaldaean Kings,* pp. 28, 69) thinks Jehoiakim may have been one of the Hatti-land kings who appeared and paid tribute to Nebuchadnezzar in the first year of his reign. However, the Chronicler speaks here of an invasion during which Jehoiakim was thrown into chains and threatened with deportation. That was not the invasion of 598/97 since Jehoiakim was dead a hundred days before the capture of Jerusalem (vs. 9). Jehoiakim remained loyal to Babylon

only so long as there was no chance of desertion, but after the
Egyptians had fought Nebuchadnezzar to a draw in 601, he with-
held tribute. The great king revamped and strengthened his army
and returned in 598, laid the city under siege and captured it on
the second of Adar, 597, 15/16 of March by our calendar (Wiseman, *op. cit.*, p. 73—from the Babylonian Chronicle). The Chronicler's assessment of Jehoiakim coincides with that of Kings and
Jeremiah. There is no reference to his death and burial (cf. Jer
xxii 19, xxxvi 30).

[The reign of Jehoiachin, 9–10]: While the Chronicler omits
some of the details about Jehoiachin—his mother's name, the
given name of Zedekiah-Mattaniah, and the catalogue of classes
exiled—he presents others with great accuracy. The list of Jehoiachin's seven sons is given in I Chron iii 17–18. The Weidner texts
report five. The phrase "at the turn of the year" corresponds with
the new data given in the Babylonian Chronicle; the "heavy
tribute" of the latter supports the reference to the costly articles of
the house of God; and the Babylonian Chronicle's "king of his own
choice" is in line with the statement about Nebuchadnezzar's in-
vesting of Zedekiah as his vassal king over Jerusalem and Judah.
Jehoiachin was deported to Babylon, where he was apparently well
treated and finally released from custody (Jer lii 31–34).

On the Babylonian Chronicle, cf. Wiseman, *Chronicles of Chaldaean Kings,* pp. 34, 73; Noth, ZDPV 74 (1958), 133–57; F. X.
Kugler, *Von Moses bis Paulus,* 1922, pp. 147–50; A. Parrot, *Babylon and the Old Testament,* 1958, pp. 89 f.; Albright, BA 5 (1942),
49–55. Incidentally, the royal treatment received by Jehoiachin in
captivity encouraged the people of Judah to hope for his return to
power (Jer xxviii 4) and they probably looked on Zedekiah as
merely a regent. The seals bearing the inscription "Eliakim steward
of Yaukin" may refer to King Jehoiachin and thus indicate that the
royal property remained intact, administered for him by Eliakim.
Cf. W. F. Albright, JBL 51 (1932), 77–106 and BA 5 (1942),
50 f. Another seal with the same inscription impressed on a jar handle
has turned up at Ramat Rahel (*The Israel Digest,* Vol. 4, No. 18,
September 1, 1961, p. 8).

42. THE REIGN OF ZEDEKIAH (598–587 B.C.). THE EXILE
(xxxvi 11–21)†

XXXVI ¹¹Zedekiah was twenty-one years old when he became king and he reigned eleven years at Jerusalem. ¹²He too did what was evil in the sight of Yahweh his God; he did not humble himself before the prophet Jeremiah who spoke for Yahweh. ¹³Furthermore, he rebelled against King Nebuchadnezzar who had compelled him to swear [loyalty] by God. He became stubborn and set his mind resolutely against returning to Yahweh God of Israel. ¹⁴Even the chiefs of ᵃJudah,ᵃ the priests, and the people committed more and more offences, which were just like the abominations of the nations, and rendered unclean the house of Yahweh which he had consecrated at Jerusalem. ¹⁵Yahweh God of their fathers continuously sent [word] to them through his messengers because he had compassion on his people and on his dwelling place. ¹⁶But they ridiculed the messengers of God, despised his words, and mocked his prophets until the wrath of Yahweh became so violent against his people that there could be no redress. ¹⁷So he brought up against them the king of the Chaldeans, slew their young men with the sword in the house of their sanctuary, without compassion for young man, or virgin, or old man, or the infirm; he gave them all into his hand. ¹⁸All the articles of the house of God, both large and small, the treasures of the house of Yahweh, the treasures of the king and his officials, all of them he brought to Babylon. ¹⁹He burned down the house of God and broke down the wall of Jerusalem; he burned with fire its palaces and destroyed all its precious articles. ²⁰Those who es-

† II Chron xxxvi 11–21 ‖ II Kings xxiv 18–xxv 12.

ᵃ–ᵃ Add with LXX.

caped the sword he exiled to Babylon and they became slaves to him and his sons until the rise of the kingdom of Persia— [21] to fulfill the word of Yahweh through Jeremiah. Until the land had compensated for the neglect of its sabbaths, all the days of its desolation, it rested until the seventy years were complete.

NOTES

xxxvi 20. Cf. Jer xxvii 7 and vss. 22, 23 below (Sec. 43).

COMMENT

Only the barest outline of the history of Zedekiah is given. He was a full younger brother of Jehoahaz (II Kings xxiv 18; Jer lii 1) and hence the uncle of Jehoiachin. In a way, the important item about Zedekiah is that he too was a son of the revered Josiah, and doubtless picked in part for that reason. His eleven-year reign marked a period of vacillation and indecision due to the circumstances surrounding the status of Jehoiachin; the pro-Egyptian elements also may have had something to do with it since they may have been inspired by Psammeticus II and Hophra, both of whom had designs on Syria.

As always, the Chronicler is interested chiefly in the theological aspects of the story. This is the sermon of the writer informing his hearers of the reason for exile and at the same time pointing out the plan of Yahweh in which they are the participants. Chief blame for the debacle falls upon the king because he consistently refused to follow the directions of the prophets, notably Jeremiah (cf. Jer xxxvii 2). Although there is some indication in the Book of Jeremiah that Zedekiah was the captive of his own officials and vacillated considerably, the Chronicler rightly interprets the over-all picture, the king having lacked the strength to make any unequivocal declaration for Yahweh. The sum (and substance) of the matter was simply that the persistent preachments of the prophets met with equally persistent ridicule. Associated with the king were the officials (vs. 14)—really the powers behind the throne. They had relapsed into the same errors (cf. Jer xxxii 30–35) prevalent before Josiah's reform (cf. Ezek viii for an excellent illustration of idolatrous practices). In addition there was Zedekiah's rebellion against Nebuchadnezzar, who was declared by the prophets to be the instrument of Yahweh to chastise his people (cf. Ezek xvii 11–21; Jer xxv 19, xxvii 6–9). Thus Jerusalem was destroyed, the temple leveled, and the people taken into exile because of the wrath of Yahweh kindled by the refusal of king and officials to listen to his word. That was precisely what Jeremiah had predicted again and again (vs. 21). Whatever may be the precise significance of vs. 21b, the general import appears to be that the future was not without hope. The Exile was a purifying process carried out in line with the law (Lev xxvi 34 f., 43 f.) and the prophets (Jer xxv 11 ff., xxix 10). After the seventy years' rest, God moved again on behalf of his people. See R. Borger, JNES 18 (1959), 74; O. Plöger, "Siebzig Jahre," in *Festschrift Friedrich Baumgärtel*, 1959, pp. 124–30; W. F. Albright, FSAC, 1957, p. 18.

43. THE DECREE OF CYRUS (ca. 538 B.C.)
(xxxvi 22–23)†

XXXVI 22 In the first year of Cyrus, the king of Persia—to
fulfill the word of Yahweh through Jeremiah—Yahweh aroused
the spirit of Cyrus, the king of Persia, to make a proclamation
throughout all his kingdom which he also put in writing as follows: 23 "Thus has Cyrus the king of Persia said: Yahweh God
of the heavens has given me all the kingdoms of the earth and
he has appointed me to build for him a house in Jerusalem which
is in Judah. Whoever among you belongs to all his people, may
Yahweh his God be with him and let him go up."

† II Chron xxxvi 22–23 ‖ Ezra i 1–4.

NOTES

xxxvi 22. *Persia*. This is the first mention of Persia in any of the
historical and prophetical books, apart from Ezekiel (xxvii 10, xxxviii 5)
where the references are clearly to the Persia before the conquests of
Cyrus and before its emergence as a world power. Cf. the similar
references to Persia in the Assyrian inscriptions of the ninth–seventh
centuries B.C.

COMMENT

This is the connecting link between Chronicles and Ezra, where
these verses are repeated. Cyrus acts in harmony with the predic-
tions of Jeremiah (xxv 11 ff., xxix 10), only this time for salvation,
that is, the return and rehabilitation of the people. Verse 23 may
allude vaguely to Isa xliv 28.

APPENDIXES

APPENDIX I: PARALLELS

I Chronicles

i 1–4	Gen v
i 5–7	Gen x 2–4
i 8–16	Gen x 6–8, 13–18
i 17–28	Gen x 22–29, xi 14–26
i 29–31	Gen xxv 13–16
i 32–33	Gen xxv 2–4
i 34–37	Gen xxv 19, 24–26, xxxvi 10–19
i 38–42	Gen xxxvi 20–28
i 43–54	Gen xxxvi 31–43
ii 1–2	Gen xxxv 23–26
ii 3–9	Gen xxxviii 2–5, 7, 29, 30, xlvi 12; I Kings iv 31 (v 11H); Josh vii
ii 10–17	Num i 7; Ruth iv 19–22
ii 18–24	I Chron ii 42–49, 50–55
ii 25–41	cf. I Sam xxvii 10, xxx 29
ii 42–45	————
iii 1–9	II Sam iii 2–5; I Chron xiv 3–7
iii 10–24	————
iv 1–10	————
iv 11–20	Num xiii 6; Judg i 13
iv 21–23	————
iv 24–43	Gen xlvi 10; Num xxvi 12; Josh xix 1–8
v 1–3	Gen xxxv 22, xlvi 9; Exod vi 14; Num xxvi 5–6
v 4–22	————
v 23–26	cf. Num xxxii 39; II Kings xv 19 f., xvii 6, xviii 11
vi 1–15	Gen xlvi 11; Exod vi 18; Num xxvi 59, 60
vi 16–30	Num iii 17–20; I Sam i 1
vi 31–53	————
vi 54–81	Josh xxi
vii 1–5	Gen xlvi 13; Num xxvi 23–24
vii 6–12	Gen xlvi 21; Num xxvi 38–40

xx 1–30	——————
xx 31–34	I Kings xxii 41–47
xx 35–37	I Kings xxii 48–50
xxi 1	I Kings xxii 51
xxi 2–4	——————
xxi 5–11	II Kings viii 17–22
xxi 12–15	——————
xxi 16–20	II Kings viii 23–24
xxii 1–9	II Kings viii 24b–29, ix 21, 27–28
xxii 10–12	II Kings xi 1–3
xxiii 1–11	II Kings xi 4–12
xxiii 12–21	II Kings xi 13–20
xxiv 1–3	II Kings xii 1–4
xxiv 4–14	II Kings xii 5–16
xxiv 15–22	——————
xxiv 23–27	II Kings xii 18–22
xxv 1–4	II Kings xiv 2–6
xxv 5–16	II Kings xiv 7
xxv 17–28	II Kings xiv 8–20
xxvi 1–5	II Kings xiv 21–xv 4
xxvi 6–15	——————
xxvi 16–23	II Kings xv 5–7
xxvii 1–9	II Kings xv 32–38
xxviii 1–4	II Kings xvi 1–4
xxviii 5–8	II Kings xvi 5
xxviii 9–15	——————
xxviii 16–21	II Kings xvi 7–9
xxviii 22–27	II Kings xvi 19, 20
xxix 1–2	cf. II Kings xviii 1–3
xxix 3–36	——————
xxx 1–27	——————
xxxi 1–21	cf. II Kings xviii 4
xxxii 1–23	II Kings xviii 13–37, xix 14–19, 35–37; Isa xxxvi 1–22, xxxvii 14–19, 36–38
xxxii 24	II Kings xx 1–3; Isa xxxviii 1–3
xxxii 25–26	II Kings xx 12–19; Isa xxxix 1–8
xxxii 27–31	——————
xxxii 32–33	II Kings xx 20–21
xxxiii 1–10	II Kings xxi 1–10
xxxiii 11–17	——————
xxxiii 18–20	II Kings xxi 17–18
xxxiii 21–25	II Kings xxi 19–24

xxxiv 1–2   II Kings xxii 1–2
xxxiv 3–7   ————————
xxxiv 8–13   II Kings xxii 3–7
xxxiv 14–21   II Kings xxii 8–13
xxxiv 22–28   II Kings xxii 14–20
xxxiv 29–33   II Kings xxiii 1–3
xxxv 1–19   II Kings xxiii 21–23
xxxv 20–27   II Kings xxiii 28–30
xxxvi 1–3   II Kings xxiii 30b–33
xxxvi 4–8   II Kings xxiii 34–xxiv 7
xxxvi 9–10   II Kings xxiv 8–17
xxxvi 11–21   II Kings xxiv 18–xxv 12
xxxvi 22–23   Ezra i 1–4

APPENDIX II. GENEALOGICAL CHARTS

A. NOAH (I Chron i 5–23)

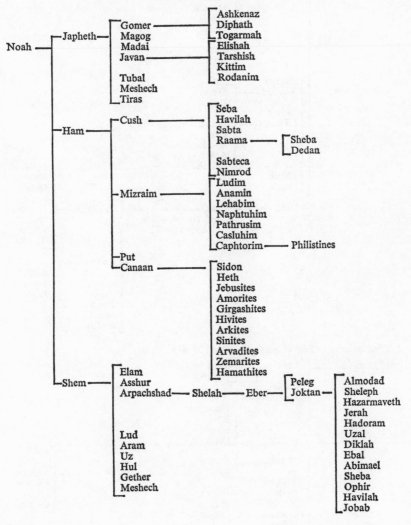

B. ABRAHAM'S DESCENDANTS

(Females designated by *italics*)

1. DESCENDANTS OF ABRAHAM (I Chron i 29–37)

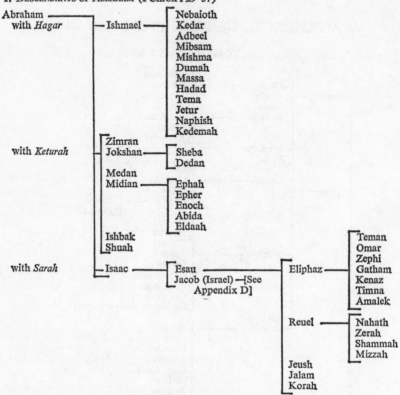

Abraham
with *Hagar* — Ishmael —
Nebaioth
Kedar
Adbeel
Mibsam
Mishma
Dumah
Massa
Hadad
Tema
Jetur
Naphish
Kedemah

with *Keturah* —
Zimran
Jokshan — Sheba, Dedan
Medan
Midian — Ephah, Epher, Enoch, Abida, Eldaah
Ishbak
Shuah

with *Sarah* — Isaac —
Esau —
Jacob (Israel) — [See Appendix D]

Eliphaz —
Teman
Omar
Zephi
Gatham
Kenaz
Timna
Amalek

Reuel —
Nahath
Zerah
Shammah
Mizzah

Jeush
Jalam
Korah

2. DESCENDANTS OF SEIR (EDOM) (I Chron i 38–42)

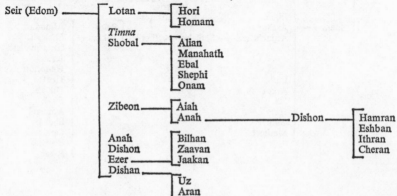

Seir (Edom) —
Lotan — Hori, Homam
Timna
Shobal — Alian, Manahath, Ebal, Shephi, Onam
Zibeon — Aiah, Anah — Dishon — Hamran, Eshban, Ithran, Cheran
Anah
Dishon
Ezer — Bilhan, Zaavan, Jaakan
Dishan — Uz, Aran

C. EDOM: KINGS AND CHIEFS

1. KINGS OF EDOM (I Chron i 43–50)

King	Father	City
Bela	Beor	Dinhabah
Jobab	Zerah	Bozrah
Husham		Teman
Hadad	Bedad	Avith
Samlah		Masrekah
Saul		Rehoboth
Baal-hanan	Achbor	
Hadad		Pai

2. CHIEFS OF EDOM (I Chron i 51–54)

Timna
Aliah
Jetheth
Oholibamah
Elah
Pinon
Kenaz
Teman
Mibzar
Magdiel
Iram

D. JACOB*

1. JACOB AND LEAH

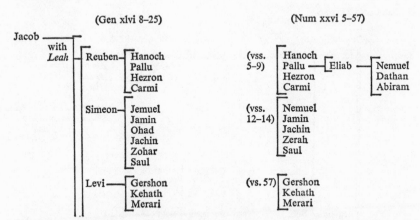

*The Chronicler gives the genealogy of each of Jacob's sons separately, as may be seen from the subsequent charts. This chart gives an over-all picture of the twelve tribes and how their lines of descent are handled in the Chronicler's sources: Gen xlvi 8–25 and Num xxvi 5–57. The order in which Jacob's sons appear in Genesis is listed at the left; the descendants of his sons, as they appear in Numbers, are listed at the right, with the verses in Num xxvi in which they occur. The order of their appearance in Numbers is as follows: Reuben, Simeon, Gad, Judah, Issachar, Zebulun, Manasseh, Ephraim, Benjamin, Dan, Asher, Naphtali, and Levi.

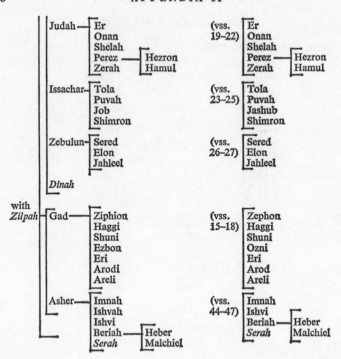

2. JACOB AND RACHEL

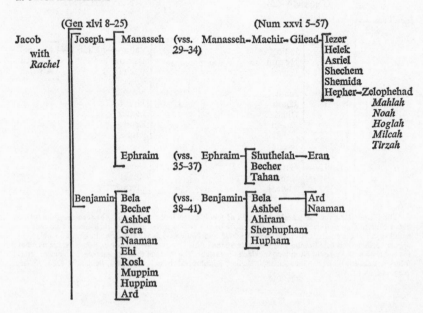

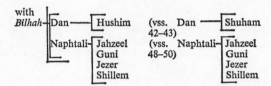

with
Bilhah—Dan———Hushim   (vss. Dan———Shuham
                          42–43)
        Naphtali—Jahzeel   (vss. Naphtali—Jahzeel
                  Guni   48–50)   Guni
                  Jezer   Jezer
                  Shillem   Shillem

E. THE LINE OF JUDAH

1. JUDAH (I Chron ii 3–8)

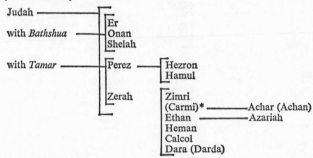

Judah ——————
                    ┌Er
with *Bathshua* ——— Onan
                    └Shelah

with *Tamar* ——— Perez ——— ┌Hezron
                           └Hamul

                Zerah   ┌Zimri
                           (Carmi)* ———————Achar (Achan)
                           Ethan ——————————Azariah
                           Heman
                           Calcol
                           └Dara (Darda)

2. ANCESTORS OF DAVID (ii 9–17)

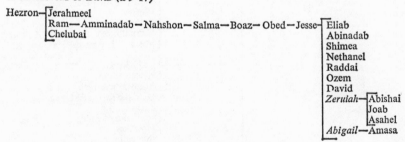

Hezron—┌Jerahmeel
        Ram—Amminadab—Nahshon—Salma—Boaz—Obed—Jesse—┌Eliab
       └Chelubai   Abinadab
                                                      Shimea
                                                      Nethanel
                                                      Raddai
                                                      Ozem
                                                      David
                                                      Zeruiah—┌Abishai
                                                                 Joab
                                                                └Asahel
                                                      Abigail—Amasa

F. CALEBITES

1. CALEBITES I (I Chron ii 18–24)

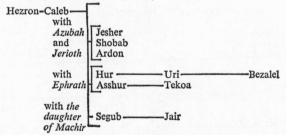

Hezron–Caleb———
    with   ┌Jesher
    Azubah   Shobab
    and   └Ardon
    Jerioth

    with   ┌Hur ———————Uri ——————————Bezalel
    Ephrath   └Asshur—————Tekoa

    with *the*
    daughter — Segub ————Jair
    of Machir

*Carmi not mentioned among the five sons of Zerah listed in vs. 6.

2. CALEBITES II (ii 42–49)

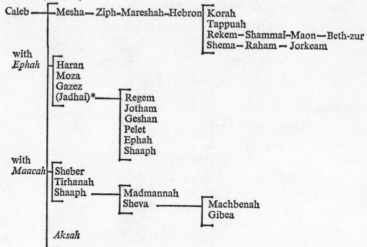

```
Caleb ——— Mesha — Ziph-Mareshah-Hebron ⌐Korah
                                         │Tappuah
                                         │Rekem — Shammai — Maon — Beth-zur
                                         └Shema — Raham — Jorkeam

         with      ⌐Haran
         Ephah     │Moza
                   │Gazez
                   │(Jadhai)* ——— ⌐Regem
                                  │Jotham
                                  │Geshan
                                  │Pelet
                                  │Ephah
                                  └Shaaph

         with      ⌐Sheber
         Maacah    │Tirhanah
                   │Shaaph ——— ⌐Madmannah
                               └Sheva ——— ⌐Machbenah
                                          └Gibea

                    Aksah
```

3. CALEBITES, THROUGH HUR (ii 50–55)

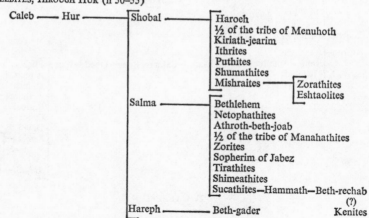

```
Caleb ——— Hur ——— ⌐Shobal ——— ⌐Haroeh
                   │           │½ of the tribe of Menuhoth
                   │           │Kiriath-jearim
                   │           │Ithrites
                   │           │Puthites
                   │           │Shumathites
                   │           └Mishraites ——— ⌐Zorathites
                   │                           └Eshtaolites
                   │Salma ——— ⌐Bethlehem
                   │          │Netophathites
                   │          │Athroth-beth-joab
                   │          │½ of the tribe of Manahathites
                   │          │Zorites
                   │          │Sopherim of Jabez
                   │          │Tirathites
                   │          │Shimeathites
                   │          └Sucathites — Hammath — Beth-rechab
                   │                                      (?)
                   └Hareph ——————— Beth-gader            Kenites
```

G. THE JERAHMEELITES (I Chron ii 25–41)

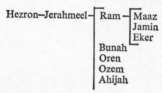

```
Hezron — Jerahmeel ⌐ Ram ⌐ Maaz
                   │       │Jamin
                   │       └Eker
                   │Bunah
                   │Oren
                   │Ozem
                   └Ahijah
```

*Jadhai not mentioned among the sons of Caleb by *Ephah* listed in vs. 46.

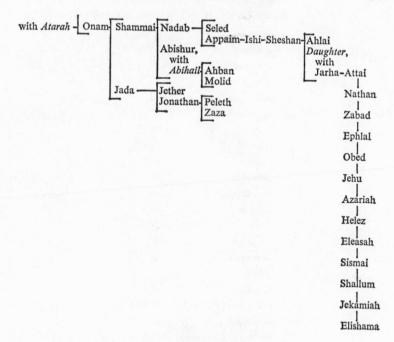

with *Atarah* – Onam – Shammai – Nadab – Seled
                                        Appaim – Ishi – Sheshan – Ahlai

Abishur,
with
Abihail – Ahban
             Molid

Jada – Jether
        Jonathan – Peleth
                     Zaza

Daughter,
with
Jarha – Attai
|
Nathan
|
Zabad
|
Ephlal
|
Obed
|
Jehu
|
Azariah
|
Helez
|
Eleasah
|
Sismai
|
Shallum
|
Jekamiah
|
Elishama

H. DAVID'S FAMILY (I Chron iii 1–9)

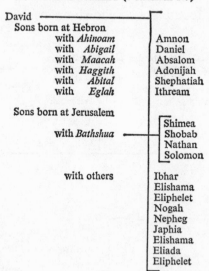

David

Sons born at Hebron

with *Ahinoam*	Amnon
with *Abigail*	Daniel
with *Maacah*	Absalom
with *Haggith*	Adonijah
with *Abital*	Shephatiah
with *Eglah*	Ithream

Sons born at Jerusalem

with *Bathshua* – Shimea
                   Shobab
                   Nathan
                   Solomon

with others – Ibhar
               Elishama
               Eliphelet
               Nogah
               Nepheg
               Japhia
               Elishama
               Eliada
               Eliphelet

I. KINGS OF JUDAH (I Chron iii 10–16)

Name	Age at Death
Solomon	?
Rehoboam	58
Abijah	?
Asa	?
Jehoshaphat	60
Joram	40
Ahaziah	23
Joash	47
Amaziah	54
Azariah (Uzziah)	68
Jotham	41
Ahaz	36
Hezekiah	54
Manasseh	67
Amon	24
Josiah	39
Jehoahaz (Jonathan)	23 +
Jehoiakim	36
Jehoiachin (Jeconiah)	18 +
Zedekiah	32

J. EXILIC AND POSTEXILIC LINE (I Chron iii 17–24)

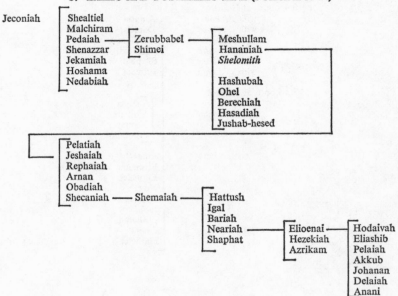

Jeconiah — Shealtiel, Malchiram, Pedaiah, Shenazzar, Jekamiah, Hoshama, Nedabiah

Pedaiah — Zerubbabel, Shimei

Zerubbabel — Meshullam, Hananiah, Shelomith, Hashubah, Ohel, Berechiah, Hasadiah, Jushab-hesed

Hananiah — Pelatiah, Jeshaiah, Rephaiah, Arnan, Obadiah, Shecaniah

Shecaniah — Shemaiah — Hattush, Igal, Bariah, Neariah, Shaphat

Neariah — Elioenai, Hezekiah, Azrikam

Elioenai — Hodaivah, Eliashib, Pelaiah, Akkub, Johanan, Delaiah, Anani

K. SOUTHERN FAMILIES

1. SOUTHERN FAMILY AT ZORAH (I Chron iv 1–2)

2.. SOUTHERN FAMILY OF BETHLEHEM (iv 3–4)

3. SOUTHERN FAMILY OF TEKOA (iv 5–10)

4. SOUTHERN FAMILY OF CALEB (iv 11–20)

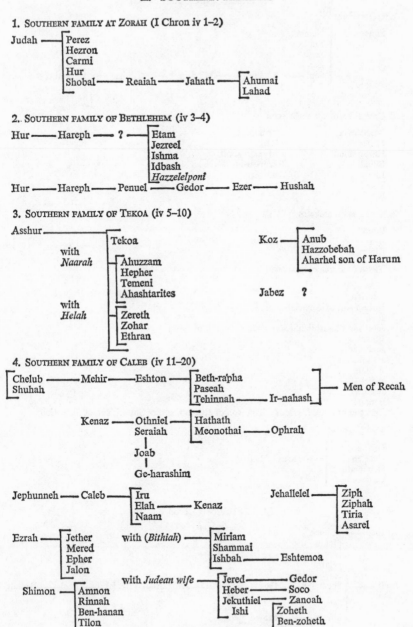

L. SIMEON (I Chron iv 24–43)

1. GENEALOGY

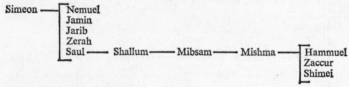

```
Simeon ──┬─ Nemuel
         │  Jamin
         │  Jarib
         │  Zerah
         └─ Saul ── Shallum ── Mibsam ── Mishma ──┬─ Hammuel
                                                   │  Zaccur
                                                   └─ Shimei
```

2. CITIES OCCUPIED BY SIMEON

Beer-sheba	Hormah
Moladah	Ziklag
Hazar-shual	Beth-marcaboth
Bilhah	Hazar-susim
Ezem	Beth-biri
Tolad	Shaaraim
Bethuel	

3. THEIR SETTLEMENTS

Etam	Tochen
Ain	Ashan
Rimmon	

4. THEIR OFFICIAL GENEALOGY

Meshobab
Jamlech
Joshah son of Amaziah
Joel
Jehu son of Joshibiah, son of Seraiah, son of Asiel
Elioenai
Jaakobah
Jeshohaiah
Asaiah
Adiel
Jesimiel
Benaiah
Ziza son of Shiphi, son of Allon, son of Jedaiah, son of Shimri, son of Shemaiah

5. THE LEADERS

```
Pelatiah ┐
Neariah  ├── sons of Ishi
Rephaiah │
Uzziel   ┘
```

M. REUBEN (I Chron v 1–10)

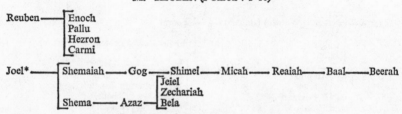

```
Reuben ──┬─ Enoch
         │  Pallu
         │  Hezron
         └─ Carmi

Joel* ──┬─ Shemaiah ── Gog ── Shimei ── Micah ── Reaiah ── Baal ── Beerah
        │                     Jeiel
        │                     Zechariah
        └─ Shema ── Azaz ── Bela
```

Territory occupied: Aroer; as far as Nebo and Baal-meon; Gilead.

*Syr. makes Joel the son of Carmi, but we cannot be sure.

N. GAD AND ½ MANASSEH

1. GAD (I Chron v 11–22)

a. Genealogy:

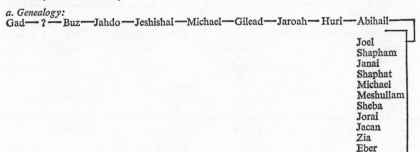

Gad— ? —Buz—Jahdo—Jeshishai—Michael—Gilead—Jaroah—Huri—Abihail—

Joel
Shapham
Janai
Shaphat
Michael
Meshullam
Sheba
Jorai
Jacan
Zia
Eber

b. Chief: Ahi, son of Abdiel, son of Guni.
c. Territory occupied: Gilead, Bashan, Sharon.

2. ½ MANASSEH (TRANSJORDAN) (v 23–26)

Chiefs: Epher, Ishi, Eliel, Azriel, Jeremiah, Hodaviah, Jahdiel.

O. CHIEF PRIESTS (I Chron vi 1–15)

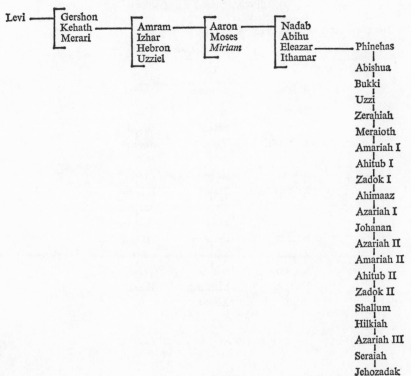

Levi — Gershon
Kehath
Merari — Amram
Izhar
Hebron
Uzziel — Aaron
Moses
Miriam — Nadab
Abihu
Eleazar — Phinehas
Ithamar

Abishua

Bukki

Uzzi

Zerahiah

Meraioth

Amariah I

Ahitub I

Zadok I

Ahimaaz

Azariah I

Johanan

Azariah II

Amariah II

Ahitub II

Zadok II

Shallum

Hilkiah

Azariah III

Seraiah

Jehozadak

P.   OTHER DESCENDANTS OF LEVI (I Chron vi 16–30)

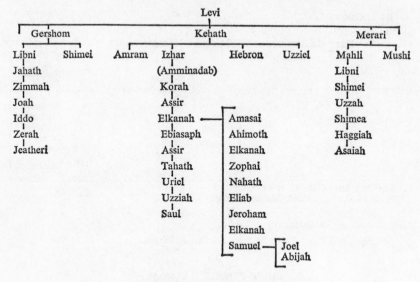

Levi — Gershom, Kehath, Merari

Gershom: Libni, Shimei
Libni → Jahath → Zimmah → Joah → Iddo → Zerah → Jeatheri

Kehath: Amram, Izhar, Hebron, Uzziel
Izhar (Amminadab) → Korah → Assir → Elkanah → Ebiasaph → Assir → Tahath → Uriel → Uzziah → Saul

Elkanah → Amasai → Ahimoth → Elkanah → Zophai → Nahath → Eliab → Jeroham → Elkanah → Samuel → Joel, Abijah

Merari: Mahli, Mushi
Mahli → Libni → Shimei → Uzzah → Shimea → Haggiah → Asaiah

Q.   SINGERS AND AARONITES

1. THE LEVITICAL SINGERS (I Chron vi 31–47)

Israel (Jacob) → Levi → Kehath, Gershom, Merari

Kehath	Gershom	Merari
Izhar	Jahath	Mushi
Korah	Shimei	Mahli
Ebiasaph	Zimmah	Shemer
Assir	Ethan	Bani
Tahath	Adaiah	Amzi
Zephaniah	Zerah	Hilkiah
Azariah	Ethni	Amaziah
Joel	Malchijah	Hashabiah
Elkanah	Baaseiah	Malluch
Amasai	Michael	Abdi
Mahath	Shimea	Kishi
Elkanah	Berechiah	Ethan*
Zuph	Asaph*	

Toah
|
Eliel
|
Jeroham
|
Elkanah
|
Samuel
|
Joel
|
Heman*

2. THE AARONITES (vi 50–53)

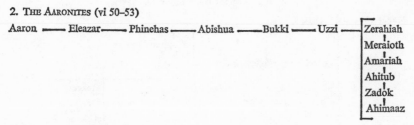

Aaron —— Eleazar —— Phinehas —— Abishua —— Bukki —— Uzzi —— Zerahiah
Meraioth
Amariah
Ahitub
Zadok
Ahimaaz

*Singers appointed by David.

R. ISSACHAR, BENJAMIN, DAN, NAPHTALI

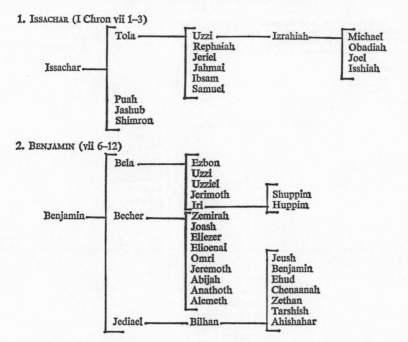

1. ISSACHAR (I Chron vii 1–3)

Issachar

Tola —— Uzzi —— Izrahiah —— Michael
Rephaiah   Obadiah
Jeriel   Joel
Jahmai   Isshiah
Ibsam
Samuel

Puah
Jashub
Shimron

2. BENJAMIN (vii 6–12)

Benjamin

Bela —— Ezbon
Uzzi
Uzziel
Jerimoth
Iri —— Shuppim
Huppim

Becher —— Zemirah
Joash
Eliezer
Elioenai
Omri   Jeush
Jeremoth   Benjamin
Abijah   Ehud
Anathoth   Chenaanah
Alemeth   Zethan
                Tarshish
Jediael —— Bilhan —— Ahishahar

3. DAN (vii 12b)?

Dan? ————Hushim

4. Naphtali (vii 13)

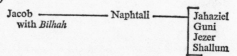

Jacob ———————— Naphtali ——— Jahaziel
with *Bilhah*   Guni
                                          Jezer
                                          Shallum

S.   MANASSEH (I Chron vii 14–19)*

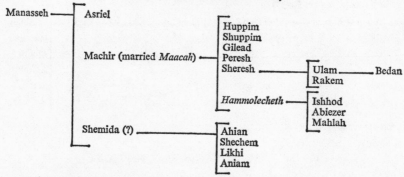

Manasseh ——— Asriel

Machir (married *Maacah*) ——— Huppim
                              Shuppim
                              Gilead
                              Peresh
                              Sheresh ———— Ulam———— Bedan
                                            Rakem

                              Hammolecheth ——— Ishhod
                                                 Abiezer
                                                 Mahlah

Shemida (?) ———— Ahian
                 Shechem
                 Likhi
                 Aniam

*It is hard to make sense of this exceedingly garbled genealogy. One example of the difficulty is that vs. 17b has the sons of Sheresh as descendants of Gilead, although vs. 16 specifically says that they are the descendants of Machir by his wife Maacah. Therefore, this chart should be considered only an approximation of the line of Manasseh as given in I Chronicles.

T.   EPHRAIM AND ASHER

1. EPHRAIM (I Chron vii 20–27)

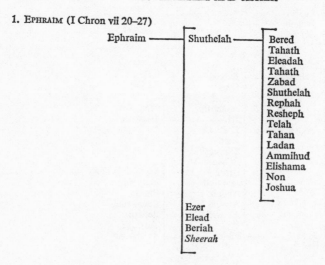

Ephraim ——— Shuthelah ——— Bered
                            Tahath
                            Eleadah
                            Tahath
                            Zabad
                            Shuthelah
                            Rephah
                            Resheph
                            Telah
                            Tahan
                            Ladan
                            Ammihud
                            Elishama
                            Non
                            Joshua

            Ezer
            Elead
            Beriah
            Sheerah

2. ASHER (I Chron vii 30–39)

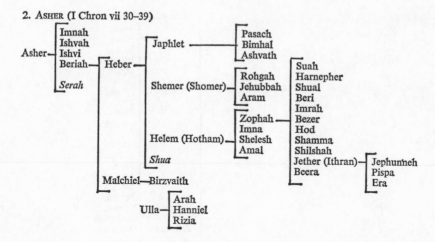

U. BENJAMIN (I Chron viii 1–32)

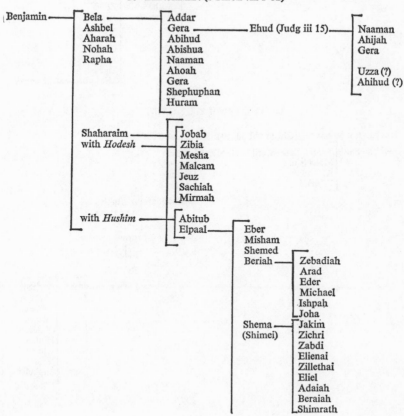

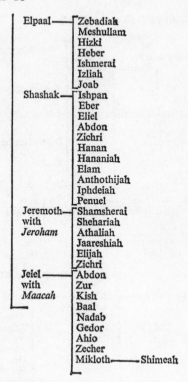

V. THE FAMILY OF SAUL

1. THE FAMILY OF SAUL (I Chron viii 33–40)

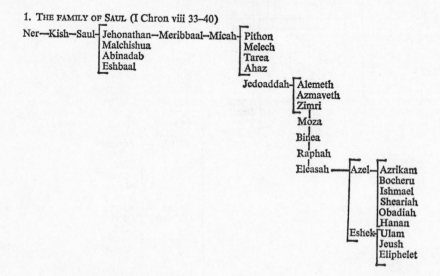

2. The Abiel Family (I Sam xiv 49–51)

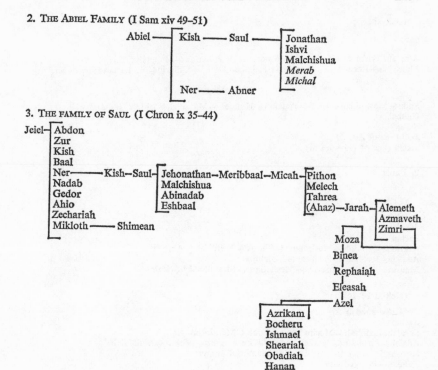

3. The family of Saul (I Chron ix 35–44)

W. RETURNEES

1. Laymen

(I Chron ix 1–9)

Judahites

Uthai Ammihud Omri Imri Bani (of the line of Perez)
Asaiah (of the line of Shelah)
Jeuel (of the line of Zerah)

Benjaminites

Sallu Meshullam Hodaviah Hassenuah
Ibneiah Jeroham
Elah Uzzi Michri
Meshullam Shephatiah Reuel Ibnijah

(Neh xi 3–9)

JUDAHITES

Athaiah←Uzziah←Zechariah←Amariah←Shephatiah←Mahalalel (line of Perez)
Maaseiah←Baruch←Colhozeh←Hazaiah←Adaiah←Joiarib←Zechariah (line of Shelah)

BENJAMINITES

Sallu← Meshullam←Joed←Pedaiah←Kolaiah←Maaseiah← Ithiel←Jeshaiah
Gabbai
Sallai
Joel (line of Zichri)
Judah (line of Hassenuah)

2. PRIESTS

(I Chron ix 10–13)

Jedaiah
Jehoiarib
Jachin
Azariah←Hilkiah←Meshullam←Zadok← Meraioth← Ahitub
Adaiah←Jeroham←Pashhur←Malchijah
Maasai←Adiel←Jahzerah←Meshullam←Meshillemith←Immer

(Neh xi 10–14)

Jedaiah←Joiarib
Jachin
Seraiah← Hilkiah←Meshullam←Zadok← Meraioth← Ahitub
Adaiah←Jeroham←Pelaliah←Amzi←Zechariah←Pashhur ←Malchijah
Amashsai←Azarel←Ahzai←Meshillemoth←Immer
Zabdiel←Haggedolim?

3. LEVITES

(I Chron ix 14–16)

Shemaiah←Hasshub←Azrikam←Hashabiah (line of Merari)
Bakbakkar←Heresh←Galal←Mattaniah←Mica←Zichri (line of Asaph)
Obadiah←Shemaiah←Galal (line of Jeduthun)
Berechiah←Asa←Elkanah

(Neh xi 15–18)

Shemaiah←Hasshub←Azrikam←Hashabiah ←Bunni
Shabbethai
Jozabad
Mattaniah← Micah←Zabdi (line of Asaph)
Bakbukiah
Abda←Shammua← Galal (line of Jeduthun)

INDEX OF PLACE AND PERSONAL NAMES

NOTES

1. The transcriptional spelling is generally that appearing in the first reference. Important variations are, however, noted where they do occur.

2. It is often difficult, perhaps impossible, to distinguish between personal and place names, especially those of the twelve tribes of Israel. The latter are all listed as personal names.

3. The general practice has been followed in transcriptions—

' = *aleph*	s = *samek*
' = *ayin*	ṣ = *tsade*
ḥ = *heth*	ś = *sin*
h = *he*	š = *shin*
ṭ = *teth*	y = *yod*
t = *taw*	

No attempt has been made to distinguish between consonants with or without *dagesh*.

PLACE NAMES

Abel-maim (*'bl-mym*) II Chron xvi 4

Adoraim (*'dwrym*) II Chron xi 9

Adullam (*'dlm*) I Chron xi 15; II Chron xi 7; Neh xi 30

Aijalon (*'ylwn*) I Chron vi 69, viii 13; II Chron xi 10, xxviii 18

Arabia (*'rb*) II Chron ix 14

Aram (*'rm*) II Chron i 17, xvi 2,7, xviii 10,30,34, xxii 5,6, xxvi 5,23

Ashdod (*'šdwd*) II Chron xxvi 6(*bis*)

Gath (*gt*) I Chron vii 21, viii 13, xviii 1, xx 6,8; II Chron xi 8, xxvi 6

Geba (*gb'*) I Chron vi 60, viii 6; II Chron xvi 6; Ezra ii 26; Neh vii 30, xi 31, xii 29

Gederoth (*gdrwt*) II Chron xxviii 18

Gerar (*grr*) II Chron xiv 12,13

Gibeah (*gb'h*) I Chron xi 31; II Chron xiii 2

Gibeon (*gb'wn*) I Chron viii 29, ix 35, xiv 16, xvi 39, xxi 29; II Chron i 3,13; Neh iii 7, vii 25

Gihon (*gyḥwn*) II Chron xxxii 30, xxxiii 14

Gimzo (*gmzw*) II Chron xxviii 18

Gur-baal (*gwr b'l*) II Chron xxvi 7

Hamath (*ḥmt*) I Chron xiii 5, xviii 3,9; II Chron vii 8, viii 4

Hamath-zobah (*ḥmt ṣwbh*) II Chron viii 3

Hassis (*ḥṣyṣ*) II Chron xx 16

Hazazon-tamar (*ḥṣṣwn tmr*) II Chron xx 2

Hebron (*ḥbrwn*) I Chron iii 1,4, vi 55,57, xi 1,3(*bis*), xii 24,39, xxix 27; II Chron xi 10

Horeb (*ḥrb*) II Chron v 10

Ijon (*'ywn*) II Chron xvi 4

Jabneh (*ybnh*) II Chron xxvi 6

Jericho (*yrḥw*) I Chron vi 78, xix 5; II Chron xxviii 15; Ezra ii 34; Neh iii 2, vii 36

Jeruel (*yrw'l*) II Chron xx 16

Jerusalem (*yrwšlm*) I Chron iii 4,5, vi 10,15,32, viii 28,32, ix 3, 34,38, xi 4, xiv 3,4, xv 3, xviii 7, xix 15, xx 1,3, xxi 4,15,16, xxiii 25, xxviii 1, xxix 27; II Chron i 4,13,14,15, ii 6,15, iii 1, v 2, vi 6, viii 6, ix 1,25,27,30, x 18, xi 1,5,14,16, xii 2,3,4,5,7,9, 13(*bis*), xiii 2, xiv 14, xv 10, xvii 13, xix 1,4,8(*bis*), xx 5,15, 17,18,20,27(*bis*), 28,31, xxi 5,11,13,20, xxii 1,2, xxiii 2, xxiv 1,6,9,18,23, xxv 1(*bis*), 23(*bis*), 27, xxvi 3(*bis*), 9,15, xxvii 1, 8, xxviii 1,10,24,27, xxix 1,8, xxx 1,2,3,5,11,13,14,21,26(*bis*), xxxi 4, xxxii 2,9(*bis*), 10,12,18,19,22,23,25,26,33, xxxiii 1,4,7,9, 13,15,21, xxxiv 1,3,5,7,9,22,29,30,32(*bis*), xxxv 1,18,24(*bis*), xxxvi 1,2,3,4,5,9,10,11,14,19,23; Ezra i 2,3(*bis*), 4,5,7,11, ii 1,68,

Ramah (*hrmh*)   II Chron xvi 1,5,6, xxii 6; Ezra ii 26; Neh vii 30, xi 33

Ramoth-gilead (*rmwt glʿd*)   II Chron xviii 2,3,5,11,14,19,28, xxii 5

Rock (*slʿ*)   II Chron xxv 12(*bis*)

Samaria (*šmrwn*)   II Chron xviii 2,9, xxii 9, xxv 13,24, xxviii 8, 9,15; Ezra iv 10,17; Neh iii 34

Sheba (*šbʾ*)   II Chron ix 1,3,9,12

Shechem (*škm*)   I Chron vi 67, vii 28; II Chron x 1(*bis*)

Shephelah (*šplh*)   I Chron xxvii 28; II Chron i 15, ix 27, xxvi 10, xxviii 18

Soco (*śkw*)   II Chron xi 7, xxviii 18

Succoth (*skwt*)   II Chron iv 17

Tadmor (*tdmr*)   II Chron viii 4

Tarshish (*tršyš*)   II Chron ix 21(*bis*), xx 36,37

Tekoa (*tqwʿ*)   II Chron xi 6, xx 20

Timnah (*tmnh*)   II Chron xxviii 18

Tyre (*ṣr*)   I Chron xiv 1; II Chron ii 10

Valley of Salt (*gyʾ hmlḥ*)   I Chron xviii 12; II Chron xxv 11

Zarethan (*ṣrdh*)   II Chron iv 17

Zephathah (*ṣpth*)   II Chron xiv 9

Zion (*ṣywn*)   I Chron xi 5; II Chron v 2

Ziph (*zyp*)   II Chron xi 8

Zorah (*ṣrʿh*)   II Chron xi 10; Neh xi 29

PERSONAL AND OTHER NAMES

Aaron (*ʾhrn*)   I Chron vi 3(*bis*), 49,50,54,57, xii 28, xv 4, xxiii 13(*bis*), 28,32, xxiv 1(*bis*), 19,31, xxvii 17; II Chron xiii 9,10, xxvi 8, xxix 21, xxxi 19, xxxv 14(*bis*); Ezra vii 5; Neh x 39, xii 47

Abdi (*ʿbdy*)   I Chron vi 44; II Chron xxix 12; Ezra x 26

Abdon (*ʿbdwn*)   I Chron viii 23,30, ix 36; II Chron xxxiv 20

Abihail (*'byhyl*)   I Chron ii 29, v 14; II Chron xi 18

Abijah (*'byh*)   I Chron iii 10, vi 28, vii 8, xxiv 10; II Chron xi 20, 22, xii 16, xiii 1,2,3,4,15,17,19,20,21,22,23, xxix 1; Neh x 8, xii 4,17

Abraham (*'brhm*)   I Chron i 27,28,32,34, xvi 16, xxix 18; II Chron xx 7, xxx 6; Neh ix 7

Absalom (*'bšlwm*)   I Chron iii 2; II Chron xi 20,21

Adaiah (*'dyh*)   I Chron vi 41, viii 21, ix 12; II Chron xxiii 1; Ezra x 29,39; Neh xi 5,12

Adnah (*'dnh*)   II Chron xvii 14

Adonijah (*'dnyh*)   I Chron iii 2; II Chron xvii 8; Neh x 17

Ahab (*'ḥ'b*)   II Chron xviii 1,2(*bis*), 3,19, xxi 6(*bis*), 13, xxii 3,4,5,6,7,8

Ahaz (*'ḥz*)   I Chron iii 13, viii 35,36, ix 42; II Chron xxvii 9, xxviii 1,16,19,21,22,24,27, xxix 19

Ahaziah (*'ḥzyhw*)   I Chron iii 11; II Chron xx 35,37, xxii 1(*bis*), 2,6,7,8(*bis*), 9(*bis*), 10,11(*bis*), xxv 23 (with Greek; MT reads *yhw'ḥz*)

Ahijah (*'ḥyh*)   I Chron ii 25, viii 7, xi 36; II Chron ix 29, x 15; Neh x 27

Ahikam (*'ḥyqm*)   II Chron xxxiv 20

Amariah (*'mryh*)   I Chron vi 7(*bis*), 11(*bis*), 52, xxiii 19, xxiv 23; II Chron xix 11, xxxi 15; Ezra vii 3, x 42; Neh x 4, xi 4, xii 2,13

Amasa (*'mš'*)   I Chron ii 17(*bis*); II Chron xxviii 12

Amasai (*'mšy*)   I Chron vi 25,35, xii 19, xv 24; II Chron xxix 12

Amasiah (*'msyh*)   II Chron xvii 16

Amaziah (*'mṣyhw*)   I Chron iii 12, iv 34, vi 45; II Chron xxiv 27, xxv 1,5,9,10,11,13,14,15,17,18,20,21,23,25,26,27, xxvi 1,4

Ammon (*'mwn*)   I Chron xviii 11, xix 2,3,6(*bis*), 7,9,11,15,19, xx 1,3; II Chron xx 1,10,22,23, xxvii 5(*tris*)

Ammonite (*'mwny*)   I Chron xi 39; II Chron xii 13 (fem.), xxiv 26 (fem.); Ezra ix 1; Neh ii 10,19, iii 15, iv 1, xiii 1,23 (fem.)

Amon (*'mwn*)   I Chron iii 14; II Chron xviii 25, xxxiii 20,21,22, 23,25; Neh vii 59

Amorite (*'mry*)   I Chron i 14; II Chron viii 7; Ezra ix 1; Neh ix 8

Amoz (*'mwṣ*)   II Chron xxvi 22, xxxii 20,32

Arabs (*'rby'ym; 'rbym; 'rbyym*)   II Chron xvii 11, xxi 16, xxii 1, xxvi 7; Neh iv 1

Aramaean (*'rmyh, 'rm*) I Chron vii 14, xviii 5,6(*bis*), xix 6,10, 12,14,15,16(*bis*), 17,18(*bis*), 19; II Chron xxii 5 (as in II Kings viii 28), xxiv 23,24

Asa (*'s'*) I Chron iii 10, ix 16; II Chron xiii 23, xiv 1,7,9,10,11,12, xv 2(*bis*), 8,10,16(*bis*), 17,19, xvi 1(*bis*), 2,4,6,7,10(*bis*), 11,12, 13, xvii 2, xx 32, xxi 12

Asahel (*'śh'l*) I Chron ii 16, xi 26, xxvii 7; II Chron xvii 8, xxxi 13; Ezra x 15

Asaiah (*'śyh*) I Chron iv 36, vi 30, ix 5, xv 6,11; II Chron xxxiv 20

Asaph (*'sp*) I Chron vi 39(*bis*), ix 15, xv 17,19, xvi 5(*bis*), 7, 37, xxv 1,2(*tris*), 6,9, xxvi 1; II Chron v 12, xx 14, xxix 13,30, xxxv 15(*bis*); Ezra ii 41, iii 10; Neh ii 8, vii 44, xi 17,22, xii 35,46

Asher (*'šr*) I Chron ii 2, vi 62,74, vii 30,40, xii 37; II Chron xxx 11

Asherah(s) (*'šrh, 'šrwt*) II Chron xv 16, xix 3, xxiv 18, xxxi 1, xxxiii 3,19, xxxiv 3,4,7

Asherim (*'šrym*) II Chron xiv 2, xvii 6

Athaliah (*'tlyh*) I Chron viii 26; II Chron xxii 2,10,11,12, xxiii 12,13,21, xxiv 7; Ezra viii 7

Attai (*'ty*) I Chron ii 35,36, xii 12; II Chron xi 20

Azaliah (*'ṣlyhw*) II Chron xxxiv 8

Azariah (*'zryh*) I Chron ii 8,38,39, iii 12, vi 9(*bis*), 10,11,13,14, 36, ix 11; II Chron xv 1, xxi 2(*bis*), xxiii 1(*bis*), xxvi 17,20, xxviii 12, xxix 12(*bis*), xxxi 10,13; Ezra vii 1,3; Neh iii 23,24, vii 7, viii 7, x 3, xii 33

Azaziah (*'zzyhw*) I Chron xv 21, xxvii 20; II Chron xxxi 13

Azrikam (*'zryqm*) I Chron iii 23, viii 38, ix 14,44; II Chron xxviii 7; Neh xi 15

Azubah (*'zwbh*) I Chron ii 18,19; II Chron xx 31

Baal (*b'l*) I Chron v 5, viii 30, ix 36; II Chron xvii 3, xxiii 17(*bis*), xxiv 7, xxviii 2, xxxiii 3, xxxiv 4

Baasha (*b'š'*) II Chron xvi 1,3,5,6

Benaiah (*bnyhw*) I Chron iv 36, xi 22,24,31, xv 18,20,24, xvi 5, 6, xviii 17, xxvii 5,6,14,34; II Chron xx 14, xxxi 13; Ezra x 25,30,35,43

Ben-hadad (*bn-hdd*) II Chron xvi 2,4

Benjamin (*bnymn*) I Chron ii 2, vi 60,65, vii 6,10, viii 1,40, ix 3,7, xi 31, xii 2,17,30, xxi 6, xxvii 21; II Chron xi 1,3,10,12,23, xiv 7, xv 2,8,9, xvii 17, xxv 5, xxxi 1, xxxiv 9,32; Ezra i 5, iv 1, x 9,32; Neh iii 23, xi 4,7,31,36, xii 34

Berechiah (*brkyh*) I Chron iii 20, vi 39, ix 16, xv 17,23; II Chron xxviii 12; Neh iii 4,30, vi 18

Bezalel (*bṣl'l*) I Chron ii 20; II Chron i 5; Ezra x 30

Boaz (*b'z*) I Chron ii 11,12; II Chron iii 17

Chaldeans (*kśdyym, ksdy'*) II Chron xxxvi 17; Ezra v 12

Chenaanah (*kn'nh*) I Chron vii 10; II Chron xviii 10,23

Cilicia (*qw'*) II Chron i 16,17

Conaniah (*kwnnyhw*) II Chron xxxi 12,13, xxxv 9

Cyrus (*kwrš*) II Chron xxxvi 22(*bis*), 23; Ezra i 1(*bis*), 2,7,8, iii 7, iv 3,5, v 13(*bis*), 14,17, vi 3(*bis*), 14

Dan (*dn*) I Chron ii 2, xxi 2, xxvii 22; II Chron ii 13, xvi 4, xxx 5

David (*dwyd*) I Chron ii 15, iii 1,9, iv 31, vi 31, vii 2, ix 22, x 14, xi 1,3(*bis*), 4,5(*tris*), 6,7(*bis*), 9,10,11,13,15,16,17,18(*bis*), 25, xii 1,9,17,18,19(*bis*), 20,22,23,24,32,34,39(*tris*), 40, xiii 1,2,5,6, 8,11,12,13(*bis*), xiv 1,2,3,8(*tris*), 10,11(*bis*), 12,14,16,17, xv 1,2,3,4,11,16,25,27(*bis*), 29(*bis*), xvi 2,7,43, xvii 1(*bis*), 2,4,7, 15,16,18,24, xviii 1,2,4(*bis*), 5,6(*tris*), 7,8,9,10,11,13(*bis*), 14, 17, xix 2(*tris*), 3,4,5,6,8,17(*bis*), 18,19, xx 1,2(*bis*), 3,7,8, xxi 1, 2,5,8,9,10,11,12,13,16(*bis*), 17,18(*bis*), 19,21(*tris*), 22,23,24,25, 26,28,30, xxii 1,2,3,4,5(*bis*), 6,7,17, xxiii 1,4,6,25,27, xxiv 3,31, xxv 1, xxvi 26,31,32, xxvii 18,23,24,31,32, xxviii 1,2,11,20, xxix 1,9,10(*bis*), 20,22,23,24,26,29; II Chron i 1,4(*bis*), 8,9, ii 2,6,11, 13,16, iii 1(*bis*), v 1,2, vi 4,6,7,8,10,15,16,17,42, vii 6(*bis*), 10, 17,18, viii 11(*bis*), 14(*bis*), ix 31, x 16(*bis*), 19, xi 17,18, xii 16, xiii 5,6,8,23, xvi 14, xxi 1,7(*bis*), 12,20, xxiii 3,9,18(*bis*), xxiv 16,25, xxvii 9, xxviii 1, xxix 2,25,26,27,30, xxx 26, xxxii 5,30,33, xxxiii 7,14, xxxiv 2,3, xxxv 3,4,15; Ezra iii 10, viii 2,20; Neh iii 15,16, xii 24,36,37(*bis*), 45,46

Dodavahu (*ddwhu*) II Chron xx 37

Eden (*'dn*) II Chron xxix 12, xxxi 15

Edom, Edomite (*'dwm, 'dwmy*) II Chron xxi 9,10, xxv 14, xxviii 17

Eliab (*'ly'b*) I Chron ii 13, vi 27, xii 10, xv 18,20, xvi 5; II Chron xi 18

Eliada (*'lyd'*) I Chron iii 8; II Chron xvii 17

Eliakim (*'lyqym*) II Chron xxxvi 4; Neh xii 41

Eliel (*'ly'l*) I Chron v 24, vi 34, viii 20,22, xi 46,47, xii 12, xv 9, 11; II Chron xxxi 13

Eliezer (*'ly'zr*) I Chron vii 8, xv 24, xxiii 15,17(*bis*), xxvi 25, xxvii 16; II Chron xx 37; Ezra viii 16, x 18,23,31

Elijah (*'lyhw*) II Chron xxi 12; Ezra x 21,26

Elishama (*'lyšm'*) I Chron ii 41, iii 6,8, vii 26, xiv 7; II Chron xvii 8

Elishaphat (*'lyšpṭ*) II Chron xxiii 1

Elizaphan (*'lyṣpn*) I Chron xv 8; II Chron xxix 13

Elkanah (*'lqnh*) I Chron vi 23,25,26,27,34,35,36, ix 16, xii 7, xv 23; II Chron xxviii 7

Ephraim (*'prym*) I Chron vi 66, vii 20,22, ix 3, xii 31, xxvii 10, 14,20; II Chron xv 9, xvii 2, xxv 7,10,23, xxviii 7,12, xxx 1,10, 18, xxxi 1, xxxiv 6,9

Ethiopian(s) (*kwšy, kwšym*) II Chron xii 3, xiv 8,11(*bis*), 12, xvi 8, xxi 16

Gad (*gd, gdy*) I Chron ii 2, v 11,18,26, vi 63,80, xii 15, xxi 9,11, 13,18,19, xxix 29; II Chron xxix 25

Gershunnite (*gršny*) I Chron xxiii 7, xxvi 21, xxix 8; II Chron xxix 12

Hadlai (*ḥdly*) II Chron xxviii 12

Hadoram (*hdwrm*) I Chron i 21, xviii 10; II Chron x 18

Hanani (*ḥnny*) I Chron xxv 4,25; II Chron xvi 7, xix 2, xx 34; Ezra x 20; Neh i 2, vii 2, xii 36

Hananiah (*ḥnnyh*) I Chron iii 19,21, viii 24, xxv 4,23; II Chron xxvi 11; Ezra x 28; Neh iii 8,30, vii 2, x 24, xii 12,41

Hashabiah (*ḥšbyh*) I Chron vi 45, ix 14, xxv 3,19, xxvi 30, xxvii 17; II Chron xxxv 9; Ezra viii 19,24; Neh iii 17, x 12, xi 15,22, xii 21,24

Hasrah (*ḥsrh*) II Chron xxxiv 22

Hazael (*ḥz'l, ḥzh'l*)   II Chron xxii 5,6

Heman (*hymn*)   I Chron ii 6, vi 33, xv 17,19, xvi 41,42, xxv 1, 4(*bis*), 5(*bis*), 6; II Chron v 12, xxix 14, xxxv 15

Hezekiah (*ḥzqyhw*)   I Chron iii 13,23, iv 41; II Chron xxviii 27, xxix 1,18,20,27,30,31,36, xxx 1,18,20,22,24, xxxi 2,8,9,11,13,20, xxxii 2,8,9,11,12,15,16,17,20,22,23,24,25,26(*bis*), 27,30(*bis*), 32,33, xxxiii 3; Ezra ii 16; Neh vii 21, x 18

Hilkiah (*ḥlqyh*)   I Chron vi 13(*bis*), 45, ix 11, xxvi 11; II Chron xxxiv 9,14,15(*bis*), 18,20,22, xxxv 8; Ezra vii 1; Neh viii 4, xi 11, xii 7,21

Hiram (*ḥyrm*)   I Chron xiv 1; II Chron ix 10

Hittite (*ḥty*)   I Chron xi 41; II Chron i 17, viii 7; Ezra ix 1; Neh ix 8

Hivites (*ḥwy*)   I Chron i 15; II Chron viii 7

Huldah (*ḥldh*)   II Chron xxxiv 22

Hur (*ḥwr*)   I Chron ii 19,20,50, iv 1,4; II Chron i 5; Neh iii 9

Huram (*ḥwrm*)   I Chron viii 5; II Chron ii 2,10,11, iv 11(*bis*), viii 2,18, ix 21

Huramabi (*ḥwrm-'by*)   II Chron ii 12, iv 16

Iddo (*ydw, y'dy, 'dw, 'dw', 'dw*)   I Chron vi 21, xxvii 21; II Chron ix 29, xii 15, xiii 22; Ezra v 1, vi 14, viii 17(*bis*); Neh xii 4,16

Imlah (*yml'*)   II Chron xviii 7,8

Imnah (*ymnh*)   I Chron vii 30; II Chron xxxi 14

Isaac (*yṣḥq*)   I Chron i 28,34(*bis*), xvi 16, xxix 18; II Chron xxx 6

Isaiah (*yš'yhw*)   II Chron xxvi 22, xxxii 20,32

Ishmael (*yšmᵉ'l*)   I Chron i 28,29,31, viii 38, ix 44; II Chron xix 11, xxiii 1; Ezra x 22

Ismachiah (*ysmkyhw*)   II Chron xxxi 13

Israel (*yśr'l*)   I Chron i 34,43, ii 1,7, v 1(*bis*), 3,17,26, vi 38,49, 64, vii 29, ix 1(*bis*), 2, x 1(*bis*), 7, xi 1,2(*bis*), 3(*bis*), 4,10(*bis*), xii 33, 39(*bis*), 41, xiii 2(*bis*), 4,6,8, xiv 2(*bis*), 8, xv 3,12,14,25, 28, xvi 3,4,13,17,36,40, xvii 5,6,7,9,10,21,22,24(*bis*), xviii 14, xix 10,16,17,18,19, xx 7, xxi 1(*bis*), 2,3,4,5,7,12,14(*bis*), xxii 1, 2,6,9,10,12,13,17, xxiii 1,2,25(*bis*), xxiv 19, xxvi 29,30, xxvii 1, 16,22,23,24, xxviii 1,4(*tris*), 5,8, xxix 6,10,18,21,23,25(*bis*), 26, 27,30; II Chron i 2(*bis*), 13, ii 3,11,16, v 2(*bis*), 3,4,6,10, vi

3(*bis*), 4,5(*bis*), 6,7,10(*bis*), 11,12,13,14,16(*bis*), 17,21,24,25, 27,29,32,33, vii 3,6,8,10,18, viii 2,7,8,9,11, ix 8,30, x 1,3,16(*tris*), 17,18,19, xi 1,3,13,16(*bis*), xii 1,6,13, xiii 4,5(*bis*), 12,15,16, 17,18, xv 3,4,9,13,17, xvi 1,3,4,7,11, xvii 1,4, xviii 3,4,5,7,8,9, 16,17,19,25,28,29(*bis*), 30,31,32,33,34, xix 8, xx 7,10,19,29,34, 35, xxi 2,4,6,13(*bis*), xxii 5, xxiii 2, xxiv 5,6,9,16, xxv 6,7(*bis*), 9,17,18,21,22,23,25,26, xxvii 7, xxviii 2,3,5,8,13,19,23,26,27, xxix 7,10,24(*bis*), 27, xxx 1(*bis*), 5(*bis*), 6(*tris*), 21,25(*bis*), 26, xxxi 1(*bis*), 5,6,8, xxxii 17,32, xxxiii 2,7,8,9,16,18(*bis*), xxxiv 7, 9,21,23,26,33(*bis*), xxxv 3(*tris*), 4,17,18(*bis*), 25,27, xxxvi 8,13; Ezra i 3, ii 2,59,70, iii 1,2,10,11, iv 1,3(*bis*), v 1,11, vi 14,16, 17(*bis*), 21(*bis*), 22, vii 6,7,11,13,15,28, viii 18,25,29,35(*bis*), ix 1,4,15, x 1,2,5,10,25; Neh i 6(*bis*), ii 10, vii 7,61,72(*bis*), viii 1,14,17, ix 1,2, x 40, xi 3,20, xii 47, xiii 2,3,28,26(*bis*)
Issachar (*yśśkr*) I Chron ii 1, vi 62,72, vii 1,5, xii 33,41, xxvi 5, xxvii 18; II Chron xxx 18

Jachin (*ykyn*) I Chron ix 10, xxiv 17; II Chron iii 17; Neh xi 10
Jahath (*yḥt*) I Chron iv 2(*bis*), vi 20,43, xxiii 10,11, xxiv 22; II Chron xxxiv 12
Jahaziel (*yḥzy'l*) I Chron xii 4, xvi 6, xxiii 19, xxiv 23; II Chron xx 14; Ezra viii 5
Jebusite (*ybwsy*) I Chron i 14, xi 4,6, xxi 15,18,28; II Chron iii 1, viii 7; Ezra ix 1; Neh ix 8
Jecoliah (*ykylyh,* Kethib) II Chron xxvi 3
Jeduthun (*ydwtwn*) I Chron ix 16, xvi 41,42, xxv 1,3(*tris*), 6; II Chron v 12, xxix 14, xxxv 15; Neh xi 17 (Kethib has *ydytwn*)
Jehallelel (*yhll'l*) I Chron iv 16; II Chron xxix 12
Jehiel (*yḥy'l*) I Chron xv 18,20, xvi 5, xxiii 8, xxvi 21,22 (*yḥy'ly*), xxvii 32, xxix 8; II Chron xxi 2, xxix 14 (Kethib has *yḥw'l*), xxxi 13, xxxv 8; Ezra viii 9, x 2,21,26
Jehizkiah (*yḥzqyhw*) II Chron xxviii 12. See also Hezekiah
Jehoaddan (*yhw'dn*) II Chron xxv 1
Jehoahaz (*yhw'ḥz, yw'ḥz*) II Chron xxi 17, xxv 17,25, xxxiv 8, xxxvi 1,2,4
Jehohanan (*yhwḥnn*) I Chron xxvi 3; II Chron xvii 15, xxiii 1, xxviii 12; Ezra x 6,28; Neh vi 18, xii 13,18,42
Jehoiachin (*yhwykyn*) II Chron xxxvi 8,9

Joash (*yw'š, yw'š*) I Chron iii 11, iv 22, vii 8, xii 3, xxvii 28; II Chron xviii 25, xxii 11, xxiv 1,2,4,22,24, xxv 17,18,20,21, 23(*bis*), 25(*bis*)

Joel (*yw'l*) I Chron iv 35, v 4,8,12, vi 28,33,36, vii 3, xi 38, xv 7,11,17, xxiii 8, xxvi 22, xxvii 20; II Chron xxix 12; Ezra x 43; Neh xi 9

Joram (*ywrm*) I Chron iii 11, xxvi 25; II Chron xxii 5,7

Josiah (*y'šyhw*) I Chron iii 14,15; II Chron xxxiii 25, xxxiv 1, 33, xxxv 1,7,16,18,19,20(*bis*), 22,23,24,25(*bis*), 26, xxxvi 1

Jotham (*ywtm*) I Chron ii 47, iii 12, v 17; II Chron xxvi 21,23, xxvii 1,6,7,9

Jozabad (*ywzbd*) I Chron xii 5,21(*bis*); II Chron xxxi 13, xxxv 9; Ezra viii 33, x 22,23; Neh viii 7, xi 16

Judah (*yhwdh*) I Chron ii 1,3(*bis*), 10, iv 1,21,27,41, v 2,17, vi 15,55,65, ix 1,3,4, xii 17,25, xiii 6, xxi 5, xxvii 18, xxviii 4(*bis*); II Chron ii 6, ix 11, x 17, xi 1,3(*bis*), 5,10,12,14,17,23, xii 4,5,12, xiii 1,13,14,15(*tris*), 16,18, xiv 3,4,5,6,7,11, xv 2,8, 9,15, xvi 1(*bis*), 6,7,11, xvii 2(*bis*), 5,6,7,9(*bis*), 10,12,13,14, 19, xviii 3,9,28, xix 1,5,11, xx 3,4(*bis*), 5,13,15,17,18,20,22,24, 27,31,35, xxi 3(*bis*), 8,10,11(*bis*), 12,13,17, xxii 1,6,8,10, xxiii 2(*bis*), 8, xxiv 5,6,9,17,18,23, xxv 5(*bis*), 10,12,13,17,18,19, 21(*bis*), 22,23,25,26,28, xxvi 1,2, xxvii 4,7, xxviii 6,9,10,17,18, 19(*bis*), 25,26, xxix 8,21, xxx 1,6,12,24,25(*bis*), xxxi 1(*bis*), 6(*bis*), 20, xxxii 1,8,9,12,23,25,32,33, xxxiii 9,14,16, xxxiv 3,5,9, 11,21,24,26,29,30, xxxv 18,21,24,27, xxxvi 4,8,10,14,23; Ezra i 2,3,5,8, ii 1(*bis*), iii 9, iv 1,4,6, v 1,8, vii 14, ix 9, x 7,9,23; Neh ii 5,7, iv 4,10, v 14, vi 7,17,18, vii 6, xi 3,4(*bis*), 9,20,24, 25,36, xii 8,31,32,34,36,44, xiii 16

Kehathite (*qhty*) I Chron vi 33,54, ix 32; II Chron xx 19, xxix 12, xxxiv 12

Kish (*qyš*) I Chron viii 30,33(*bis*), ix 36,39(*bis*), xii 1, xxiii 21,22, xxiv 29(*bis*), xxvi 28; II Chron xxix 12

Korahites (*qrhym*) I Chron ix 19,31, xii 7, xxvi 1; II Chron xx 19

Kore (*qwr'*) I Chron ix 19, xxvi 1; II Chron xxxi 14

Levite(s) (*lwy, lwym*) I Chron vi 19,48,64, ix 2,14,26,31,33,34, xii 27, xiii 2, xv 2,4,11,12,14,15,16,17,22,26,27, xvi 4, xxiii 2,3, 26,27, xxiv 6(*bis*), 20,30,31, xxvi 20, xxvii 17, xxviii 13,21;

Michael (*myk'l*)   I Chron v 13,14, vi 40, vii 3, viii 16, xii 21, xxvii
    18; II Chron xxi 2; Ezra viii 8
Miniamin (*mnymn*)   II Chron xxxi 15; Neh xii 17,41
Moab, Moabite (*mw'b, mw'by*)   I Chron iv 22, xi 22,46, xviii 2;
    II Chron xx 1,10,22,23, xxiv 26; Ezra ix 1; Neh xiii 1,23
Moses (*mšh*)   I Chron vi 3,49, xv 15, xxi 29, xxii 13, xxiii 13,14,
    15, xxvi 24; II Chron i 3, v 10, viii 13, xxiii 18, xxiv 6,9, xxv 4,
    xxx 16, xxxiii 8, xxxiv 14, xxxv 6,12; Ezra iii 2, vi 18, vii 6; Neh
    i 7,8, viii 1,14, ix 14, x 30, xiii 1

Naamah (*n'mh*)   II Chron xii 13
Nahath (*nḥt*)   I Chron i 37, vi 26; II Chron xxxi 13
Naphtali (*nptly*)   I Chron ii 2, vi 62,76, vii 13, xii 35,41, xxvii 19;
    II Chron xvi 4, xxxiv 6
Nathan (*ntn*)   I Chron ii 36(*bis*), iii 5, xi 38, xiv 4, xvii 1,2,3,15,
    xxix 29; II Chron ix 29, xxix 25; Ezra viii 16, x 39
Nebat (*nbṭ*)   II Chron ix 29, x 2,15, xiii 6
Nebuchadnezzar (*nbkdn'ṣr, nbwkdn'ṣr*)   I Chron vi 15; II Chron
    xxxvi 6,7,10,13; Ezra i 7, ii 1, v 12,14, vi 5; Neh vii 6
Neco (*nkw*)   II Chron xxxv 20,22, xxxvi 4
Nethanel (*ntn'l*)   I Chron ii 14, xv 24, xxiv 6, xxvi 4; II Chron
    xvii 7, xxxv 9; Ezra x 22; Neh xii 21,36
Nethaniah (*ntnyh*)   I Chron xxv 2,12; II Chron xvii 8
Nimshi (*nmšy*)   II Chron xxii 7

Obadiah (*'bdyh*)   I Chron iii 21, vii 3, viii 38, ix 16,44, xii 10,
    xxvi 19; II Chron xvii 7, xxxiv 12; Ezra viii 9; Neh x 6, xii 25
Obed (*'wbd*)   I Chron ii 12(*bis*), 37,38, xi 47, xxvi 7; II Chron
    xxiii 1
Obed-edom (*'bd-'dm*)   I Chron xiii 13,14(*bis*), xv 18,21,24,25,
    xvi 5,38(*bis*), xxvi 4,8(*bis*), 15; II Chron xxv 24
Oded (*'wdd*)   II Chron xv 1,8, xxviii 9
Omri (*'mry*)   I Chron vii 8, ix 4, xxvii 18; II Chron xxii 2
Ornan (*'rnn*)   I Chron xxi 15,18,20(*bis*), 21(*bis*), 22,23,24,25,
    28; II Chron iii 1

Pekah (*pqḥ*)   II Chron xxviii 6
Perizzite (*przy*)   II Chron viii 7; Ezra ix 1; Neh ix 8
Pharaoh (*pr'h*)   I Chron iv 18; II Chron viii 11; Neh ix 10

Philistine (*plštym*)   I Chron i 12, x 1(*bis*), 2,7,8,9,11, xi 13(*bis*), 14,15,16,18, xii 20(*bis*), xiv 8(*bis*), 9,10,13,15,16, xviii 1(*bis*), 11, xx 4,5; II Chron ix 26, xvii 11, xxi 16, xxvi 6(*bis*), 7, xxviii 18

Rehoboam (*rḥbʿm*)   I Chron iii 10; II Chron ix 31, x 1,3,6,12,13, 17,18(*bis*), xi 1(*bis*), 3,5,17,18,21,22, xii 1,2,5,10,13(*bis*), 15(*bis*), 16, xiii 7(*bis*)
Remaliah (*rmlyhw*)   II Chron xxviii 6

Samuel (*šmwʾl*)   I Chron vi 28,33, vii 2, ix 22, xi 3, xxvi 28, xxix 29; II Chron xxxv 18
Seir (*śʿyr*)   I Chron i 38; II Chron xx 23, xxv 11,14
Sennacherib (*snḥryb*)   II Chron xxxii 1,2,9,10,22
Shallum (*šlwm*)   I Chron ii 40,41, iii 15, iv 25, vi 12,13, vii 13, ix 17(*bis*), 19,31; II Chron xxviii 12, xxxiv 22; Ezra ii 42, vii 2, x 24,42; Neh iii 12, vii 45
Shamiraimoth (*šmrymwt*)   II Chron xvii 8
Shaphan (*špn*)   II Chron xxxiv 8,15(*bis*), 16,18(*bis*), 20(*bis*)
Shecaniah (*šknyh*)   I Chron iii 21,22, xxiv 11; II Chron xxxi 15; Ezra viii 3,5, x 2; Neh iii 29, vi 18, xii 3
Shelomith (*šlmyt*)   I Chron iii 19, xxiii 9 (Qere, Kethib have *šlmwt*), 18; II Chron xi 20; Ezra viii 10
Shemaiah (*šmʿyh*)   I Chron iii 22(*bis*), iv 37, v 4, ix 14,16, xv 8,11, xxiv 6, xxvi 4,6,7; II Chron xi 2, xii 5,7,15, xvii 8, xxix 14, xxxi 15, xxxv 9; Ezra viii 13,16, x 21,31; Neh iii 29, vi 10, x 9, xi 15, xii 6,18,34,35,36,42
Shemariah (*šmryhw*)   I Chron xii 6; II Chron xi 19; Ezra x 32,41
Shephatiah (*špṭyh*)   I Chron iii 3, ix 8, xii 6, xxvii 16; II Chron xxi 2; Ezra ii 4,57, viii 8; Neh vii 9,59, xi 4
Shilhi (*šlḥy*)   II Chron xx 31
Shilonite (*šylwny*)   I Chron ix 5; II Chron ix 29, x 15; Neh xi 5
Shimeath (*šmʿt*)   II Chron xxiv 26
Shimei (*šmʿy*)   I Chron iii 19, iv 26,27, v 4, vi 17,29,42, viii 21, xxiii 7,9,10(*bis*), xxv 3,17, xxvii 27; II Chron xxix 14, xxxi 12, 13; Ezra x 23,33,38
Shimri (*šmry*)   I Chron iv 37, xi 45, xxvi 10; II Chron xxix 13
Shimrith (*šmryt*)   II Chron xxiv 26
Shishak (*šyšq*)   II Chron xii 2,5(*bis*), 7,9

Sibbecai (*sbky*) I Chron xi 29, xx 4, xxvii 11

Simeon (*šm'wn*) I Chron ii 1, iv 24,42, vi 65, xii 26, xxvii 16; II Chron xv 9, xxxiv 6

Solomon (*šlmh*) I Chron iii 5,10, vi 10,32, xiv 4, xviii 8, xxii 5,6,7,9,17, xxiii 1, xxviii 5,6,9,11,20, xxix 1,19,22,23,24,25,28; II Chron i 1,2,3,5,6,7,8,11,13,14,16,18, ii 1,2,10,16, iii 1,3, iv 11,16,18,19, v 1(*bis*), 2,6, vi 1,13, vii 1,5,7(*bis*), 8,10,11(*bis*), 12, viii 1,3,6,8,9,10,11,12,16,17,18(*bis*), ix 1(*tris*), 2(*bis*), 3,9, 10,12,13,14,15,20(*bis*), 22,23,25,28,29,30,31, x 2, xi 3,17(*bis*), xii 9, xiii 6,7, xxx 26, xxxiii 7, xxxv 3,4; Ezra ii 55,58; Neh vii 57,60, xi 3, xii 45, xiii 26

Sukkiim (*skyym*) II Chron xii 3

Tilgath-pilneser (*tlgt-pln'sr, tlgt-plnsr*) I Chron v 6,26; II Chron xxviii 20

Tobiah (*twbyhw, tbyh*) II Chron xvii 8; Ezra ii 60; Neh ii 10,19, iii 35, iv 1, vi 1,12,14,17(*bis*), 19, vii 62, xiii 4,7,8

Tyrian (*ṣry*) I Chron xx 4; II Chron ii 13; Ezra iii 7; Neh xiii 16

Uri (*'wry*) I Chron ii 20(*bis*); II Chron i 5; Ezra x 24

Uriel (*'wry'l*) I Chron vi 24, xv 5,11; II Chron xiii 2

Uzziah (*'zyh*) I Chron vi 24, xxvii 25; II Chron xxvi 1,3,8,9,11, 14,18(*bis*), 19,21,22,23, xxvii 2; Ezra x 21; Neh xi 4

Uzziel (*'zy'l*) I Chron iv 42, vi 2,18, vii 7, xv 10, xxiii 12,20, xxiv 24, xxv 4, xxvi 23; II Chron xxix 14; Neh iii 8

Zabad (*zbd*) I Chron ii 36,37, vii 21, xi 41; II Chron xxiv 26; Ezra x 27,33,43

Zadok (*ṣdwq*) I Chron vi 8(*bis*), 12(*bis*), 53, ix 11, xii 29, xv 11, xvi 39, xviii 16, xxiv 3,6,31, xxvii 17, xxix 22; II Chron xxvii 1, xxxi 10; Ezra vii 2; Neh iii 4,29, x 22, xi 11, xiii 13

Zaham (*zhm*) II Chron xi 19

Zebadiah (*zbdyh*) I Chron viii 15,17, xii 8, xxvi 2, xxvii 7; II Chron xvii 8, xix 11; Ezra viii 8, x 20

Zebulun (*zblwn*) I Chron ii 1, vi 63,77, xii 34,41, xxvii 19; II Chron xxx 10,11,18

Zechariah (*zkryhw*) I Chron v 7, ix 21,37, xv 18,20,24, xvi 5, xxiv 25, xxvi 2,11,14, xxvii 21; II Chron xvii 7, xx 14, xxi 2, xxiv

KEY TO THE TEXT

Chapter	Verse	§	Chapter	Verse	§
i	1–17	1	xxi	1	22
	18	2		2–20	23
ii	1=17	2	xxii	1–9	24
iii	1–17	3		10–12	25
iv	1–22	4	xxiii	1–21	25
v	1	4	xxiv	1–27	26
	2–14	5	xxv	1–28	27
vi	1–42	6	xxvi	1–23	28
vii	1–10	7	xxvii	1–9	29
	11–22	8	xxviii	1–27	30
viii	1–18	9	xxix	1–36	31
ix	1–28	10	xxx	1–27	32
	29–31	11	xxxi	1–21	33
x	1–19	12	xxxii	1–23	34
xi	1–23	13		24–33	35
xii	1–16	14	xxxiii	1–20	36
xiii	1–23	15		21–25	37
xiv	1–14	16	xxxiv	1–33	38
xv	1–19	17	xxxv	1–19	39
xvi	1–14	18		20–27	40
xvii	1–19	19	xxxvi	1–10	41
xviii	1–34	20		11–21	42
xix	1–11	21		22–23	43
xx	1=37	22